TRIBES

A New Way of Learning and Being Together

TRIBES

A New Way of Learning and Being Together

By Jeanne Gibbs

in collaboration with

Teachers and Administrators Extraordinaire

CENTER
SOURCE
S Y S T E M S

Windsor, California

Published in the United States of America by

CenterSource Systems, LLC
7975 Cameron Drive, Suite 500, Windsor, California 95492

Library of Congress Cataloging in Publication Data
Gibbs, Jeanne
TRIBES: A New Way of Learning and Being Together
Includes index and bibliography.

1. Cooperative learning; 2. Classroom environment;
3. Academic achievement; 4. Social learning;
5. School improvement.

ISBN 0-932762-40-9 • CIP 93-73135

Illustrations: Pat Ronzone, Sausalito, CA
Photographs: Nita Winter Photography, Sausalito, CA

PRINTED IN THE UNITED STATES OF AMERICA

10   9   8   7

One learns by doing the thing, for though you think you know it, you have no certainty until you try.

—*Sophocles*

Table of Contents

Preface

Throughout the years, the same inquiry is made. "Tribes? What is Tribes?" Our response is never quite the same. It keeps changing as more and more schools report the impact that the process of Tribes TLC®–Tribes Learning Community–brings to their school communities. In the early years schools were delighted to find that...

• membership in active learning groups (tribes) motivates students;
• discipline problems fade away and teachers have more time to teach;
• the caring community culture promotes respect for diversity and character values;
• the climate of the school becomes safe and non-violent.

We based our response to inquiries on those results. Now we realize that it is a bit like reporting on the development of a growing child from infancy into his or her young adult years. Today it is known that the process of Tribes is a way to...

• re-culture and restructure the whole school as a learning community;
• develop teacher collegiality, reflective practice and collaborative planning;
• focus on the socialization of students as well as intellectual development;
• and raise levels of academic achievement.

Tribes is not a curriculum, not a program or list of activities. It is a "process"–a way to establish a positive culture for learning and human development throughout a school community. The process as described in this book is based on a synthesis of studies on children's development, cooperative learning, cognition, systems theory, multiple intelligences, human resilience and the skills needed for the 21st century. Hundreds of teachers, administrators, resource people, researchers and colleagues have contributed over the years to make Tribes what it is today. Particularly, we want to thank the teachers, trainers and administrators who have contributed articles to this edition. We also are delighted to have new chapter pictures from the nationally acclaimed photographer, Nita Winter, who captures joy, vitality and hope in the faces of children. Once again we appreciate the winsome artistry of Pat Ronzone for the new book cover and illustrations. Thank you one and all!

We welcome you as a new friend and colleague into the growing international Tribes Learning Community. May something herein lighten and brighten your days–and the futures of the children who come your way. This is really what the process known as "Tribes" is all about.

Jeanne Gibbs
Developer & Author

1
A New Pattern of Interaction

1

A New Pattern of Interaction

Who are these people? We're teachers, parents, administrators, business people, service organizations, and students who have come together to figure out how to change our school—so that everyone is excited about learning.

We're asking ourselves:

What if

. . . we created a safe and caring environment in our school?

. . . everyone respected individual differences and the diversity of our cultures?

. . . our teachers designed learning experiences to reach students who learn in different ways?

. . . students became responsible for themselves and each other?

. . . we knew how to educate all of our students for success in the 21st century?

. . . our families became more actively involved in the education of their children?

. . . we could awaken a love of learning in everyone?

Toward a New Pattern of Interaction

"What if" questions like these are being asked by thousands of parents and educators throughout school communities. They recognize the need to prepare students with the knowledge, skills, and personal qualities to do well in a world of rapid change. They realize that they have much at stake, not just the health and well-being of their own children, but of all children. There are no easy answers, and certainly no single program or curriculum can revitalize a school. The complexity of change can only be met through an ongoing process that engages teachers, administrators, parents, community members, and students over several years of time. All must begin to relate, plan, and act out of a new pattern of interaction toward common goals on behalf of children. As you move through this book, you will discover a trusted process to use not only within classrooms but throughout the whole school community. It is a synthesis of concepts, agreements, and strategies woven into a new pattern of interaction to create caring environments for human growth and learning.

The first custom of the Tribes process, no matter where it is used, is to invite people to reflect upon and share their own experiences. This step is called "inclusion." In order to involve you, the reader, right away— we would like you to take a moment to reflect upon your own heartfelt experiences of being a student in school. The first question is, "When did you go to school? Was it in the 1980s, 70s, 60s, 50s, 40s, or 30s? What did you enjoy? What was difficult? What did teachers do? Did the days ever seem very long?"

The different decades of our experience really do not matter very much. Nine chances out of ten, most of us spent years hearing these or similar words:

> *"Be quiet."*
>
> *"Pay attention to the teacher."*
>
> *"Give the right answer."*
>
> *"Don't share your work with others—that's cheating."*
>
> *"Those with the right answer get A's."*
>
> *"Don't talk to your neighbor."*
>
> *"Work alone."*

We also heard teachers say:

> *"This is our classroom"*—but decisions were made by the teacher.
>
> *"You are in charge of yourself"*—but lots of rules were on the board.
>
> *"Everyone is special"*—but culture and ethnicity were ignored.

> "
>
> *The way organizations are now is a product of how we think and interact. They cannot change in any fundamental way unless we can change our basic patterns of thinking and interacting so that learning can be a way of life.*
>
> — Peter Senge
>
> "

"No one is favored"—but the smart kids were called on more.

"New Americans are welcome"—but bilingual education was nonexistent.

"Creativity is important"—but the approach was already defined.

"We live in a democracy"—but not when in school.

The words, the structure, the roles, and the pattern of interaction between teachers and students has changed very little over the past 150 years. The pattern, which also dominated the management of schools, is one of command and control. Its message to students has been that the teacher gives out information, students listen and speak only when called on, some people are smart and valued, and some people just can't learn. Most of all, people have to compete to be recognized, to have status and get rewards. The pattern, whether in traditional classrooms or school meetings, looks like this:

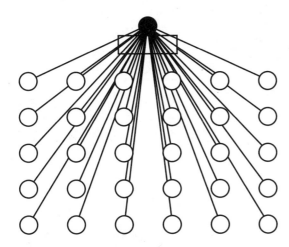

The people-management pattern began in the 19th century to control factory workers at the beginning of the Industrial Age. When large numbers of people moved from farm areas to jobs in cities, the "little red school house" was relegated to the nostalgia of the disappearing Agricultural Age. With it went the caring, sharing, mutual support, and participation so longed for today. Factories needed workers who were punctual, could do repetitive tasks, and wouldn't make changes. Meeting the needs of the factory system became the role of schools. Students were seen as the raw material to be shaped into standardized products, out of standardized texts, taught by standardized teachers. The ability to memorize and repeat facts spelled success.

Although massive funds for school improvement, restructuring, and reform have flowed through school districts for more than 20 years, the traditional pattern of interaction between teachers and students has changed very little.

> "
>
> *Pouring more money into the factory model of education is, for the most part, foolish. It does no more good to spend more money on teacher talk than it does to increase the amount of time that students have to sit in class listening to it. ...Schools clinging to this mode for learning are using a 19th-century model to prepare kids for a 21st-century world.*
>
> —Edward Fiske
>
> "

What Results Are We Getting?

The question that is being asked by thousands of school communities is, What results are we getting from this model of education? Even a few sobering statistics help to overcome denial:[1]

80% of students entering school feel good about themselves. By the 5th grade only 20% do. Only one out of five high school students has positive self-esteem.

68% of major business firms report educational shortcomings in their employees.

Only one in five 21-25 year-olds can read a bus timetable or draft a job application letter.

More than 25% of high school students fail to graduate. Some high schools never graduate more than 50% of their students.

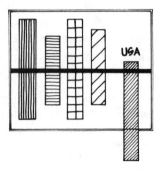

THIS IS *SERIOUS!*

90% of U.S. students are dismally behind international averages in math and science.

36% of American companies spend an estimated $20 billion per year on remedial courses in math, reading, and writing.

Letting Go and Catching On

Few would disagree that improving the quality of education requires letting go of assumptions that no longer are working well. However, before letting go of a weak perch, it's good to examine the new one attracting your attention. Though the word "paradigm" seems to be getting overworked these days, we're going to use it just as some folks at the Department of Education in Hawaii have done. The following lists point out the dramatic change taking place in many schools today.[2]

Traditional Paradigm	Emerging Paradigm
Emphasis on teaching	Emphasis on learning
Emphasis on parts	Emphasis on the whole
Isolated knowledge and skills	Integrated knowledge and skills
Student as passive recipient	Student as active constructor of meaning
Teacher as information giver	Teacher as co-learner and facilitator
Limited view of intelligence	Teaching to multiple learning styles
Sorting and weeding out of students	Equal access to instruction and content for all
Learning as an individual activity	Learning also as a social activity—collaboration enhances learning
Only teacher-directed learning	Also student-directed learning
Homogeneous grouping	Heterogeneous grouping
Emphasis on product and content	Emphasis on process, metacognition—learning how to learn
Primary emphasis on form	Primary emphasis on meaning
Learning decontextualized	Learning grounded in "real world" contexts
Language as separate skill— covered only in English	Reading, writing, thinking, communicating across the curriculum
One answer-one way, correctness	Open-ended, non-routine multiple solutions
Western bias	Multicultural, global views
Criteria, goals given by teacher; not explicit or public before instruction	Shared development of goals and criteria for performance
Tests that test	Tests that teach

"

In America's best classrooms, again, the emphasis has shifted. Instead of individual achievement and competition, the focus is on group learning. Students learn to articulate, clarify, and then restate for one another how they identify and find answers. They learn how to seek and accept criticism from their peers, solicit help, and give credit to others. ...This is an ideal preparation for life-times of symbolic analytic work.

—Robert Reich

"

A New Way Of Learning Together

The great news is that thousands of schools are making the big shift—learning how to create the new pattern of interaction and structures that support the emerging paradigm. The pattern of interaction in classrooms (and also faculty meetings) looks like this now:

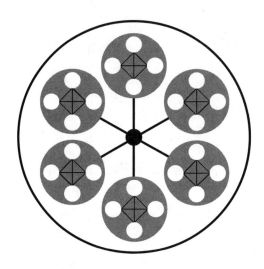

"What, you mean kids can work together on the same math problems?"

"That's right! They've always heard that many heads are better than one, but we never let them prove it to us before."

At best, the traditional structure may give each student five to ten minutes a day to speak about academic topics or respond to questions from the teacher. Dialogue with peers in groups can provide ten times that amount of 'air time.'

At best, the traditional structure may give each student five to ten minutes a day to speak about academic topics or respond to questions from the teacher. Dialogue with peers in groups can provide ten times that amount of "air time." At the same time, students are practicing an essential set of collaborative skills that people need in order to work well together. The ability to listen attentively, express ideas, solve group problems, resolve conflict, make decisions, research and analyze material, and encourage others are the democratic skills needed within families, work settings, government, and all organizational systems.

The new pattern of interaction changes the role of the teacher in a dramatic way. Teachers now see themselves as learners, facilitators, researchers, and designers of curricula. When teachers work in collegial groups their inherent isolation from each other disappears. No matter what the group approach may be called—cooperative learning, authentic instruction, student team learning, group investigation, co-op co-op, active learning, jigsaw, complex instruction, group work, or Tribes Learning Community—the benefits of cooperative instruction are documented by hundreds of research studies.[3] The traditional competitive system awards the few, but loses many. Students, even those considered to be slow learners, become motivated when able to work with peers.[4] At a time when school failure is a critical problem jeopardizing the country's future, cooperative learning is heralded as one of the most promising instructional strategies to dramatically improve academic achievement.[5]

What Is Tribes?

Tribes? You smile and wonder when you hear the name. Twenty years ago, teachers in several northern California schools began to refer to the training groups that they were experiencing as "our tribes."[6] They were participants in a pilot project using small learning groups to increase participation and peer support. The purpose of the project was to call forth the unique potential of every student. The story of the on-going development of the Tribes process is contained in the Appendix of this book.

Tribes is a democratic group process, not just a curriculum or set of cooperative activities. A "process" is a sequence of events that lead to the achievement of an outcome. The outcome of the Tribes process is to develop a positive environment that promotes human growth and learning. How does this happen? Can anyone do it? Yes! It requires learning how to build community through three stages of group development using four agreements among the students or adults with whom you are working.

Community Agreements

- Attentive listening
- Appreciation/no put-downs
- The right to pass
- Mutual respect

Throughout the process people learn to use specific collaborative skills, and to reflect both on the interaction and the learning that is taking place. The Tribes process not only establishes a caring environment for cooperative learning, but provides structure for positive interaction and continuity for working groups whether in the classroom, the faculty, the administration or the parent community.

TRIBES LEARNING COMMUNITY

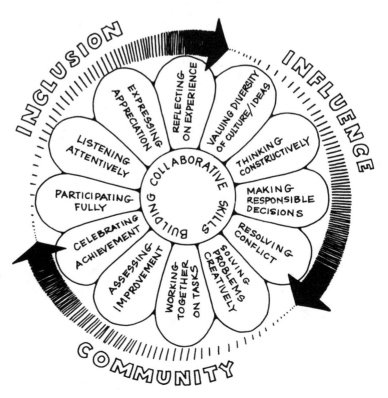

The power of being included and valued by peers motivates students to active participation in their own learning.

Tribes in the Classroom

Tribes are formed sociometrically to distribute boys and girls, students of high and low peer acceptance, and people of heterogeneous abilities. Although students have the opportunity to name others whom they would like to have in their tribe, the teacher determines who will be in each group. People are seated together in a small circle or square of desks, or at the same table. Unlike many cooperative learning approaches being used in schools today, Tribes stay together over a long period of time.

A tribe can consist of three to six students who work together each day throughout the school year. The size of the tribe varies depending upon the age of its members and its purpose. Preschool children, ages three to five, do very well when clustered in groups of three. Teachers using cooperative learning structures prefer groups of four, and high school/adult classes using the process for group projects or study groups prefer having the resources of five to six members.

The power of being included and valued by peers motivates students to active participation in their own learning. Positive expectations and support from an ongoing group of peers is the reason that students in Tribes Learning Communities (TLC) become excited about learning.

A Shared Mission and Goal

The mission of Tribes is

> *to assure the healthy development of every child*
> *so that each has the knowledge, skills, and resiliency*
> *to be successful in a rapidly changing world.*

Children's learning and development are influenced by the key systems of their lives—family, school, friends, and community. Schools working toward this developmental goal encourage all of the systems involved in learning to use the same caring Tribes process and collaborative skills.

The goal for a Tribes school is

> *to engage all teachers, administrators, students, and families in*
> *working together as a learning community that is dedicated to*
> *caring and support, active participation, and positive expectations*
> *for all students.*

STUDENTS

who maintain long-term membership in classroom tribes will

- Actively participate in the learning process
- Communicate and work well with others
- Value diverse abilities and cultural differences
- Assume responsibility for their own behavior
- Develop critical thinking and collaborative skills
- Improve their sense of self-worth and mastery of academics

PARENTS

who become involved in the school community will report

- Their children like school better than before
- Positive behavior carries over into the home
- Strengthening protective factors to foster children's resiliency
- Appreciation of their involvement with other parents and the staff of the school
- A new recognition of their own role in their children's education

**TRIBES TLC®
A New Way
of Learning and
Being Together**

TEACHERS

who are long-term members of faculty planning groups and fully implement the Tribes process in their classroom will

- Spend less time managing student behavior
- Have more time for creative teaching
- Notice that students are retaining what they learn
- Enjoy professional dialogue and supportive colleagues
- Reduce their own levels of stress
- Enjoy teaching more than they have before

ADMINISTRATORS

who use the Tribes process to organize and support their students, staff, and parent community will

- Have fewer student behavior problems
- Benefit from significant and supportive parent involvement
- Over time, improve academic achievement
- Achieve recognition for transforming the school to excellence

A Tribes school is a learning community

where teachers, administrators, students, and parents all enjoy
the mutual respect and caring essential for growth and learning

Using the Tribes process, the interactive systems have a way to work collaboratively to attain the shared goals they have for children in their circle of concern. The graphic on the previous page defines the outcomes that a school community can achieve over a period of time.

The essence of a "learning community" approach is described by Peter Senge, author of the book *The Fifth Discipline, The Art and Practice of the Learning Community*. In a recent interview Senge stated:

> *It's true that there is no substitute for individual caring and commitment, but I have come to think that the real generative point in moving toward a learning organization is in small groups that form around commitments. These are groups of people who are really committed to something larger than themselves and larger than their own personal desires. They support each other in the way that real friends support each other. They tell the truth to each other and they are continually in a mode of inquiry, knowing that nobody knows and everybody can learn continually.*"[7]

How the Tribes TLC Process Changes the Pattern

The process changes the traditional pattern in classrooms because

- The classroom is student-centered (people no longer relate primarily to the teacher, but work with peers)

- The teacher becomes a facilitator, using the proven group development process

- Everyone belongs to a long-term membership group and feels included and valued for their unique contribution

- Students themselves are involved in classroom management (defining agreements, problem-solving, choosing tasks, and sustaining the positive learning environment)

- Teachers use multiple strategies to reach and teach students of multiple cultures, intelligences, and abilities

- Students learn both critical thinking and collaborative social skills along with academic content

- Individual and group accountability is assessed jointly by students and teacher

- Inherent in the Tribes process are the protective factors that foster resiliency: caring/sharing, active participation, and positive expectations.

The Opportunity to Practice Democracy

Critical in the shift to the emerging paradigm of education is the need to encourage active participation and give students more choice about what and how they learn. If we only chop up lesson plans for coopera-

tive group learning and teach collaborative skills but fail to use democratic processes, everyone including our country as a whole will be
short-changed. Moreover, we believe that cooperative learning will be
seen as one more fleeting technique to teach academics. The important
question is, After we announce that we are now practicing democracy,
how much choice and control will we really give students? Alfie Kohn
believes that "it is the integration of two values, community and choice,
that defines democracy." He writes:[8]

> It needs to be said that allowing people to make decisions about what
> happens to them is inherently preferable to controlling them. ...Apart from
> the skills that will be useful for students to have in the future, they ought
> to have a chance to choose in the present. Children after all are not just
> adults-in-the-making. They are people whose current needs and rights and
> experiences must be taken seriously. Put it this way: students should not
> only be trained to live in a democracy when they grow up; they should
> have the chance to live in one today.

Questions to consider with your faculty

- How can we help students formulate their own learning goals?

- How will students take part in defining rules and agreements?

- How can students help teachers design stimulating learning
  experiences?

- How can they help to assess progress toward learning objectives?

There is much evidence that when children are given more opportunity
to participate in decisions about schoolwork they miss school less, are
more creative, put in more time on task, and complete tasks in less
time.[9] Self-determination and a sense of self-worth and civic responsibility could well be the by-products of giving students authentic opportunities to use the democratic skills that they are being taught.

The Whole School Community

Picture all of the students, faculty, parents, and support and resource
people in your school community. (It takes wide-screen vision!) Everyone is included and involved in a group of their own peers—even those
parents who are usually so hard to find. (Don't worry now about how
to do it.) Picture all of the small groups: teachers with teachers of their
same grade level, parents with other parents whose children are in the
same classroom, students with other students in the same classroom,
and so on. All of the groups are learning and using the same caring
process and collaborative skills. All are developing ways to optimize the
conditions that support the development of competency and resiliency
for every student in the school community. It's as though a whole
chorus once singing many different tunes finally is harmonizing and
singing the same song! Impossible? No, it can become a reality once the
old pattern begins to change.

> "
> *We teach reading,
> writing, and math by
> having students do them,
> but we teach democracy
> by lecture.*
> —Shelly Berman
> "

2

Finding Our Way to the Future

2

Finding Our Way to the Future

The time is 7:30 P.M. and the meeting of the Middleton Middle School Restructuring Committee is called to order by Thelma Brown, the parent chairperson. "Friends, the purpose of our work tonight is to finalize the plan." Les Aldridge, principal, coughs. "First," he says, "I need to remind you of the District's mandate that our restructuring plan is not only to be innovative, but financially and organizationally sound as stipulated by the District's criteria." Heads nod. "Yes," says Thelma, "but now is the time you've been waiting for. Tonight we will select the immediate programs and policies to improve the school." The words are no sooner spoken than a flurry of hands begin to wave wildly.

Trudy Armstrong, teacher: *"Our test scores will go up if you all will finally vote to have the new math curriculum."*

Polly Crabtree, parent: *"No, teachers just need to give more homework, and we should go back to tracking."*

Donna Gonzales, parent: *"But that simply isn't enough!"*

Tony Salvatore, parent: *"I agree with Donna. What about upgrading computer equipment and doing more teacher training?"*

Les Aldridge, principal: *"My priority is to have guards on the playground, and a tougher discipline policy."*

John Pasquale, parent: *"Sure, and how about the dress code we discussed?"*

Jerry Lingo, teacher: *"We should consider school-site management, like some schools are doing."*

Trudy: *"No, what's important is just getting the new math curriculum."*

Parent (no one knows her name for sure): *"What about eliminating field trips?"*

Tony: *"Now you're talking...that's a good idea!"*

What we need today is a third wave that builds on the prior efforts, looking beyond both external factors and the roles of teachers, parents, and administrators. We need a comprehensive effort that places the student at the center of educational reform.[1]

—William Greider

Beyond the Quick-Fix Approach

If you have ever experienced a school planning meeting that in any way resembled this Middleton Middle School parody, and if you managed not to feel frustrated...there's really no use reading any further. Across America groups of dedicated, well-meaning people become caught in the quick-fix approach to school improvement, jumping to partial solutions rather than asking, What developmental outcomes do we want for our students? Ultimately, the principal or district administrators sort out the confusion and distribute a written plan that probably reflects little of the Planning Committee's influence...after all those meetings! Yet, the need for change remains.

Waves of Reform

There are, however, clues that point a way. During the past ten years, American schools have moved through two waves of school reform. Following the release of *A Nation at Risk* in 1983 by the U.S. Department of Education, the focus of school reform was on such external factors as higher standards, competency statements, the strengthening of teacher certification, discipline policy, dress codes, and attendance rules. Five years later the next wave of reform, still current in many places, focused on changing the roles and interaction of adults: teacher empowerment, parental choice, school-site management, and the adoption of schools by local business groups. Attention shifted from mandated activities to collaborative efforts.

A New Set of Questions

Centering on students rather than adults raises entirely different questions, which require new knowledge, research, and a richer discussion among school planning groups. Our friends from Middleton will have to ask:

- What kind of world are we preparing kids for?

- What knowledge, skills, and competencies do students need in order to do well in these rapidly changing times?

- What are our children really like?

- How do they learn? Do they all learn the same way?

- What do **they** want to learn?

- Should we have developmental goals beyond academics?

Unless these questions are seriously considered, child-centered goals supported by effective learning strategies cannot be well defined. Those many unrelated quick-fix solutions will continue to drive and sabotage the planning that needs to happen to prepare students for a 21st-century world.

Looking at Our Changing World

If we are to plan how to educate kids for a future we're only beginning to imagine, it is important to look at some significant changes.

Let your mind wander and jot down some of the most important changes that took place during the last twenty, thirty, or forty years.

1.

2.

3.

4.

5.

6.

7.

8.

9.

10.

Now review your list and star the changes that you believe most affect how we educate kids. How many of the changes that you listed fall into the following major categories?

From	To
Industrial Age	Information Age
Homogeneous culture	Multicultural diversity
Socialization by family	Socialization by media, peers, and school
Individualism	Community

From the Industrial Age to the Information Age

It boggles the mind when we realize that there have been only two other times in the history of humankind when massive transitions totally changed the world: first, from the Age of Nomadic Hunter-Gatherers to the Age of Agriculture; then from the Age of Agriculture to the Industrial Age; and now from the Industrial Age to the Information Age.

Information Age

Age of Nomadic Hunter-Gatherers

Age of Agriculture

Industrial Age

"

When resources came out of the ground, the United States was a rich country. Now that resources come out of people's heads, we are a developing country.

—John Sculley
former CEO
Apple Computer

"

Moving between ages means giving up hand-held plows for tractors, the abacus for calculators—the Pony Express for fax machines, cellular equipment, and satellite communication. Upheaval, chaos, and uncertainty inevitably accompany global change throughout every realm of society for many years. It is the process of letting go of old forms and creating new ones.

The Industrial Age of the past 150 years was based on a technology of centralized workplaces in which people worked on individual tasks without much influence over the end-product or service. It had time clocks, authoritarian management, and prescribed methods. To meet the needs of the Industrial Age, schools were organized to train people to be punctual, to do repetitive tasks, and not to make changes. Now as we move to the Information Age we begin to realize that ever-changing data combined with rapidly changing systems and situations require critical thinking and collaborative skills. During the 1991 Gulf War we learned that even the U.S. Army depends upon ground troops that can think critically...to analyze data flowing from computers, to synthesize a complexity of information, to relate it to the task at hand, to plan and to work cooperatively with colleagues as a team. There is no doubt about it—this is a high tech/high touch era.

A 1991 U.S. Department of Labor document entitled *What Work Requires of Schools,* made the challenge very clear.[2]

"More than half of our young people leave school without the knowledge or foundation required to find and hold a good job. These young people will pay a very high price. They face the bleak prospects of dead end work interrupted only by periods of unemployment."[3]

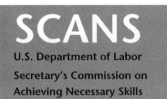

SCANS
U.S. Department of Labor
Secretary's Commission on
Achieving Necessary Skills

The report emphasizes that schools must teach a new set of skills so that young people entering the work force know how to identify and organize information and resources, relate well with others in work teams, and understand social and organizational systems.

Skills for the 21st Century

BASIC SKILLS	THINKING SKILLS	PERSONAL QUALITIES

Reads, writes, performs arithmetic and mathematical operations, listens and speaks well

Thinks critically, makes decisions, solves problems, visualizes, knows how to learn and reason

Displays responsibility, self-esteem, sociability, self-management, integrity, and honesty

◆ **Reading**
locates, understands, and interprets written information in prose and in documents

◆ **Writing**
communicates thoughts, ideas, information, and messages in writing, and creates documents such as letters, directions, manuals, reports, graphs, and flow charts

◆ **Arithmetic/Mathematics**
performs basic computations and approaches practical problems by choosing appropriately from a variety of mathematical techniques

◆ **Listening**
receives, attends to, interprets, and responds to verbal messages and other cues

◆ **Speaking**
organizes ideas and communicates orally

◆ **Creative Thinking**
generates new ideas

◆ **Decision Making**
specifies goals and constraints, generates alternatives, considers risks, evaluates and chooses best alternative

◆ **Problem Solving**
recognizes problems, devises and implements a plan of action

◆ **Seeing Things in the Mind's Eye**
organizes and processes symbols, pictures, graphs, objects, and other information

◆ **Knowing How to Learn**
uses efficient learning techniques to acquire and apply new knowledge and skills

◆ **Reasoning**
discovers a rule or principle underlying the relationship between two or more objects and applies it when solving a problem

◆ **Responsibility**
exerts a high level of effort and perseveres toward goal attainment

◆ **Self-Esteem**
believes in own self-worth and maintains a positive view of self

◆ **Sociability**
demonstrates understanding, friendliness, adaptability, empathy, and politeness in group settings

◆ **Self-Management**
assesses self accurately, sets personal goals, monitors progress, and exhibits self-control

◆ **Integrity/Honesty**
chooses ethical course of action

From Homogeneity to Multicultural Diversity

When the United States was originally founded to provide haven and opportunity to people from many countries, the metaphor of a cultural melting pot came into being. Now we realize that expecting all people to be assimilated into our dominant Western European culture has contributed to conflict, prejudice, and unequal opportunity for multi-ethnic populations. Our cities and the majority of suburbs already have rich diversities of people from many races and cultures. By the year 2000, white people will constitute only 55.9 percent of the U.S. population, down from 75.5 percent in 1980. Throughout the world by that same year 5 billion of the 6 billion people on earth will be people of color. The need for multicultural education, tolerance, and respect is apparent.

If we could shrink the earth's current population of 5.2 billion to a village of precisely 1,000 and all of the existing human ratios remained the same, it would look like this.

There would be:

564 Asians and Oceanians

210 Europeans

86 Africans

80 South Americans

60 North Americans

moreover

820 would be people of color;

180 would be white.

50% of the entire world's wealth

would be in the hands of only 60 people

700 would be unable to read; 500 would suffer from malnutrition

600 would live in substandard housing[4]

As a nation, we need to prepare young people to work and live in the realities of today's world. The challenge is articulated well by Mako Nakagawa, a multicultural educator.

If we are to succeed as a nation both in international trade and in leadership for democracy, we need to use the diverse cultural laboratory of our own country as a training ground for producing citizens who value differences, respect the validity of our own perspectives, understand the independence of people, and who have the interpersonal skills to effectively communicate across all spectra of ethnicity, nationality, language, culture, gender, values, and even political ideology.

"

It is less important for students to learn to appreciate ethnic foods than it is for students to understand equal rights.

—Mako Nakagawa

"

It is less important for students to learn to appreciate ethnic foods than it is for students to understand equal rights. Yet, much of what we have taught under the rubric of multicultural education has fallen into the trap of "Tacos on Tuesdays." That is, the trap of teaching about cultures and about cultural differences without teaching an understanding of how cultural differences, or gender, class, and other differences, contribute to the unified whole of a democratic nation.[5]

If we want to give all kids a chance, we agree that schools across the nation need to embrace the concept of what Nakagawa calls "cooperative pluralism." It is a perspective that focuses on the linkages between and among people, coupled with the harmonious networking of all groups. It expands multicultural education from simply learning about a specific culture to learning about our whole system, how we interact, and how we can build everyone's skills and opportunities for active participation and power. Such a philosophy fosters unity and global harmony out of diversity.

Bonnie Benard of the WestEd Research Laboratory writes, "An attitude that celebrates diversity is, therefore, the foundation upon which a school can be culturally transformed and the principle around which all school change efforts are organized." From her review of the extensive literature on multicultural education, she defines five components as essential to creating a culturally transformed school community:

- Active involvement of the entire school community

- A mission policy/statement centering on diversity

- Redistribution of power and authority within the school and classrooms

- High expectations by teachers

- Theme focused multicultural curriculum, cooperative learning, respect for individual learning styles, and multiethnic, well-trained teachers[6]

> *An attitude that celebrates diversity is, therefore, the foundation upon which a school can be culturally transformed and the principle around which all school change efforts are organized.*
>
> —Bonnie Benard

The melting pot metaphor of assimilation grew out of the naiveté of two hundred years ago and is now an insensitive anachronism. Multiculturism is a reality and can become a great strength for this country due to the diversity of our people resources. We need to think in terms of alternative metaphors, such as an orchestra of many fine instruments or a salad bowl composed of many wonderful vegetables all contributing to the whole. The richness of the salad comes from the diversity of colors and flavors. The more the better! What holds it together? Of course, the dressing. It's called "inclusion."

From Socialization by the Family to Socialization by Peers

One of the greatest changes, of course, has taken place within American families. The average American family moves every two to three years, and each time loses whatever support systems it may have had. Twenty-five percent of American families are one-parent families. Of the remaining two-parent families, in 80 percent both parents work. It is startling to read in a national poll that the average family spends 27 minutes per day together. The one-time sense of family history, values, and expectations has largely disappeared. Grandparents, aunts, uncles, and cousins rarely live in the same area. A majority of families, due to various stressful situations, are no longer helping their own children to

- Gain a sense of identity and self-worth
- Learn shared cultural values
- Bond to significant others

The dramatic changes in our families have caused youngsters to rely on peers for socialization. As they do so, a very different set of values and behaviors evolves. Of course, far too many are being socialized by television sets, more often than not filling the vacuum with negative social behaviors and values.

This leaves one more critical challenge up to the school since it is the system that has children for the greatest number of hours each day. Out of necessity schools must teach pro-social attitudes, principles, and skills. If for no other reason, so that students can learn how to read and write, and get along well with others. This fact alone calls for a new curriculum, a curriculum that develops identity, self-worth, social responsibility, and bonding to positive groups. You guessed it! This is especially what Tribes is about!

Individualism to Community

The Agricultural Age depended upon people helping each other. Images of a barn-raising, a quilting bee, and a town meeting spelled *community*. Things changed with the onset of the Industrial Age. People moved to cities to work in factories, families began to scatter, gold was discovered, the West and its natural resources were "conquered," and rugged individualism was heralded. Independence, competition, and domination were the cornerstones for survival in the 17th to 19th centuries to establish our independence as a new country. Extended into this century we became a "do it yourself" population...neighbors isolated from neighbors, freeways filled with solitary commuters twice a day, and people afraid to reach out to each other. Proud of our independence, we learned how to be competitive but not interdependent. We know how to operate but not cooperate. We have lost the basic habits of the heart of caring and sharing as a community.[7]

> "
> *Given the incredible stresses the family is now experiencing, school has become a vital refuge for a growing number of children.*
>
> —Bonnie Benard
>
> "

From all sides of the globe people recognize that survival now depends upon our capacity for cooperation, interdependence, conservation, and respect for a diversity of people and nations. It means

- Negotiation rather than hostility

- Cooperation, not just competition

- Sharing and conserving resources

- Community building through consensus

- Decentralized rather than authoritarian management

- Work teams and staff support groups

- People coming together to help one another do what few can do alone

Many believe that contemporary civilization is threatened by a loss of the sense of community that characterizes tribal peoples. David Maybury-Lewis, author of *Millennium: Tribal Wisdom and the Modern World*, points out that our emphasis on individualism has led to the isolation of individuals within mass society, and a deep longing for connection and community.

It has been the caring community that has assured personal and cultural survival throughout all of history. People giving each other support, respecting diversity, working in cooperation to achieve shared visions and goals. The slogans of yesterday may have been "I will take care of me" and "go it alone," but what about something like "together we can" for today and the world of tomorrow? [8]

With few exceptions the solitary animal is, in any species, an abnormal creature...The dominant principle of social life is not the struggle for existence, but cooperation...If we would seek for one word that describes society better than any other the word is cooperation.

—Ashley Montagu

Implications for Schools

What conclusions can be drawn from these four major changes in our world? The explosion of information makes a fallacy of having students memorize facts and concepts from standardized curricula. Students (and teachers) need to learn how to access information relevant to interests, themes, and tasks at hand. Explorers together, they will become constructors of knowledge, using their own creativity to replace irrelevant curricula with meaningful learning experiences. No longer simply passive consumers, they will be producers, creating and contributing new ideas, knowledge, products, organizations, and systems. Since people no longer will work alone, but in groups composed of a rich diversity of cultures and skills, an understanding of cultural pluralism, cooperation, and human systems is essential.

Teachers will do more than teach—they will reach. They will call forth multicultural populations of students of multiple intelligences through multiple kinds of learning experiences. Static curricula will disappear.

Based on these major changes taking place, we need to ask, What learning experiences students should have today in schools? Here is a partial list for you and your school community to consider or revise:

Change	Learning Experiences Need to Include:
Information Age	Critical thinking skills (reasoning and creativity) Collaborative/social skills Reading, writing, and mathematics Knowing how to learn (multiple intelligences) Seeing things in the mind's eye (visual/spatial learning)
Multicultural	Knowledge of, and respect and appreciation for, a diversity of cultures Understanding cultural pluralism, ways to foster unity, communication, collaboration, and empowerment Group problem solving, decision making, and conflict management Knowledge of systems (group dynamics, systems change, Tribes group development process) Philosophy of mutual respect and cooperation
Socialization by Peers and School	Pro-social skills Knowledge of the characteristics of resiliency How to develop active participation, peer groups, parent involvement
Community	Community building Interdependence and individual accountability Cooperation and collaboration Individual and group creativity Pro-social principles: altruism, empathy, social support, and respect for diversity

The implications for educational systems are enormous yet very exciting. The basic 3 Rs, Reading, 'Riting and 'Rithmetic, may have been sufficient for an age gone by, but our entry into a high tech/high touch age requires the addition of 3 social Rs, Relatedness, Respect, and Responsibility. These are the basic habits of the heart so desperately needed throughout our schools, families, communities, nation, and workplace.

It's just a thought. But what if we all took off our comfortable old hats and launched out on our own to learn again? Yes, teachers, administrators, parents, and community leaders. We would have to look at the 21st-century skills again and ask ourselves: Do we know how to work together well? Do we have an understanding of multiculturalism, human systems, group and organizational development, ways to problem solve, negotiate, and be kind to each other?

DO we know how to make cooperation a reality?

If not, how can we reach or even teach this new generation in our care?

A Perspective on Children's Development

What skills do our students need to be successful in the 21st century? That is the first question that a restructuring committee should discuss. Beyond that they need to ask, How do we go about developing the unique gifts and full potential inherent in each child? What do we know about the dynamics of human development? A shared philosophy and perspective are needed to guide an effective approach.

Many teachers and some parents in your community will have learned something about child development. They may be familiar with the stages listed on the following chart. These stages, however, do not tell the whole story. Children's development is not a neat, predictable path, but is affected by:

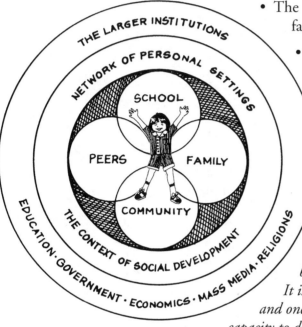

- The child's interaction in the settings of his/her daily life: family, school, community, and peer groups

- The cultural norms, languages, beliefs, and mores within surrounding systems

- The larger forces of institutions, government, economics, mass media, and religion[9]

Urie Bronfenbrenner, professor of human development and psychology, widened the perspective of our work with Tribes by stating that:

Human development is an ongoing transaction between each of us and the surrounding systems. It is one's conception of an ever-widening world and one's interaction with it, as well as a growing capacity to discover, sustain, or change it.[10]

Looking at child development as a process that is interactive with the surrounding systems means that people in those child-rearing systems must learn how to challenge and support the child's ever-widening experiences, interests, and explorations in the world beyond self.

Think of it this way. A baby's world is limited to what sustains her physical well-being...a relationship with Mom, crib, and toys. Soon she is out of the crib, maybe in a playpen, then crawling about the house discovering, and most likely changing things. Her growing capacity to discover becomes more exciting to her and more challenging to Mom and Dad each day. She has begun her pattern of life-long learning. As a young child her world centers on "me" and "mine." But by seven or eight years she moves into a new mental world of ideas. The identification with her body, her things, and her ideas is a natural progression within the world of "me." Our mode of thinking and capacity to relate well beyond the smaller world of childhood depend upon moving from a "me" identification to a "we" identification with others and our common good.

The Stages of Development in Children and Youth

Age/Grade	Key Systems	Cognitive Development	Social Development	Implications
2-4 **Preschool**	Family	**Preoperative Stage** • magical thinking • circularity in thinking • difficulty dealing with more than 1 or 2 causes • concrete mental operations	• emphasis on self • oriented to parents • needs limits, secure environment • developing motor skills	• build self-esteem • support pro-social development (sharing, taking turns, asking questions) • provide safe, caring environment
5-7 **Kindergarten to 1st Grade**	Family School	**Preoperative Stage** • magical thinking • circularity in thinking • difficulty dealing with more than 1 or 2 causes • concrete mental operations	• emphasis on self • identifies with own gender • enjoys group play • oriented to parents	• build self-esteem • support pro-social development • involve parents in activities, knowledge, social stages, and resiliency • encourage sharing, caring behavior • use cooperative learning groups
7-11 **2nd to 5th Grade**	Family School Neighborhood Peers	**Concrete Operations** • begins to think relationally and to generalize • becomes capable of integrating several variables (causes and relationships)	• oriented to parents • enjoys group play and same gender peer relationships • often competitive or has difficulties with peers • often unaware of behavior effect on others • impressed by older role models • learns behavior from parent/ peer role models • more concerned about physical image than social	• train parents and teachers in development of resiliency • teach collaborative skills • use cooperative learning groups • provide feedback on behavior • teach decision making and problem solving

[11] *This chart is based on a synthesis of stages described by child development theorists Jean Piaget and Erik Erikson.*

The Stages of Development in Children and Youth

Age/Grade	Key Systems	Cognitive Development	Social Development	Implications
12-16 **6th to 10th Grade**	Family Peer group School	**Normal mental operations** • capable of cognitive problem solving • can think abstractly and hypothetically • integrates multiple factors to understand concepts	• oriented to present rather than future • preoccupied with self— presentation, acceptance by peer group, physical maturity • seeks initial sexual intimacy • seeks peer role models • motivated by social effects of drug use • seeks independence in decision making • differentiates between self and environment • feels awkward in social skills	• oriented to peers • teach collaborative skills • peer role models teaching refusal skills • use cooperative learning groups • encourage responsible decision making • promote peer leadership, peer helping programs • involve in community service activities • involve in environment
16-18 **11th to 12th Grade**	Peer group School Work Family Community	**Relativistic thinking:** • capable of synthesizing wide range of relational material	• primary concern: individual identity, financial independence, deepening relationships, self-explora- tion, distancing from family and making own decisions	• provide opportunities for leadership • involve in business ventures, community projects, and drug-free alternative activities • self-directed learning, inquiry with peers, and exploration of own emerging interests

Yet there are so many adult people living in worlds still narrowly focused on "me and mine." Persistent identification with our own bodies, objects, and ideas leads to misunderstandings, intolerance, conflict, nationalism, and war. It perpetuates the exclusion of those identified as different, or outsiders. Understanding human development from a systems perspective gives insight into pathological problems, alienation, violence, depression, alcohol/drug use...and hopelessness.

What was it that limited the worlds of so many kids in our country today? Were they the ones who were never challenged and supported to discover their own identification in a world of "we" as well as "me?" Did they find school irrelevant and restrictive? Did their teachers and parents fail to understand their unique ways of learning? Studies on pre-schoolers have shown that a child who, at an early age, can demonstrate that he is capable of changing a frustrating situation, later tends to be active and competent in grade school.[12] Those who stay passive, self-centered, and resigned to circumstances that they consider beyond their control have difficult lives. What if education were about this: truly calling forth every child's human development beyond just getting grades, a diploma, a job, or going on to college.

More than four decades ago, John Dewey also believed that a primary task of education was to enable people to influence their environment and to gain the insight needed to make choices beyond their past experiences.

We urge you to challenge the next planning committee in your school to become a *learning committee* or a *learning community*. Take the time to envision what you hope students in your school will become at their fullest potential. What characteristics and attitudes would they have? What capacity would they have to discover, sustain, or change the complexity of systems they will face in their lives?

An Assurance Policy Called Resiliency

"But," as a teacher you say, "so many of these kids come from terrible neighborhoods and families with overwhelming problems. Poverty, unemployment, lack of health care, inadequate childcare, juvenile problems, community crime, divorce, alcoholism, drug abuse, and stress surround many of the kids in our classrooms." True, today's world has become a harsh one for America's children.

Yet, there are those who somehow live through deprivation, adversity, and stress more easily than others. Why does one child in a family, though raised in the same conditions as siblings, do well though the others fail? Why do some become competent and successful even though raised in the same overwhelming environment?

"

We must move beyond a focus on the risk factors in order to create the conditions that will facilitate children's healthy development.

—Bonnie Benard

"

The answer is to be found in the exciting research on human resiliency, which (to the credit of Bonnie Benard) is being brought to the attention of schools throughout the nation.[13] Unlike the typical problem-focused, or "pathology," approach to identifying risk factors, the research on human resiliency identifies the protective factors that create competency, wellness, and the capacity to overcome stress. The lives of children who were considered to be at high risk (due to conditions of poverty, neglect, war, parental schizophrenia, abuse, physical handicaps, depression, alcoholism, and criminality) were followed by longitudinal studies. Throughout the years, a percentage of the high-risk children did develop various problems, but to the amazement of the researchers, a greater percentage became healthy and competent adults. Somehow, the larger percentage had become resilient enough to withstand difficulties and do well though they were raised under the same stressful conditions as others who developed problems. Profiles of the resilient children emerged.

The resilient children had the following attributes:

- **Social competence:** pro-social behaviors such as responsiveness, empathy, caring, communication skills, a sense of humor

- **Problem-solving skills:** abstract and reflective thinking, flexibility

- **Autonomy:** an internal locus of control, a strong sense of independence, power, self-esteem, self-discipline, and control of impulses

- **A sense of purpose and future:** healthy expectancies, goal directedness, orientation to the future, motivation to achieve, persistence, hopefulness, hardiness, belief in a bright and compelling future, a sense of anticipation, and a sense of coherence

It was learned that the greater the number of these attributes, the greater a person's capacity to be resilient and invincible—even in the midst of severe stress. Resiliency is the capacity to survive, to progress through difficulty, to bounce back, to move on positively again and again in life.

Take time out now and think of those times in your own life when you were somehow able to move through a difficult situation or period of time, when you were able to face the stress and bounce back because of your own resilient attributes.

The question is, How did you develop such resiliency? The studies tell us an abundance of "protective factors" must have surrounded you. Protective factors are the positive (or health-enhancing) behaviors and conditions within schools, families, and communities that supported the development of those resilient attributes within you.

A consistent set of protective factors in the immediate care-giving environments has been identified. These factors are listed in the chart below:

PROTECTIVE FACTORS

Family

- Develops close bonding with child

- Is nurturing and protective

- Uses a high warmth/low criticism parenting style (rather than authoritarian or permissive)

- Values and encourages education

- Manages stress well

- Spends quality time with children

- Has clear expectations

- Encourages supportive relationships with caring adults beyond the immediate family

- Shares family responsibilities

School

- Expresses positive expectations

- Encourages goal setting and mastery

- Encourages pro-social development (altruism and cooperation)

- Provides opportunities for leadership and participation

- Fosters active involvement for all students (whatever their learning style or capability)

- Trains teachers in cooperative learning

- Involves parents

- Staff views themselves as caring people

Community

- Provides opportunities for participation

- Involves youth in community service

- Provides supportive social networks

- Leaders prioritize community health, safety, and quality of life for families

- Provides access to resources (health care, housing, daycare, job training, employment, education, and recreation)

Bonnie Benard has summarized the protective factors into three helpful categories:

- **caring and support**
- **positive expectations**
- **active participation**

Learning about this research has been exciting because it indicates that the Tribes process is a good way for school communities to go about fostering resiliency in students. The Tribes process activates Benard's three categories. It promotes inclusion (caring), influence (participation and being valued by others), and community (positive expectations and support).

Resiliency is not a basic skill we can teach. It is what we do to change the human systems (families, schools, communities, peer groups, workplace) surrounding children. What better effort could schools and families work toward than to assure that all children in their care live within daily environments humming with an abundance of protective factors. Friends, it's the best way to give each and every child the capacity, the resiliency, he or she will need to meet inevitable life stress and to succeed in spite of it.

Everyone Creating the Learning Environment

Having a student-centered focus of human development and resiliency brings coherence to planning and the curricula of the school. Once all teachers, administrators, families, and community caregivers (the systems) appreciate the focus and learn some how-to-do-it knowledge, everyone can participate in creating healthy environments. School reform, restructuring, revitalizing...whatever we may call it, will not happen unless the systems determining children's development have a shared child-centered vision, and the courage to improve the systems themselves. Then, and only then, will the often quoted African saying "It takes the whole village to raise a child" become a reality in America.

AT THE HEART OF RESILIENCY ARE THE RELATIONSHIPS BETWEEN US

Defining the Basics for Today's Schools and Families

The human experience of

- Growing into ever-widening environments
- Being capable of interacting beyond "me" to "we," to community, to nation, to the world
- Having the resiliency to deal with it all

is what education can be all about. For the transactional model of human development to work well, all of the systems must communicate, collaborate, and cooperate. Not just schools alone, but all systems working toward their shared goal.

The more the school community understands and initiates many protective factors, the more it assures a positive future for all of the children within their care.

As one of the key systems, the school must examine its own environment, or climate. School climate is the spirit that prevails for teachers, students, administrators, resource people, and parents. It is the music underlying the words—an energy that either contributes to or inhibits learning. A positive classroom climate evolves out of

- An atmosphere of trust
- A sense of belonging and community
- Involvement in decision making
- Kindness and encouragement from peers
- The teacher's energy and morale
- The teacher's authenticity and nonjudgmental attitude
- Clear expectations, goals, learning outcomes
- Fairness and equity in participation

A positive climate is built through inclusion, sharing and caring, encouragement of participation, and high expectations for each and every child. In the same way, families need to zero in on these very same climate and protective factors. Everyone can finally learn to sing the same song.

The more the school community understands and initiates many protective factors, the more it assures a positive future for all of the children within their care.

"

Resiliency requires changing hearts and minds.[14]

—Bonnie Benard

"

Back to the Middleton Middle School Restructuring Committee

It's 7:30 P.M. Three weeks later.

Thelma Brown, parent chairperson: *"I am glad we took these extra weeks to define our student-centered human development approach, and to agree that over the next three years we all will work together to foster resiliency for each and every student. Tonight we will hear from our cooperative learning study committee."*

Tony Salvatore, parent: *"We're so excited. We not only discovered that we're on the right track, but that a lot can be brought about through cooperative learning—using small groups in classrooms."*

Trudy Armstrong, teacher: *"And we realize that we already have eight teachers trained and using a cooperative learning process called Tribes."*

Tony: *"You'll be as excited as we are, once you hear about the hundreds of studies verifying what can happen for students. John Pasquale and Les Aldridge put this chart together and want to tell you about it."*

John began the presentation by saying that the information comes from the work of Drs. David and Roger Johnson of the University of Minnesota, who have summarized more than 600 studies reporting the significant benefits of learning through cooperation.[15]

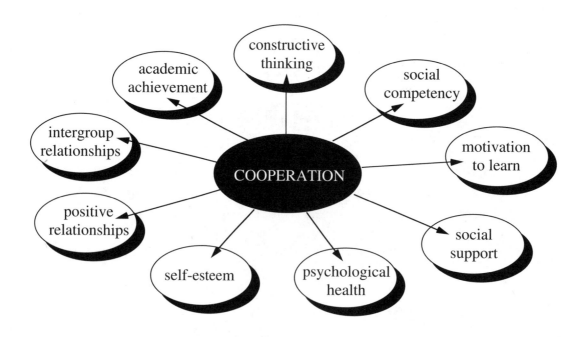

Benefits of Cooperation

The benefits of cooperation are

- **Greater productivity and academic achievement**

- **Constructive thinking skills:** planning, inferring, analyzing, gathering data, and strategizing

- **Social competency:** trust in others, perspective taking, sense of personal identity, awareness of interdependence, sense of direction and purpose

- **Motivation:** high expectations of success and achievement; high commitment and persistence

- **Social support:** constructive management of stress; high quality relationships that extend life and help people recover from illness

- **Psychological health:** the ability to develop, maintain, and improve one's relationships and situation in life; success in achieving goals

- **Self-esteem:** improved due to positive peer relations and to improved academic achievement

- **Positive interpersonal relationships:** acceptance of diversity; appreciation for peer contributions, skills, and efforts

- **Intergroup relationships:** caring concern; acceptance of multicultural diversity; commitment to the common good

These benefits are the healing components that build community and a caring democracy. We doubt that the many problems of youth—alienation, violence, drug abuse, gangs, school dropouts, suicide, delinquency, and despair—will ever lessen unless school, family, and community systems teach and model cooperation rather than competition. The isolated and alienated must be included, not excluded.

If you are trying to convince your school board, administrators, parents, or other teachers that cooperative learning works, we urge you to share the research on cooperative learning. Using the Tribes Learning Community (TLC) process not only can bring the benefits of cooperation to classrooms, but can introduce a new pattern of interaction into all groups of the school learning community.

The move to cooperative learning is an ever-growing phenomenon as more and more educators and parents realize that the learning environ-

"

Our work is not about a curriculum or a teaching method...it is about nurturing the human spirit with love.[18]

—Ron Miller

"

ment must change. Martin Wolins asserts that schools need an environment that is "reclaiming...one that creates changes that meet the needs of both the young person and society."[16] Bronfenbrenner calls for "a curriculum of caring."[17] The resiliency studies highlight environments of caring/sharing, participation, and high expectations. Tribes doesn't just suggest what a positive learning environment should be...it makes it happen!

The best journeys begin with a vision, a knapsack, and some friends. So call up a few friends and grab your backpacks. This tribal community journey meets kids in a new way in the next chapter.

3

How Children Learn

3
How Children Learn

The busyness taking place in Mrs. Johnson's 7th grade classroom this morning may at first look like a reenactment of Santa's workshop. Hearing the excitement, the principal has just slipped into the back of the room. Six groups of 7th graders are huddled together at tables filled with fascinating geometric designs. Some people in each group are measuring surface areas of the creations that people in their Tribes have made. Other pairs are estimating real-time construction costs. Architect workers are snipping, stapling, and taping posterboard together. The best surprise of all are the three people in one corner who are trying out a song they have written...a song about "Polyhedraville."

"Ah, Mrs. Johnson," the principal says, "is this the math lesson for today?" "Oh no," she answers, "Polyhedraville began three weeks ago, and it isn't just about math. Our theme is planning quality urban environments. The students have been designing a whole town...taking into consideration the many human, environmental, and facility needs. Each Tribe is working with budgets to design and construct their particular buildings for the town. The task depends upon each person creating a building and the tribes coming to a consensus on total costs for all of their buildings. Every person's creativity, participation, and skills are important. I'm the facilitator and the consultant on call as needed. The students are the ones planning the town and helping each other to learn."

What Mrs. Johnson Had to Learn

Two questions: First, What did Mrs. Johnson have to give up in order to teach this way? And second, What did she have to learn in order to involve and excite this class of typically bored 7th graders? This note from the *Wall Street Journal* addresses the question of what she had to give up:

> *"Across the curriculum, up and down the grade ladder, a new wave of teachers is casting out textbooks, cursing standardized tests, killing drills and preaching a new creed of student engagement."*—Wall Street Journal, *September 11, 1992.*[1]

She also had to give up

- Trying to pour standardized curriculum into the heads of nonstandardized students

- Talking endlessly except to ask for right answers

- Awarding just the kids who had the right answers

- Praising boys more than girls

- Having low expectations for students of different cultures

- Teaching subjects in unrelated boxes

- Wanting a quiet, orderly, straight-row classroom that she had to control all day long

To make her classroom come alive, Mrs. J. had to learn what thousands of other teachers are learning today:

- How to make classrooms student-centered rather than teacher-centered

- How to use cooperative learning methods

- How to reach and involve students of multiple learning styles

- How to create and sustain a positive learning environment

- How to design interactive learning experiences

Developing resiliency and the potential of all types of children in our schools cannot become a reality unless teachers learn to make the critical shift from 19th-century methods to those that are effective with 21st-century people. If we acknowledge that the force feeding of textbooks and seat time has failed for too many children who simply do not learn that way, then it is time to find out how young people do learn. Once we're clear about that, environments and methods that support the development of all kids—no matter their culture, race, gender, or way of learning—can become a reality within a school.

Moving from the Teacher-Centered Classroom

It all begins for many teachers when they just get tired of talking to apathetic students. One day Mrs. J. really saw her standardized self and was startled with the emotion she felt. She was lonely. There seemed to be an impenetrable wall between her and the beautiful people sitting in rows in front of her. She had been noticing the wall ever since her faculty heard a presentation by a Tribes TLC® trainer several weeks earlier. She saw and heard about this diagram.[2]

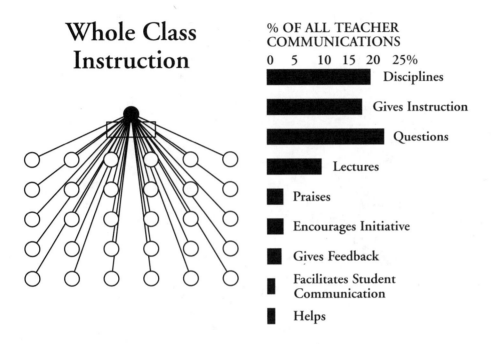

Whole Class Instruction

% OF ALL TEACHER COMMUNICATIONS

0   5   10   15   20   25%

- Disciplines
- Gives Instruction
- Questions
- Lectures
- Praises
- Encourages Initiative
- Gives Feedback
- Facilitates Student Communication
- Helps

Studies verify that when teachers depend upon "whole class instruction" they themselves talk more than two-thirds of the time, and more than 70% of their "teacher talk" is spent disciplining, lecturing, giving instructions, and asking questions. Students are expected to sit passively, to refrain from interaction with each other, and to listen to the teacher. When teachers use whole class instruction, only 30% of their time can be devoted to doing what the majority want to do...to praise, encourage initiative, give feedback, facilitate student communication, and help students.

Traditional class structures cause students to be competitive more than cooperative. The illusion is that since this traditional approach was effective one hundred years ago it will always be effective though today's students, born out of many cultures, learn in very different ways. The failure of American education should be proof enough that teacher-centered classes, standardized textbooks, and competition perpetuates educational mediocrity and too many failures. Of course, several popular motion pictures exhort teachers to become dramatic actors like Robin Williams in *Dead Poets Society*, or tough challengers like James Olmos in *Stand and Deliver*. True, some students may become motivated, but these "sage on the stage" models are also teacher-centered rather than student-centered. Missing is

- The transfer of responsibility to students themselves for their own learning

- A realistic way to help each student develop his or her own unique set of intelligences and gifts

- Opportunities for students to use inquiry, to construct meaning, and apply concepts learned

- A process to awaken each and every child to the joy of learning

The "teacher talk" approach ignores the fact that we are social creatures stimulated and motivated by social interaction...which, of course, is ruled out in traditional classrooms. What if students discovered that learning was truly an exciting process when people entered into it together? What if school was not about who could get the most A's in the class, but how we can help each other to

- Listen
- Generate creative ideas
- Resolve conflicts
- Stay on task
- Synthesize information
- Conceptualize a drama

- Write a song
- Set goals
- Figure out a formula
- Think through a complex problem
- Care and share

Think about it...what if?

Creating a Student-Centered Classroom

In contrast to the previous diagram, the same studies show that when classrooms are reorganized into student learning groups, "teacher talk" time lessens from 70% to 25%.[3]

Interactive Learning

Teacher as Facilitator

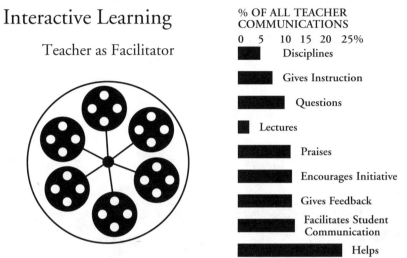

% OF ALL TEACHER COMMUNICATIONS

0 5 10 15 20 25%

Disciplines

Gives Instruction

Questions

Lectures

Praises

Encourages Initiative

Gives Feedback

Facilitates Student Communication

Helps

When students become responsible to each other, accountability for performance and behavior is shared by the students and the teacher. The wall between teacher and students melts away.

Then 75% of the teacher's time can be spent in praising, encouraging initiatives, giving feedback, facilitating student communication, and helping students. The transfer of responsibility to student groups for gathering information, interpreting, and applying it makes the dramatic difference. When students become responsible to each other, accountability for performance and behavior is shared by the students and the teacher. The wall between teacher and students melts away. This is not to say that teachers should never use the lecture/question format, but if it is not integrated with interactive group learning, eyes will glaze over again.

Once a teacher changes his or her role to that of a "facilitator," meaning "one who makes it easy," the classroom becomes alive. The image of the classroom changes from austere rows to something like this:

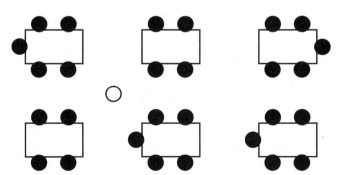

Tables often replace desks and desks become centered so that four or five students can face each other and work together. Altering the physical environment is step one toward making the classroom student-centered. Gradually, as cooperative learning tasks and much of the classroom management are transferred to students themselves, the teacher has time to encourage initiative, give feedback, facilitate student communication, suggest resources, help and praise students. Cooperation replaces competition and individualistic desk work, and the impressive, immense benefits of cooperation discussed in our last chapter become real for today's children.

Getting Beyond the One Right Answer

To switch from a teacher-centered classroom to student-centered learning, Mrs. Johnson also had to give up asking for the one right answer.

What grade are you teaching? Well, here's an interesting experiment to try. Someday, put a large dot on an empty chalkboard.

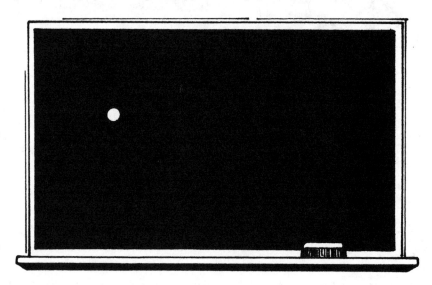

Then ask the class "What is it?" The book *A Whack on the Side of the Head* by Roger von Oech tells the story of a teacher of a sophomore English class who did this.[4] After she asked, "What is it?" the class just sat there and looked and looked in silence at the dot. Finally, someone said, "It's a chalk dot." The teacher looked rather sad and replied, "You know, I did this with a group of kindergarten children yesterday, and they said "It's an owl's eye, a cigar butt, a squashed egg, a pebble. They just went on and on." The important question is, What happened between the years of five to sixteen to kill expression and imagination?

Just think about the imprint of eleven school years—of being asked to repeat back or write down the right answer. The lecture/question format awards those who can call out right answers. And who wins? Right! The verbal/linguistic kids. The shy, low-self-image, and non-verbal learners lose. Gradually spontaneity and creativity, two qualities essential to our more complex, fast-moving information world, are killed off.

Stephen Schneider, MacArthur Award scientist, echoes our own concern:[5]

> *Creativity isn't simply learning the textbook. It is finding new ways to think and act...Somehow we have to get kids participating creatively in the process of their education. Because if they continue to think that truth comes only from the front of the room, and that learning is a product that can be standardized, we are going to end up with sheeplike, uninformed citizens who are not capable of conducting public debate on difficult issues. And that will leave the "solutions" to the spin doctors, advertisers, elites, and lobbyists.*

Instead of teaching kids to regurgitate right answers, teachers are learning to use open-ended questions, group brainstorming, student inquiry, and group investigation projects. They are cheering the diversity of ways that students within cooperative groups (tribes) handle a task or solve a problem.

Creating Equal Opportunities for All Students

Expression, creativity, self-image, and love of learning also are diminished between kindergarten and high school for students who are culturally different. Race, color, culture, gender, disabilities, and appearance all add up to being labeled and treated differently from the majority within a system. The pain of being called a name or ridiculed for being different is devastating. The exclusion of not being called on because you are not expected to have the "right answer" is damaging to self-image. The curriculum that does not accurately portray one's own culture or ignores it completely is an insult. The inner-city multi-ethnic or rural Native American school that still has a majority of white teachers models institutional racism.

Admittedly, the exclusion and perpetuation of inequity is often unconscious on the part of teachers. For instance, studies show that teachers call upon boys more than girls when many hands are waving in a classroom.[6] To gain attention, many boys not only wave a hand but jump up and down to be called upon. They are five times more likely to receive attention from teachers. They are eight times more likely to call out in class, except when the teacher is a woman, and then they are twelve times more likely to be speak out. Boys also receive more words of praise for responding. Boys out-talk girls in the classroom three to one. Jane Kahale, president of the National Association for Research in Science Teaching, refers to this behavior as "risk taking."[7] Whether negative or positive, risk taking gets teachers' attention. Why do we wonder that girls, who are not as active in risk taking, are far less likely to volunteer responses in class?

Generalizations and labels also sabotage learning. How often have you heard

   "You think like a girl."   "You're as wild as an Indian."

"You throw like a girl."   "He's just being a boy."

"Black kids have rhythm."   "Special Ed kids can't make it."

"Girls have trouble with   "The boys all have sloppy papers."
math; the boys do well."

Comparisons like "the girls are working harder than the boys" or "the Asians are smarter than the Latinos in math" not only are hurtful put-downs but pit one group against another. "We" versus "they," the "in group" and the "out group," the "jocks" and the "nerds." Different expectations for behavior, language, and academic performance sentence some groups to years of unfair treatment. Bias and inequity are devastating to children's development and learning. They promote hostility, alienation, poor school performance, failure, and despair.

Equal opportunity for learning must begin with a recognition that multiculturism is a national reality in the United States. At its best it not only includes the experiences of particular individuals and groups but fosters interconnectedness between groups for unified action on shared interests and concerns.

We're committed to equity for all students, but how do we go about implementing a gender equity/multicultural focus?

Once teachers begin to use the Tribes TLC® process, which promotes inclusion and deep respect for individual uniqueness and diversity, classrooms are well on the way to equity for all students. There is a fine article, "How can we make multicultural education effective?" in Chapter 7 of this book. It was written for you by Gail Whang, a teacher in a multicultural city school, and it tells her experience in using the Tribes TLC® process with her students.

You can also

- Awaken staff consciousness by having your faculty use the *Matrix for Achieving Equity in Classrooms.* See the next page.

- Arrange training for the staff on multicultural and equity issues.

- Make a plan that includes a review of current curricula and incorporates the five components suggested in Chapter 2, page 35, by Benard.

Giving Up Boxes for Integrated Themes

Creativity is also sabotaged all day long in American schools through the factory model system of keeping things in separate curriculum boxes. Fifty minutes for English, fifty for math, then political science, history, biology, etc., all in chunks interrupted by clanging bells. Whose needs does this procedure best serve? Right! The school system's need for control, standardization, and convenience.

Yet our challenge is to educate people to understand and solve multi-disciplinary problems crossing multicultural, multinational, and

Matrix for Achieving Equity in Classrooms

Use the following matrix to assess six forms of bias in a classroom or a school community. Strategies for reducing bias are included in each component.

	Linguistic Bias	Stereotyping	Invisibility/Exclusion	Unreality	Imbalance/Selectivity	Fragmentation/Isolation
What To Look For	Language which is dehumanizing or denies the existence of females or males; e.g. Japs, mankind.	Members of a group portrayed in one role or with one characteristic.	The lack of representation of a group.	Misinformation about a group, event or contribution.	Single interpretation of an issue, situation or conditions.	Separating contributions of females and ethnic groups from the mainstream.
Policy What To Do	Review policy for biased language.	Ensure nondiscriminatory discipline policy.	Recognize teaching performance which fosters equity.	Design proactive mission statement which corrects past bias.	Earmark money for equity classroom materials and training.	Design staff evaluations inclusive of equity criteria.
Instructional Strategies	Pluralize subjects to avoid a gender pronoun.	Encourage males and females to express a wide range of feelings responses and sensibilities.	Encourage contributions from females and ethnic minorities.	Discuss controversial topics of discrimination and prejudice.	Engage students in analyzing and debating an issue.	Call on students equitably. Use cooperative learning.
Curriculum Content	Set expectations for students to use non-sexist language.	Select readings that have the females and ethnic minorities in responsible, exciting leadership positions.	Have students count the numbers of male, female and ethnic group members to determine the proportion in relation to a population.	Engage students in conducting research.	Introduce collaborative ways to solve problems and make decisions.	Stress that learning is the result of collaborative efforts and contributions by many.
Management (School and Classroom)	Engage all members in noticing and correcting biased language.	Intervene when slurs or jokes are made at another's expense.	Nurture cooperation among males, females and ethnically diverse students.	Facilitate shared decision making.	Create a supportive climate for differing perspectives to be discussed.	Establish ways of integrating groups during free time.
Family and Community Involvement	Attend council meeting and have students present on the use of non-biased language in newspapers, on road signs, etc.	Invite nontraditional role models to teach a lesson on their area of specialization.	Provide students with shadowing opportunities.	Examine the history of discrimination within local laws and history.	Establish community advisory groups that are balanced by sex, ethnicity and disability.	Solicit volunteers from diverse groups to work with students.

"

To control and sort young people for the sake of institutional efficiency is to crush the human spirit.[7]

—Ron Miller

"

multirelational boundaries. Issues such as peace, toxic pollution, urban violence, equity employment for women and people of color, integrated community services, conversion of defense industries, and educational change are not box topics! They are themes requiring integration of the sciences, mathematics, history, biology, composition, and the capacity to access and interpret information. We spend years teaching students about the boxes and then wonder why they have trouble synthesizing the diverse contents of the boxes when they are finally out in this world of complex issues.

Mrs. Johnson's Polyhedraville project required student groups to investigate, research, discuss, and apply information from such subject areas as math, English, social science, science, and art. They were not only learning and applying subject area content, but living collaborative group skills of interdependence and individual accountability. Most important is the fact that each student got the clear message that they were needed and respected for their unique skills and contributions. The integration of curricula into themes has repeatedly been proven to energize student learning.

Throughout the last ten years we have appreciated the work of Susan Kovalik and her associates who are training teachers to move beyond textbooks developed by publishers from afar...to develop their own classroom curricula based on a unifying yearlong theme. Susan asserts that the selected theme must

- Have substance and real application to the world

- Have readily available resources

- Be age appropriate and meaningful to students

- Be worthy of time

- Flow from month to month and "back to center" (ongoing support of the concepts of the yearlong theme)[8]

- Have a title that is "kid grabbing" (You Can't Fool Mother Nature, The Time Bomb, Passport to Adventure, etc.)

One of the most exciting benefits is that the integration of disciplines into themes enhances the pattern-seeking operation of the brain, which in turn increases intelligence.

We urge schools interested in thematic instruction to use the ITI model. It is well researched, comprehensive, and in use in thousands of classrooms throughout the world. See Chapter 12, Resources.

Reaching Students Who Learn in Different Ways

Do you remember the story about the Animal School? It went something like this:

Once upon a time there was a school for animals. The teachers were certain it had a very comprehensive curriculum, but somehow all the animals were failing. The duck was the star in the class for swimming, but was flunking tree climbing. The monkey was great at tree climbing, but was getting F's in swimming. The chickens excelled in grain research, but disrupted the tree climbing class so much they were sent to the principal's office daily. The rabbits were sensational in running, but had to have private tutoring in swimming. Saddest of all were the turtles, who, after many diagnostic tests, were pronounced "developmentally disabled." Yes, they were sent to a special class in a remote gopher hole. The question is, Who were the real failures?

Like the animals in the story, each student is a unique creation...a person who has a different set of talents, intelligences, and ways of learning. It is time to take seriously the fact that the predominant focus of American education favors students who are adept in verbal and logical/mathematical skills and those ways of learning, but discourages those who have different innate intelligences. One might ask, All are not tree climbers, but are great swimmers or runners doomed to failure simply because they are in a system designed solely for a different type of animal?

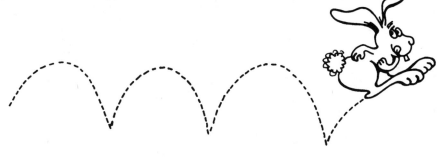

Nine Intelligences

The work of Howard Gardner and other scientists has identified nine intelligences that are common to all human beings and that vary in degree in each person. The multiple intelligences, ways of learning, and knowing, are as follows.[9]

Verbal/Linguistic
Thinks and learns through written and spoken words; has the ability to memorize facts, fill in workbooks, take written tests, and enjoy reading

Logical/Mathematical
Thinks deductively; deals with numbers and recognizes abstract patterns

Visual/Spatial
Thinks in and visualizes images and pictures; has the ability to create graphic designs and communicate with diagrams and graphics

Body/Kinesthetic
Learns through physical movement and body wisdom; has a sense of knowing through body memory

Musical/Rhythmic
Recognizes tonal patterns and environmental sounds; learns through rhyme, rhythm, and repetition

Interpersonal
Learns and operates one-to-one, through group relationships, and communication; also depends on all of the other intelligences

Intrapersonal
Enjoys and learns through self-reflection, metacognition, working alone; has an awareness of inner spiritual realities

Existential
Is concerned with ultimate life issues—love, death, philosophy
Learns in context with meaning

Naturalist
Loves nature and the out-of-doors
Enjoys classifying species—flora and fauna

Remarkably enough, only two of the nine intelligences, verbal/ linguistic and logical/mathematical, are developed in the majority of schools in the Western world. However, before our children enter school, they are usually busy developing the other intelligences. As a result, school can make many feel inadequate as they struggle to deal with the two less familiar intelligences. Their active, physical, rhythmic, imaginative, and relational selves must be anesthetized during school hours. This applies all the way through school for children coming from other than Western Caucasian cultures, namely: Native Americans, Asians, and Latino, Hispanic, and Black populations.

In infancy and early childhood children begin learning through what Gardner calls "raw patterning" to perform simple tasks as the foundation of a given intelligence. Walking, running, and jumping are the basics of body/kinesthetic intelligence; just as learning the alphabet is basic to verbal/linguistic intelligence. As children grow they move to greater levels of pattern complexity called "symbol systems," in which they may develop the ability to draw various shapes (visual/spatial intelligence) or make different tones (musical/rhythmic). Each intelligence has its own "notational language" that not only can be taught and can also be learned by others, but can also be recorded in some form, such as a musical composition (musical/rhythmic) or an understanding of group process (logical/mathematical). Finally, a stage is reached (generally in the secondary or college years) where an intelligence evolves into a "vocational or avocational" career path.

David Lazear writes:

> If we provide students the opportunity to develop the full range of their intellectual capacities and teach them how to use their multiple ways of knowing in the learning task, they will learn the things we are trying to teach more thoroughly than if we only permit them to learn in the more traditional verbal/linguistic and logical/mathematical ways.[10]

Lynn Stoddard, author of the very fine book *Redesigning Education: A Guide for Developing Human Greatness,* deplores the fact that "our fixation on curriculum development instead of human development is the enormous dam blocking educational reform."[11] It has caused us to ignore the work of those who reveal the individuality of human nature, how young (and even older) brains work, and how children learn. Moreover, the discovery and development of each child's intelligences and gifts go unattended. In Chapter 8 we will revisit the multiple intelligences and look at many ways to support the development of all of the intelligences in students.

From a Teacher's View

· · · · · ·

Jill Hay, M.Ed.

is the Elementary Education Specialist with the Bethel School District in Spanaway, Washington. As a certified Tribes TLC® Trainer and Special Education administrator, Jill enjoys taking the time to share how she utilizes the process of Tribes for inclusion and community building with staff and students.

Patty Harrington

has been an educator for 20 years. She is a certified Tribes TLC® Trainer and Susan Kovalik associate. Patty trains teachers thoughout the U.S. and Europe in both programs. She believes Tribes is a way of life and is essential for the bodybrain compatible learning environment for children and adults.

How Does Tribes Support Brain Compatible Learning?

It comes as a shock to be told that there is a new epidemic among too many children of the world today. An inestimable number of children are suffering physical brain damage from bad life experiences. The symptoms include aggression, language failure, depression, asthma, epilepsy, high blood pressure, immune system dysfunction and diabetes. The symptoms are generated by poverty, violence, sexual abuse, family break-up, neglect, drugs, lack of good stimulation and too much of the wrong stimulation. Studies on how the human brain functions report that severe conditions and experiences can, in time, organize the trillions of constantly active connections between the brain cells into *diseased networks*.[12] We need not deplore, *"We can do nothing,"* because at this same time research on how the bodybrain learns is providing exciting direction to educators and parents.

New approaches for teaching are referred to as *bodybrain compatible learning and bodymind based education* by noted educators Susan Kovalik, Eric Jensen[13] and Renate and Geoffrey Caine[14]. All agree that one of the most important things educators can do is to create caring classroom and school environments, places of learning that the bodybrain perceives as non-threatening and capable of nurturing reflective

thinking. By understanding a bit about how the bodybrain works we will know why the Tribes Learning Community process is respected as an effective approach.

The body and brain work in an inseparable partnership (of course!) to the ultimate goal of survival. Sensory information is gathered through our eyes, nose, mouth, ears, skin, hands, feet and more. As the bodybrain processes that information it has two possible pathways for reaction. When there is no sense of danger, information travels on a slow pathway to the thalamus (sensory relay station), the hippocampus (learning and memory) and then to the cerebral cortex (rational thinking and long term memory).

A sense of imminent danger sends data on a fast pathway to trigger

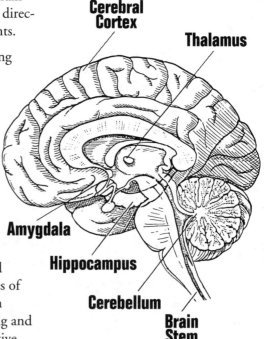

mechanisms for survival. The sensory input travels directly to the thalamus which sends immediate input to the amygdala (center of all fear, threat and passion), hypothalamus (internal regulator), pituitary gland and adrenal gland. These glands release cortisol, a stress hormone, that rapidly moves thoughout the body and brain via the bloodstream and activates fight or flight behaviors. The "hijacking" of the rational cerebral cortex destroys emotional balance in the situation. In heated moments of anger a person usually regrets what was said or done only moments after the incident. With persistent stress, cortisol can be devastating to the hippocampus, which regulates the memory system. It is no wonder that Eric Jensen, author of *Teaching with the Brain in Mind,* states that excess stress and threat in the school environment may be the single greatest contributor to impaired academic learning. He also considers poor student relationships as a salient stressor. We need to provide our students with places of learning that the brain perceives as non-threatening.

It is through an awareness of our students' emotions and needs that we are able to be effective educators. Cortisol produced through stress can be neutralized by positive and empowering experiences. The caring community Tribes process allows students to reflect and "cool down."

Most of us are aware that exercise and movement decrease stress. A part of bodybrain compatible learning includes movement through energizers and other active teaching strategies. The body produces chemicals that enhance learning and memory when we move, laugh and even talk.

The stunning research on how the brain functions and learns helps us to understand why the Tribes Learning Community process is such a timely approach for addressing the emotional well being of America's children. Whenever the Tribes agreements of mutual respect, appreciation, listening and no put-downs are utilized in a classroom, a safe emotional place in which to learn is created. The kindness of peers to each other supports the development of social/interpersonal skills, enabling students to deal with the challenges in their daily and future lives. Today, there is an urgent need for a new way of learning and being together in the thousands of classrooms across this country. The goal of each teacher and school is to raise student achievement. The main culprit is stress. Tribes provides the antidote by giving teachers ways to enhance students' sense of self worth within a caring community. Join us in meeting the challenge by creating brain compatible classrooms in your school...through the Tribes process.

Creating a Positive Learning Environment

No, our friend Mrs. Johnson didn't just start Polyhedraville out of the blue the first week of school. First she and her students created a Tribes TLC® (Tribes Learning Community) environment in the classroom. She knew that learning is a social phenomenon and that people not only had to know each other before working on tasks, but had to feel valued for the unique contributions they brought to their tribes and to the class.

So...Mrs. J. bought some books and attended Tribes TLC® training with teachers of her school, and together they began to focus on developing the gifts of each and every student in their school. Sounds complex? Not really. How they did it and how you can transform your classroom and school community is the content of the rest of this book.

Are you ready? Great! Grab your backpack again...we're heading down the Tribes trail!

4
What Tribes Are
and How They Work

4

What Tribes Are and How They Work

A Native American teacher, Paula Swift Robin, is talking with four other teachers during a luncheon conference in eastern Washington. "What is the most exciting thing you are doing in your classroom?" asks one of her new friends. Paula leans forward excitedly. "You'll never believe the gift that came my way. Two years ago I went to the annual used book sale at our town library. As I looked around, my eye was attracted to a worn book called Tribes. *Must be about Native Americans, I said to myself. It was on the ten-cent table. What could I lose for ten cents? I bought it along with some other books and took it home. Surprise! It's about using small groups, called tribes, as a way to involve kids themselves to help each other learn, to feel good about themselves, and learn to enjoy learning. Just what our kids need, I said to myself. Well, I followed through the chapters each day and started building tribes. Our students took to it right away, and we wove in studies about our Native American tribes throughout the year. It's made amazing changes for our kids. It's the caring and challenge they long for...a lot like the closeness that our own people have depended upon throughout time."*

Yes, this is a true story. What Paula didn't realize was that the teacher at the table who kept beaming a big smile back at her while she talked was also a Tribes TLC® Trainer.

When looking for a classroom program that was culturally compatible with First Nation beliefs and values, Tribes was recommended. It surpassed our expectations. Tribes honours the sacred circle in which all people come together. The influence of First Nation beliefs is seen throughout the philosophy, norms and activities. Tribes has helped us teach the children how to be kind. It has helped the children own their responsibilities. It is helping us to talk and listen to one another, as the old ones still do.

Laura Horton
Native Student Retention Coordinator
Fort Frances-Rainy River
Board of Education
Ontario, Canada

About Calling the Process "Tribes"

At times our Native American friends have asked why this interactive learning process is called Tribes. It's hard to remember exactly when it happened. Throughout the years people who experienced the caring, community-building process kept saying, "This is like being in a family...not a team but a tribe." People appreciated the social support, the respect for individual differences, and the sense of belonging that native tribes seem to have. The word "team" never fit because it denoted competition. "Tribes" symbolized the affection and caring that so many of us in Western society long for today.

Richard Burrill, author and anthropologist, has graciously written the paragraph on the next page to give a perspective on the cultural values of tribes, not only for Native Americans but for indigenous peoples since the beginning of time.

The Meaning of Tribes to Indigenous Peoples
By Richard Burrill

Many Native Americans today are experiencing a rebirth as tribal peoples. They realize that they carry insights and virtues that urbanized, industrial civilizations have allowed to fall to the wayside. They honor the Old Ways belief that human beings, animals, plants, and the earth elements are all part of the same one; all part of an interdependent web of life. "Family" includes the land and all living things. It is their way of organizing a caring society.

Consider how, according to the Old Ways, a tribe's members are linked to the land, to the animals, and to each other. "We are all one family," says story-philosopher Grizzly Bear Heart. "We know our place is to protect the web by being guardians of the Great Round House in the sky, our planet Earth. People are not favored over the animals. Animals are not favored over the trees and plants."

In contrast, modern Westerners feel separated from the natural world with their notion that only "We are gods," and the rest of nature is not. Modern science touted humankind as masters of nature, that the people's place is to make nature produce. Focus turned to class ranking, and individuals became servants to the wants of the empire. In modern society, things are the valuables. In tribal societies, people are valuable. Human beings who are the protectors of the land walk in balance. Human beings who live to exploit the land walk out of balance. As far as making the modern world a better place, reclaiming ourselves as earth people, as opposed to empire people, cannot happen fast enough.

Richard Burrill, M.A., is the author of the new book Protectors of the Land: Teachings of the California Indians, *as well as* Ishi, River of Sorrows, *the* Human Almanac *and other books of anthropological significance. He leads groups in cooperative games and songs, and sports workshops that build self-worth and community. Richard's counsel on multicultural education and human development is deeply valued by the author of this book.*

The Tribes Agreements–
A New Way of Being Together

Building the positive environment for a Tribes Learning Community, whether in a small group, a classroom, staff of whole school begins by replacing unspoken norms of the school with explicit positive agreements. All groups and organizations have tacit norms that affect behavior by conveying "this is how we do things around here." In a dispassionate impersonal school the norms may be:

Nobody listens anyway   The more put-downs the more fun

No one respects me or my things   Don't ask for help!

Never let on how you feel!   Appreciation—what's that?

There is no way to support, let alone reach and teach any age group of children, when negative norms are operant every hour of every day throughout a school.

Admonitions by teachers and attempts of outer control do not stop relational abuse. We have to engage students themselves to agree upon kinder new rules–agreements that they make and monitor with each other. Inherent in our goal of adolescent development is the encouragement of self-responsibility and the internalization of ethical social principles. It begins by transferring the responsibility of students to help each other live caring social agreements. It becomes intrinsic in behavior when kids' hearts as well as heads come to appreciate and commit to a better way of being with peers and others. The four agreements are:

1. **Attentive Listening:** To pay close attention to one another's expression of ideas, opinions and feelings; to check for under standing; and to let others know that they have been heard

2. **Appreciation/No Put-Downs:** To treat others kindly; to state appreciation for unique qualities, gifts, skills and contributions; to avoid negative remarks, name-calling, hurtful gestures and behaviors

3. **Right to Pass:** To have the right to choose when and to what extent one will participate in a group activity; to observe quietly if not participating actively; and to choose whether to offer observations later to a group when asked to do so

4. **Mutual Respect:** To affirm the value and uniqueness of each person; to recognize and appreciate individual and cultural differences; and offer feedback that encourages growth

Some schools or classes may want to add additional agreements beyond the four. For example, schools concerned with student violence have elaborated on the second and fourth agreements. Treat people as you want to be treated/no hitting or violence. It is important, however, that the list isn't longer than five agreements or students will be more likely to forget or overlook them and not reinforce them with each other.

Tribes agreements are very important and need to be posted in prominent places in classrooms and throughout the school. One dedicated leader, a bus driver of a Navaho reservation school, has the four agreements on the steps going up into his bus. He smiles and says now he is enjoying his riders, they all have a "new way of being" on the bus. The riders, of course, are the "agreement enforcers." Through practice and monitoring, and many strategies in classroom community circles, the new way or better way of being together begins to happen. Whenever the tribes begin work together, the teacher not only reminds everyone of the Tribes agreements again, but transfers the responsibility to the tribes to maintain them. Transforming the classroom or school into a positive, caring learning climate is dependent upon everyone internalizing these positive agreements.

A major difference between Tribes and some of the other classroom group methods is that people maintain membership in the same group for an extended period of time. This is based on research indicating that[1]

- People perform better on learning tasks when they are members of "high cohesion" rather than "low cohesion" groups

- Students who feel comfortable with their peers utilize their academic abilities more fully than those who do not

The difference between using randomly organized task groups and creating on-going tribes looks something like this:

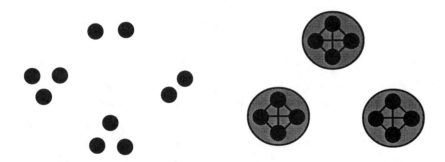

Random Learning Groups   **The Tribes Learning Community**

Random groupings produce a scattered energy, and since they do not provide ongoing inclusion (trust, safety, and a sense of belonging), it is more difficult for students to work together. The system of long-term membership in the Tribes process assures support for all members within each small group and within the classroom. This **intentionally created environment** supports development and achievement for students of all abilities.

Stages of Group Development:
The Tribes Trail

The strange map on the following page is one of the main secrets to the magic that happens in Tribes. OK, we know you think our map looks more like the cross-section of a gopher-infested garden! It really is our attempt to detail the important synchronization that takes place between the teacher-facilitator and the development of small groups. The success of any group's life together and the individual achievements its members can make depend upon the teacher-facilitator's knowledge and ability to orchestrate activities appropriate to the group's particular stage of development. It strikes us as sad that though all living takes place in groups, we seldom are taught how to make groups work well together. Families, labor unions, churches, parent-teacher associations, management staffs, faculties and classrooms...all are in search of positive participation and a reliable democratic process.

*"The meeting will come to order. Tonight's agenda was mailed to you. The secretary will read the minutes. The executive committee **has decided** that all members will..."*

Ignorant of any group development process, a majority of organizations struggle in limbo somewhere between the Great Man theory of leadership and democratic process, waving Robert's Rules of Order to maintain control. As a member, you may never feel as involved as the leaders are. You may wonder why you are there at all, and how the group will ever really know what unique talents, skills, or resources you have to contribute. YOU, the real special "you," are seldom invited to express your expectations or opinions and may never become a possible resource to the organization. In time your interest wanes and you drift onward, hoping for more recognition, support, and a way to make a contribution in some other group.

The reason that people become drop-outs—whether from their families, staff, organization, or for that matter from other relationships is because they do not feel **included** and **of value** to the others. Paid employees (yes, even teachers and administrators) also manage to drop out, but in subtle ways, such as not following through on responsibilities, taking leave days, sabotaging a department's plans, caucusing with other disgruntled peers, manipulating meetings, or being apathetic. Students drop out by gradually moving to "flight or fight." Apathy, boredom, lack of participation, shyness, absenteeism, inability to complete tasks are some of the ways of taking flight. Those that fight, or initiate behaviors (such as teasing, hitting, stealing, using foul language, etc.), are delivering the same message: **"I don't feel included ...nobody cares about me."** Few leaders are aware of a basic principle:

If a person does not feel included, he/she will create his or her own inclusion by grabbing influence—attracting attention, creating a controversy, demanding power, or withdrawing into a passive belligerence.

"

When one has no stake in the way things are, when one's needs or opinions are provided no forum, when on sees oneself as the object of unilateral actions, it takes no particular wisdom to suggest one would rather be elsewhere.

—Seymour Sarason

"

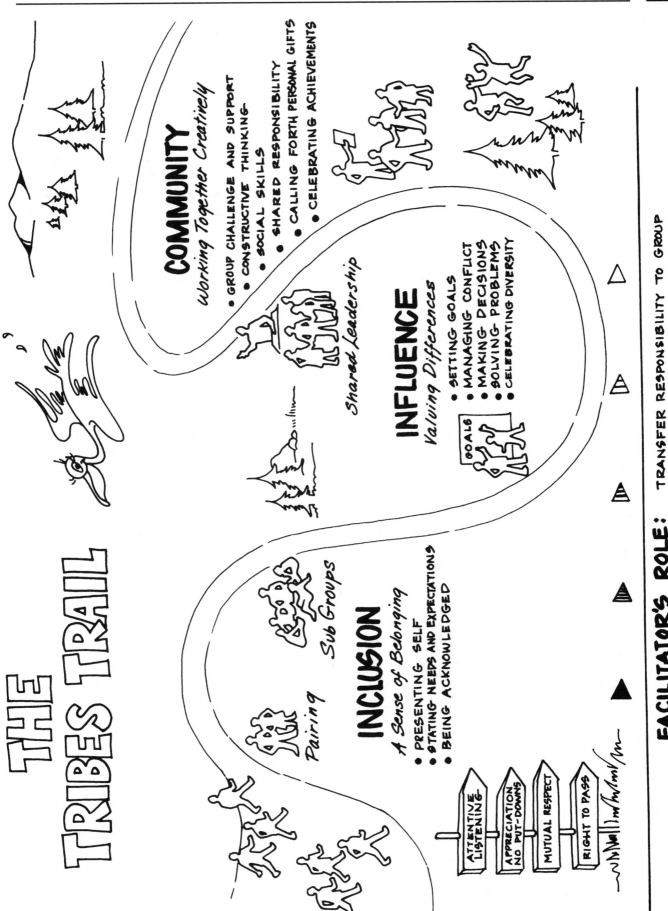

THE TRIBES TRAIL

COMMUNITY
Working Together Creatively
- GROUP CHALLENGE AND SUPPORT
- CONSTRUCTIVE THINKING
- SOCIAL SKILLS
- SHARED RESPONSIBILITY
- CALLING FORTH PERSONAL GIFTS
- CELEBRATING ACHIEVEMENTS

Shared Leadership

INFLUENCE
Valuing Differences
- SETTING GOALS
- MANAGING CONFLICT
- MAKING DECISIONS
- SOLVING PROBLEMS
- CELEBRATING DIVERSITY

GOALS

Sub Groups

Pairing

INCLUSION
A Sense of Belonging
- PRESENTING SELF
- STATING NEEDS AND EXPECTATIONS
- BEING ACKNOWLEDGED

ATTENTIVE LISTENING

APPRECIATION NO PUT-DOWNS

MUTUAL RESPECT

RIGHT TO PASS

FACILITATOR'S ROLE: TRANSFER RESPONSIBILITY TO GROUP

This organizational **dis-ease** is a veritable plague in any system still managed through top-down authoritarian methods that only provide inclusion and influence for the manager, principal, boss, or leader. Negatively outspoken teachers on the faculty or strident parents in the P.T.A. need to feel included and, lacking that, seek undue influence. We need to get past thinking of individual student behavior problems as hopeless, uncontrollable, or pathological. The majority are in need of inclusion and affection from teachers, family, and peers. **If school and family systems can learn how to help all kids feel included and of value to significant others in their lives**, one of this country's major concerns, anti-social youth behavior, will be turned around.

All guides taking people into a wilderness need a map so that the community of people traveling together arrives at their hoped-for destination. As a classroom group facilitator, it is essential that you understand some simple stages of group development and the major issues that are bound to arise as your students learn to work well in groups.

The Tribes Trail Map

The Tribes Trail Map illustrates the sequential stages of group development that you, the teacher-facilitator, will lead your flock through. Notice the bottom line. It shows a gradual shift in your role from being directive, providing much structure, to becoming less directive and transferring leadership to tribes within the community. After initial activities that develop inclusion for everyone in classroom tribes, you will be encouraging students to assume leadership in their tribes and within the classroom. The net effect of this subtle process is that responsibility is transferred to students themselves. This is why the Tribes process is known as one that calls forth the potential talents and resources of group members. This provides the learning community or organization with a multiplicity of resources, and enables tasks to be accomplished by all in satisfying and creative ways.

It is this intentional transfer of leadership in the midst of a positive and caring environment that makes the Tribes program different from other cooperative learning methods. This transfer, this calling forth, is the big secret to building self-worth and motivation among people. No matter what the age level, it gives a loud and clear message—you are capable people who can indeed manage yourselves and help each other!

The Stage of Inclusion

Now let's look a bit closer at how this works. Notice on the Tribes Trail Map the separate individuals coming into a classroom, or into a staff or organization's meeting. As mentioned earlier, the scale at the bottom of the map indicates the degree of structuring that the leader, or teacher-facilitator, needs to provide for people as they come from their many separate paths. Each person entering the group is unique in his/her life experience and perceives the new classroom situation or meeting out of a personal complex of diverse needs and expectations. All newcomers to any group feel an initial anxiety and have many unspoken questions:

- I wonder if I'll like this classroom?

- Will the teacher and other kids like me?

- How will they get to know me? I feel scared.

- Why am I nervous?

- What will we be doing?

- I wish this were the end of the day, not the beginning.

Knowing this, your responsibility is to live up to the name "facilitator," which means "one who makes it easy." If people stay immersed in these initial anxieties, they cannot learn and in time will demonstrate acting-out or dropping-out behaviors. Remember how the brain works? In fear or anxiety, the brain downshifts into a lower state and is not available to reason or learn. Immersed in anxiety, students will take to their own comfort zones...which may not be positive for either themselves or others. A student may simply show restlessness, shuffle papers, get a stomach ache, or in time become regarded as one more learning disability. A teacher who never feels comfortable in her faculty may be inattentive at meetings, irritable with students, and simply suffer through to the end of the year.

Tribes is a process...

the music for all

of the words!

INCLUSION

In order to have **inclusion**, three opportunities must be provided:

1. Each person needs to be able to **introduce herself,** not just by stating a name but offering a short description of her feelings, interests, resources, talents, or special qualities.

2. Each person needs to be able to **express his hopes or expectations for** what will happen during the group's time together.

3. Each person needs to **be acknowledged** by the group as having been heard, appreciated, and welcomed.

In a classroom it may take several days or weeks for all students to present themselves to the total class or within a small group. In organizational settings (like faculty meetings), initial **inclusion** means gaining adequate recognition and the same opportunity to present oneself prior

Invite the pelican that soars over the Tribes Trail to be your constant companion. Her name is Reflection. She will tell you, rather immodestly, that she makes the Tribes process work well anywhere. At times, you will want to ignore her calls: "timeout," "stop the action, teacher," "time to reflect," or "what's happening now?" Reflection knows that if you watch from the bird's eye view, classroom management goes more smoothly. Reflection is a wise bird who can describe just what she saw or heard while people worked together. You will find her questions on the pages of every Tribes strategy. Reflection clears up confusion and helps everyone soar to greater heights.

to tasks and agendas. It means **balancing persons and tasks**. This is what makes the big difference in how people finally are able to work together.

As soon as possible the facilitator begins to model and discuss the basic four agreements that make the Tribes process work well. By having people first meet in small temporary groupings (pairs or triads), initial anxiety is alleviated and inclusion begins to happen. Observe any organization of more than six people. People very naturally sub-group or arrive at a meeting with one or two others in order to feel less anxious. The intentional use of small temporary groups (sometimes called "trial tribes") early in a meeting makes it easier for all to feel included at least with a few others before relating to a larger group of people. Using our process, leaders of large conferences sub-group hundreds of people early in the gathering just to guarantee that no one is isolated. Agenda items can even be submitted from all of the small groups in order to include everyone's expectations.

Inclusion is a basic human need, and unless it is met people feel vulnerable and defensive. The saying "a camel is a horse designed by a committee" most certainly refers to a committee whose members attempted to undertake a task without first having achieved inclusion together. Time spent up front, building inclusion and trust is the most valuable commitment a group can make. Although it takes a bit longer at first, the pay-off in achievement makes all the difference!

The Stage of Influence

As mellow as the stage of inclusion can be, in time a very natural restlessness will be seen throughout the community. The restlessness is a good sign, because it means people do feel included and are ready to work together. You will begin to notice that

- Members are taking more initiative and speaking up to you; they may be making suggestions, asking confronting questions, and even criticizing the current leadership

- People are discussing or questioning group goals, ways to work together, and how decisions are being made

- People are not being as polite or as patient with each other

- Conflicts are beginning to arise

Rather than panic and decide that groups just don't work, recognize these indicators as positive signals. The new restlessness means that the time spent in building inclusion, trust, kindness, and a sense of belonging has been achieved. People are now ready to really work on tasks together...the stage of influence has arrived. Congratulations!

The **influence stage** centers on these questions:

- How can each person influence the goals, tasks, and decision-making process of the group?

- How can members assert their individuality and value in the midst of the group?

- How can leadership be shared so that the resource and potential of each member is called forth?

To feel "of influence" is to feel of value (worth, power, individual resource to the group). To the extent that each person does not feel important in a classroom or organization, commitment and motivation decrease.

To feel "of influence"

is to feel of value.

INFLUENCE

Rather than allowing group members to wrestle for ways to have influence, the skilled facilitator provides a selection of strategies that help people to

- Express diverse attitudes, opinions, positions, and personal feelings

- Put forth ideas without others passing judgment; help people to respect individual differences

- Use participatory methods for decision making so that all members feel they are influential and of value to the group

- Help members share leadership responsibility

The role of the teacher-facilitator is also to provide methods for resolving the inevitable different issues and concerns. Conflicts and misunderstandings are a natural part, a vital dynamic, of the process and cannot be ignored. They can be resolved through a variety of strategies, such as

- Reflecting on and discussing the incident or situation that is happening

- Helping people to state their feelings clearly

- Assisting the group to give constructive feedback

- Facilitating problem-solving methods

- Role-playing, using role-reversal techniques

- Negotiating the priorities of individual members

If issues are ignored, the energy of the group is deflected away from its capacity to accomplish tasks together!

The sensitive classroom teacher recognizes that continuing to focus on subject matter in the midst of interpersonal or group issues is neither academically nor emotionally helpful. Having people meet in their tribes to resolve a disruptive issue not only transfers responsibility to the class, but promotes a sense of value for the students. Once the conflict has been resolved by students, people will go back to their work on tasks with renewed energy.

During the **influence stage** the facilitator supports the tribes to work as much as possible on their own. Maintain contact with the groups by requesting periodic reports and circulating among the tribes to determine whether assistance is needed. If the facilitator sits down within a group, the dynamic changes immediately. Group members will once again center on the teacher and cease to participate with each other. As the influence stage progresses and issues become resolved, shared leadership begins to emerge from group members. What a delight it is to see the shy child of the class lead an activity in her tribe! And what a relief it is to see the dominant member sit back as the others in the tribe demonstrate their unique skills and talents. Some folks have called the Tribes process **magic**...but we call it a reality that can be achieved by any committed teacher.

The Stage of Community

Who does not long for a sense of community in the midst of a city, an organization, a staff, a school, the classroom...the impersonal crowd? The deep human longing is our need to be known, to belong, to care and be cared for. Community is the esprit that happens when many minds and hearts come together to work toward a common good. Community happens through inclusion and the appreciation of individual differences. One can tell when community has become a reality. It is the delightful surprise one day that those we are with (no matter what the difference in age, gender, race, culture, intelligence, or talent) are indispensable and beautiful.

The possibility for community, whether in a classroom, school, or any organization, depends upon the assumption that interdependence and connection to others is key to human development, learning, and the accomplishment of task.

> "
>
> *You will know that you are in a community if you often hear laughter and singing. You will know you are in an institution or bureaucracy if you hear the silence of long halls and the intonations of formal meetings.*
>
> —John McKnight
>
> "

FIVE INDICATORS OF COMMUNITY

John McKnight, author, points out five indicators:[2]

Capacity: Communities are built upon recognizing the whole depth, the strengths, weaknesses, the unique capacities of each member.

Collective Effort: They share responsibility to achieve goals for the common good, and engage the diversity of individual talents and skills to do so.

Informality: Transactions of value are based on consideration; care and affection take place spontaneously.

Stories: Reflection upon individual and community experiences provide knowledge about truth, relationships, and future direction.

Celebration: Activities incorporate celebration, parties, and social events. The line between work and play is blurred as people enjoy both at once.

At this point in the Tribes process, the classroom, faculty, or school community needs to ask itself the following:

- How well do we know the unique strengths and weakness of each of our members?

- Do we share responsibility for accomplishing goals for the good of the whole community using our diverse talents and skills?

- Are we freely expressing our caring and consideration for one another?

- Do we take time to tell stories and reflect on our experiences together?

- Do we laugh, play, and enjoy each other as we create new approaches or solve old problems together?

- How well do we recognize contributions and celebrate our community accomplishments and shared traditions?

The caring community we long for doesn't just happen; it can be intentionally developed. It depends upon any group of people deliberately creating *inclusion* for all members, and working through the nitty-gritty issues of *influence*.

COMMUNITY

Creating community requires

• Dedication to resolving rather than avoiding uncomfortable problems and conflicts that begin to separate members

• Learning and practicing the skills that enable collaboration

• Agreements about how we will treat each other

• Time to reflect on how well we are doing

Once a group has gone through adversity together, its members become filled with confidence that they can handle whatever comes their way. This is the path to resilient relationships, creativity and outstanding results!

The Spiral of Renewal

Each time the members of a learning community or classroom tribe come together they need some type of inclusion activity before they begin to focus on task; and influence issues will always need to be addressed. A helpful way of visualizing the continuing growth and evolution of a tribe is to imagine an ascending spiral that moves up through the levels of inclusion, influence, and community as it rises. One full "loop" represents a group meeting, so that each time the spiral completes a cycle it goes through the three stages again. But each time a tribe meets, though it still needs to begin with inclusion, it moves on to a slightly higher level of positive interaction. The spiral is continuous and a never-ending process. Graphically, it looks something like this:

The repeated sequence of inclusion, influence, and community enables the group to experience increasingly more profound interaction the longer they are together.

Although we have been experimenting and evaluating this process for many years, there is still so much to learn. It is gratifying to hear students, teachers, administrators, and parents say that they emerged a bit more **special in their own self-worth** because they had the opportunity to be part of a tribe somewhere. It does take a commitment and time to integrate the Tribes cooperative learning process into a classroom or school community, but a surprising array of benefits do come about whenever **inclusion** leads the way.

5

Creating the Learning Community

5

Creating the Learning Community

Here they come! Twenty-six 3rd, 4th, and 5th graders are entering their classroom this snowy day in November. Teacher Brad Allen observes the chaos as hats, coats, gloves, and boots find their way to shelves and racks. Every snowy day Brad wonders again why he didn't take that job in the sunshine of San Diego, and the same answer keeps coming back to him: It's these kids...this bunch of kids from this community. One by one the waiting circle of chairs is filled. The 5th graders, who have had two years with Brad, are helpful with the younger 3rd graders. They keep the positive energy going. "There's hardly a put-down anymore, no teasing, pushing, or shoving," Brad muses. He raises his hand, and one by one people raise their hands and the chatter stops. "Good morning and congratulations," Brad says. "We're all here in spite of the storm. To build our community inclusion today, let's go around the circle and share anything amusing, crazy, or special that happened to you this morning. We'll just do one-sentence stories so that everyone has a turn. Remember, you have the right to pass if you would rather not share at all." One by one people begin to speak:

"I found my lost skateboard under a bush when my dad and I were shoveling a path to our car this morning."

"My grandma came out and out-shoveled my mom."

"I brought that pulley that our tribe needs for our project."

"I dropped my lunch in a snowdrift and found it except for one banana."

"I got to wear my brother's boots today."

A few say they would like to pass. No one pressures them to participate. Everyone is listening attentively to those who do share. Brad nods, comments, and laughs now and then. The day has begun.

Why is this community circle so important each morning, each day? Brad Allen would say there are three big reasons:

- I want to help these students make a transition from whatever has gone on in their lives outside of school to the classroom.

- I want to have them feel included in the classroom community before working on tasks.

- I want to involve them in creating and sustaining a positive learning environment.

The Community Circle

The special spirit of community doesn't just happen in a classroom or organization by having people work in small groups, or by using randomly selected cooperative learning activities. Building community is a deliberate process that a teacher or leader facilitates over a period of time. It begins by creating inclusion for every person within the intended learning community and by practicing the set of positive Tribes agreements:

- Attentive listening

- Appreciation/No put-downs

- Right to pass

- Mutual respect

It takes several weeks for all students within a new class to be able to know everyone else. The purpose of the time is to give students many opportunities to present themselves in positive ways. During this time, the teacher not only will be selecting many of the Tribes inclusion strategies from this book, but will be teaching collaborative social skills and engaging students in honoring agreements. She will also be modeling the skills and agreements.

Experienced Tribes teachers may have students meet several times each day in a community circle for sharing, discussions on curricula, learning collaborative skills, reflecting on the day, and celebrating.

The daily community circle is step one in implementing the essential protective factors that foster resiliency: caring and sharing, participation, and positive expectations.

At the same time that a teacher begins to help students become familiar with the community circle process, he also begins to have people get together in pairs, triads, and groups of four or five, as an additional way to promote inclusion and to begin working together on academic topics.

Inclusion example: *"Find two people you still do not know very well and for five minutes share your favorite summer outdoor activity."*

"

When I first heard about Tribes, I said, 'Good. It's about time that non-native people realize how much Anishnoabe people have to offer.' The community circle is like our Healing Circle. It allows everyone a chance to be seen, to speak, and to be heard. Each of us has a different way of looking at things. We can learn from each other. It's good to listen and watch. When you watch, you see everything. You learn to give to other people and you see different ways to deal with problems.

"

—Anne Wilson, Ojibwe elder, Manitou Rapids First Nation, Ontario, Canada

Academic example: *"Turn to a neighbor and for a few minutes discuss what you would have done if you had been Rosa Parks in her situation."*

This use of temporary small groups helps to make the transition to long-term Tribes membership groups. It also gives the teacher an opportunity to see how different combinations of students work together.

Getting Started

So there you are with twenty-six faces looking up at you expectantly. How do we get started? Remember the Tribes Trail Map? Yes, here in the beginning it is up to you to be directive...to help all become comfortable and feel included. Your primary responsibility is to make it safe for people to share and for you to affirm how glad you are that they are part of the learning community. The quality of the classroom environment is strongly influenced by your personal style, the behavior that you model and expect from your students. What is talked about during a community circle session is usually less important at this point than how the group interacts together.

Here's an example of the community circle experience. You have chosen the strategy "Five Tribles." First, be sure that all people are sitting in a circle large enough so that each person can see all the other faces. Your students will probably chatter among themselves while the circle is being formed. Be patient and observe their interactions. Soon they will settle down and you can get started.

Tell them, "This year our class will be working together in some new ways—in small groups, so that people can help each other learn and learn from each other. We will meet often as a whole class, talking together in a community circle like this."

Somewhere during this first introduction, raise your hand and tell the class that this is how you will ask for attention. It is a non-verbal signal. Whenever people see the teacher's raised hand it means that everyone also raises his or her hand and stops talking. You might state that using the signal means they will never have to hear you shout.

"Now how many people would like that? (Ask for a show of hands.) It is also a great test of our awareness, or consciousness. Are the same people the first to notice?"

Giving Instructions

Describe the activity or task that the community will be doing, and give the purpose for doing it. For example: "Look at the faces of these five little creatures, called "Tribles," and choose one that seems to be what you feel like this morning. It's is important for us to hear how everyone is today before we begin to work together." Manage the time by asking students to make their statements in one or two sentences, a phrase or word. Some initial strategies, other than the "Five Tribles," that may be appropriate for your students are Community Circle Topics, Zoo Animals and JOY. Check the Tribes Strategy Grid in Chapter 11 to make selections for age, grade level and population groups. The primary purpose of Tribes active learning strategies is for teachers to use them as structures (formats) for the active learning of academic material.

Initiating Sharing

The teacher-facilitator initiates sharing by saying something like, "This morning I feel like the middle Trible, quiet but not excited. I think that is because I was up rather late last night." Then, "Let's go around the circle starting with you Jennifer." Remind everyone they have the right-to-pass. When someone does pass, openly acknowledge the person with a nod or smile to convey that it is all right. After going around the circle once, facilitate a second go-around to give those who hesitated to speak the first time a second opportunity. It is often helpful to pass a physical object such as a feather, bean bag, "talking pencil," stuffed animal, etc., from speaker to speaker. This helps younger children and special learners, who may have shorter attention spans. It also works well with those folks of any age who cannot stop talking even if no one is listening. Set a time limit for holding the physical object.

Keeping Things Moving

It is best not to repeat, paraphrase or comment on anyone's contribution. Make mental notes on things you way to bring up later. However, if someone gets put down by the group (derisive laughter groans, etc.) deal with the incident in a direct but matter-of-fact way. "People, remember the agreement that we made about not putting anyone down." Or ask the group "Which agreement do we seem to be ignoring?" And let the class identify it rather than you.

Learning and Practicing the Tribes Agreements

The second purpose of the community circle is to teach and practice the Tribes agreements and other basic social skills. Announce the skill to be practiced for a certain time: "Class, we will be practicing attentive listening during our ten minutes of sharing." Be sure that the time

The Daily Pledge of Fifth Grade Class D203

The democratic group process of Tribes has provided us with a systemic approach to creating a climate where the responsibility for learning is shared with all members of the class. In our classroom, we have a "Constitution" that is displayed and recited in unison every morning. It is a pledge to honor the Tribes agreements. After determining what we wanted our learning community to be like for the year, the document was written by the students. We used the Tribes strategy, "An Ideal Classroom" to gather everyone's ideas. As I continue to use the Tribes process in my classroom, I know that the constructive social skills my students are gaining enable them to sustain community in our classroom every day. I believe the meaningful learning will allow them to create and sustain democratic group learning communities throughout their school years—and well into their future adult lives.

Our Classroom Constitution

We the people, in order to form an ideal classroom and establish attentive listening, mutual respect, appreciation, no put-downs, participation, the right to pass, and safety, do ordain this Constitution for our class.

Article 1: Attentive Listening

We will listen with our eyes, ears, and heart.

Article 2: Mutual Respect

We will treat people the way we want to be treated.

Article 3: Appreciation/ No Put-Downs

We will speak kindly to others and think of other people's feelings.

Article 4: Right to Participate/Pass

We have the right to pass in certain activities, and know that the more we participate the more we gain.

Article 5: Safety

We will always think of safety first.

From a Teacher's View

• • • • • • • •

Teri Ushijima, Ed.D

is a 5th grade teacher at Mililani Mauka Elementary School in the Central Oahu District. She has been actively involved in the Tribes assessment initiatives the last three years and has done extensive training throughout the district. Teri uses the Tribes process with children and adults of all ages.

is well within your students' abilities. Begin transferring responsibility to the class by asking one or two people to keep track of the time, and later have them ask "How well did people listen to each other?" The class can also discuss and post "Spotlight Behaviors" that time-keepers select and look for during circle time. At the close of the circle discussion the time-keepers can identify people who demonstrated a "Spotlight Behavior." The rest of the class can guess which behaviors were spotlighted. Kids love this, and try to demonstrate all of the behaviors during circle time.

Defining Community Agreements

It is important for the students in your classroom to enter into a discussion of what they need in order to feel safe, or trusting, in a group. Take the time to do this rather than simply posting the Tribes agreements. This can be done as a brainstorm in small groups or as a community circle discussion. Typically, people will say things like

"I don't like it when people call me names."

"I don't want to get pushed around."

"I don't want to do something just because everyone else does."

"I don't want our group to fight and hassle all the time."

"I want people to like me."

"I want people to listen to me when I talk."

After the brainstorm, synthesize and summarize similar statements that are as close as possible to the basic four Tribes agreements introduced in the last chapter:

- Attentive listening

- Appreciation/No put-downs

- Right to pass

- Mutual respect

> "
>
> *No matter what my voice and eyes are saying, if my heart isn't present, I remain separate from my students and they will know it.*
>
> —Vicki Stewart
>
> "

It's OK if the class feels it needs one more agreement. However, since the purpose of these agreements is to build a positive learning environment and to have students become responsible for sustaining the agreements, the list should be brief—actually no more than five. It must not become just another version of school or teacher rules. The agreements are relational, defining how we want to relate to each other. *Such rules as No Running in the Halls or No Pushing in the Bus Line are not what is meant by relational agreements.* In time such behaviors will lessen due to the agreements of mutual respect and no put-downs being internalized by students. The point is to have your students "own" the agreements as much as possible. Even though you may have a beautiful graphic of the agreements ready for posting, save it for the next day or have the class make posters after this important discussion.

Of course, this initial activity may not be possible with younger children or all populations. In that case, do your graphic ahead of time, and have it posted in a prominent place in the classroom. Tell the class that these agreements help people get along well together and create a classroom that everyone will enjoy.

Your own modeling is absolutely the most essential factor in teaching the new Tribes agreements. Modeling comes through to kids as authentic when it is congruent and heartfelt. Vicki Stewart once said, *"No matter what my voice and eyes are saying, if my heart isn't present, I remain separate from my students and they know it."* Creating the Tribes environment begins with you, the facilitator, owning and living the agreements yourself. It also means

- Setting aside a lesson plan long enough to tune into a student's concern or pain

- Being non-judgmental, patient, and caring even with the more difficult ones

- Avoiding subtle put-downs in the midst of frustration or stress

- Standing on your own rights...to pass, to state your feelings, to say "No, I choose not to do that. It would not be good for me."

- Affirming through warm eye contact or a gentle touch on the shoulder

- Laughing at your own mistakes; conveying your own fallibility and commitment to lifelong growth and learning

It means being there in an authentic way, consciously present in the existential moment...touching, speaking, and listening with head and heart.

Attentive Listening

Attentive listening is probably the most important social skill to be taught and practiced by everyone in the learning community. Unfortunately, for many students (and adults) the experience of being listened to in a caring way rarely happens.

ear — you — eyes — undivided attention — heart

Attentive listening is a gift to be given. It depends upon

- Acknowledging the person who is speaking with full attention and eye contact

- Withholding one's own comments, opinions, and need to talk at the time

- Paraphrasing key words to encourage the speaker and to let them know they have been heard

- Affirming through body language that the speaker is being heard

- Paying attention not only to the words but also to the feelings behind the words

Too often we half-listen to each other, running the words through our heads that we want to say as soon as it is our turn. Most teachers assume that kids have learned at home how to listen. Most adults assume that we all do it well—though we may never have been taught the principles.

The skill of attentive listening needs to be considered a priority within every school's curriculum because it affects children's ability to learn academic material. This is especially important as classrooms move toward cooperative educational methods. Some of the listening skills that should be practiced include:

- Attending (listening silently with full attention)

- Non-verbal encouragement (nodding "Uh-huh")

- Paraphrasing ("What I heard you say was...")

- Reflecting feelings ("You sound angry...")

Begin with these strategies:

- Teaching listening

- Teaching paraphrasing

- Reflecting feelings

Appreciation/No Put-Downs

If one of our main objectives is to develop a sense of self-worth and self-esteem in children, school systems and families must find ways to eliminate the scores of derogatory and negative remarks that bombard young people each day. Unfortunately, put-down remarks are a basic form of communication among children and adults themselves; at times they are used in families to convey affection: you goof-off, you jerk, you crazy kid. Though off-hand or flippant, they not only damage self-esteem but undermine the level of trust within a group. A positive climate that builds self-worth cannot develop unless you, the teacher-facilitator

- Challenge students themselves to prohibit put-down remarks

- Encourage students to exchange statements of appreciation (positive regard and recognition)

Eliminating put-downs can be a tedious process until students themselves begin to object when they hear one. When calling attention to a put-down, remind people that the class has made an agreement not to use them.

One way to encourage your class to confront put-down statements is to teach them to respond with I-Messages: *"I feel sad when I'm called 'stupid,' Aaron. It's a put-down and hurts!"* The next chapter contains instructions for teaching I-Messages.

Minimizing put-down statements is half of the step toward building student self-esteem. Put-downs need to be replaced with statements of appreciation. You might want to tell the class that as we quit hurting people with put-downs, we will discover that just as a coin has two sides, our put-down agreement has a secret on its other side that will help everyone feel great. It's called *appreciation*. Helping people of any age to express appreciation often can feel like swimming against a strong current. It is a sad commentary on our society that in the course of a day we make five times as many negative comments as statements that affirm how we value each other.

Statements of appreciation are invited after every strategy and are modeled by the teacher throughout the day. It is very important that you search for truths to say. Kids know when something doesn't ring true—is not sincere and honest. To help people begin making statements of appreciation, use such sentence starters as these:

"I liked it when...(describe the situation)."

"I felt good when you..."

"I admire you for...(describe the quality)."

After completing a group activity, write the sentence starter on the chalk board and invite people to make statements. Your own modeling encourages the sharing of positive statements perhaps more than anything. It is important that you model being both a good giver and a good receiver.

Examples

"I appreciate your kindness, Joel."

"The ideas that you came up with, Sandy, made our project special."

"I felt honored when you gave me a copy of your own poem."

The Right to Pass

The right to pass means that each person has the right to choose the extent to which she or he will share in a group activity. It is the essence of our democratic system not to be coerced, to have a right to one's privacy, and to take a stand, if necessary, apart from the majority. Without such guarantees, individual freedom within a group is not protected. Choosing the right to pass means that the community member prefers not to share personal information or feelings, or to actively participate in the group at the moment. It may be their choice to remain quiet and to be an observer for a short period of time. This right must be affirmed repeatedly by teachers and peers: *"OK, you do have the right to pass. It's just fine to do so."* Being a silent observer is still a form of participation and can also lead to greater learning.

It is a sad commentary on our society that we make five times as many negative comments in the course of a day as statements that affirm how we value each other.

This protective agreement is essential within all organizational and group settings because it provides control to members. It encourages students to be self-determining and responsible for their own well-being among peers. It gives members the practice and courage to stand back from situations that are uncomfortable or contrary to their own values. Drug abuse prevention programs for secondary students have emphasized the teaching of refusal skills, and the slogan "Just Say No" has become popular over the last few years. However, we are convinced that the teen years are a bit late to begin learning refusal skills: By this time admonishing kids to just say "No" is somewhat simplistic. They need to be able to assert their right to pass throughout all their developmental years. To be "me" and to know that "I" do not have to go along with the crowd is an essential resiliency strength for life.

Many teachers are anxious that if this agreement is used in classrooms, students will pass on learning subject matter. First of all, the agreement does not apply when individual accountability is required on learning tasks. Students do not have the right to pass on homework, taking tests, responding to the teacher, etc. They do, however, have the right to pass on peer-led interaction. It is important to keep in mind that

- Temporarily withdrawing from activity does not mean a student is not learning

- You can count on the tribe, or peer group, to draw the person who usually passes back into an active working role

Healthy human development and resiliency depend upon young people becoming inner-directed rather than remaining dependent upon outer control from others.

Mutual Respect

The purpose of the mutual respect agreement is to assure everyone that their individual cultural values, beliefs, and needs will be considered and properly honored. It also means respect by adults for children's rights, needs, and differences. The rich multicultural diversity of our population is an invaluable resource for this country's future. Within a school community this agreement means respect for

- Others—no matter what their race, gender, age, color, or learning ability

- Newcomers from other cities, states, or countries

- Teachers, parents, and other caring adults

- Personal property and individual privacy

- Individual skills, talents, and contributions

This new agreement for the Tribes process was expanded from one once called "confidentiality/no rumors-no gossip," which we regard as one of the important aspects of mutual respect. Students will continue to need assurance of confidentiality—to know that others in their group will not disclose personal confidences. For students in classroom tribes, No Gossip does not mean that a student should not go home and tell her parents what she said or did in her tribe. It does mean that she does not have group members' permission to disclose what someone else may have said.

One way to teach this part of the agreement is to have each tribe make lists of how people feel when someone gossips about them. Help them to see that it is OK to share your own secret elsewhere, but not another's. Example questions:

> *"How did you feel when someone told Amy what you were going to give her for her birthday?"*

> *"Was a surprise ever spoiled for you due to someone's sharing?"*

> *"Do you think gossip always hurts people?"*

Building Collaborative Skills Through Stages of Group Development

The Tribes process with its sequential stages of group development—inclusion, influence and community—is a pathway for the development of the essential collaborative skills that students (and all of us) need in order to live, love, play, and work well together. Collaborative skills don't just happen, even though we may use cooperative learning groups in classrooms, or have the intent to collaborate with others on a work project. The skills must be taught and practiced over and over in relation to others who share a common purpose and meaning in their lives. This could be a class, faculty, a work team, a board of directors, a neighborhood group, or city council. Whenever human systems do not work well or fall apart, these vital human skills are missing. Collaborative skills are the constructive thinking and social skills set forth in the U.S. Secretary of Labor's report as necessary skills for the 21st Century. Business leaders say that more jobs are lost due to the inability to work well with others than due to a lack of knowledge among American workers.

The graphic on the next page illustrates the twelve skills taught and strengthened during the sequential stages of group development in a Tribes classroom. Inclusion skills prepare the class to handle the influence stage. The essential collaborative skills learned in the influence stage become the foundation for a vital community...working together with others from diverse backgrounds, solving problems, assessing for improvement, and celebrating their achievements. The ongoing practice of these key collaborative skills creates a classroom with high levels of participation on the part of all students and establishes a positive climate for teaching and learning.

"

Placing socially unskilled students in a learning group and telling them to cooperate obviously will not be successful. Students must be taught the social skills needed for collaboration, and be motivated to use them.

—David and Roger Johnson

"

TRIBES Learning Community

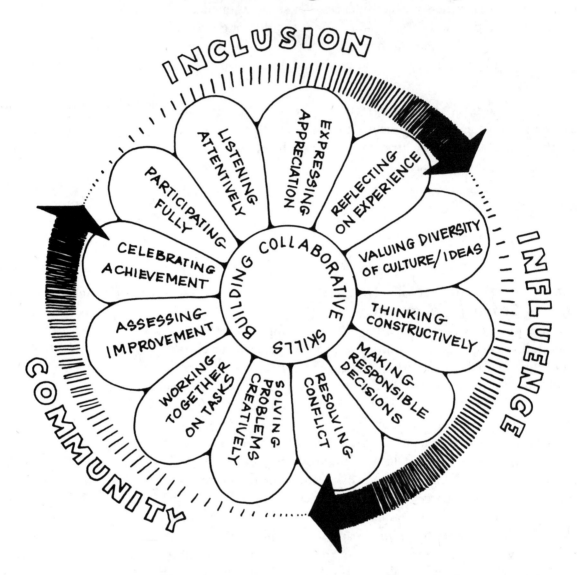

Seven Steps in Teaching Collaborative Skills

1. Engage students in identifying the need for the skill (using discussion, role-play, story, or situation).

2. Teach the skill (using the Looks/Sounds/Feels-Like structure or other strategy).

3. Practice the skill regularly, and have students give feedback on how well it was used.

4. Transfer the responsibility to the tribes to remind each other to use the skill.

5. Ask reflection questions about the use of the skill in tribes, the class, the playground, at home, etc.

6. Point out times when you notice people using the skill well.

7. Notice and celebrate when the skill is "owned" as a natural behavior in the classroom or school.

Teaching Community Agreements

In addition to the four Tribes agreements, many faculties (and families) choose a universal collaborative skill each month for the whole school to work on. These are human values such as honesty, self-responsibility, truth, unselfishness, kindness, and justice. A good way to teach these (as well as the four Tribes agreements) is to call students together in a community circle. Pre-sketch or sketch the following grid on the blackboard and have the class fill in the specific examples:

AGREEMENT: LISTENING		
LOOKS LIKE	**SOUNDS LIKE**	**FEELS LIKE**
heads together	*talking one at a time*	*great*
eyes looking	*encouragement*	*I'm important*
people nodding	*good idea*	*people care*
leaning forward	*uh-huh*	*I'm smart*
smiling	*yes!*	*we're friends*

1. Invite discussion on the need for the skill or agreement. Remember the cooperative learning way: Meet them where they are. Don't lecture or talk at them. Invite students to share what they already know and then add to it.

2. Ask people to call out words for the grid: *"What does listening look like?"*

3. Then: *"What does it sound like?"*

4. And: *"What does it feel like?"*

The four agreements should be posted in a prominent place and reviewed whenever the community circle or tribes meet. When learning the Tribes agreements, affirm the behaviors whenever you see them happening, and in time ask students to do the same.

Example: *"I can tell the Zoomer tribe is listening well to each other... people are talking one at a time and their heads are together."*

Now and then you may inadvertently overlook one of the agreements yourself. Do encourage the class to bring this to your attention. Accept such reminders graciously and without defensiveness. Kids can be great agreement and social skills reinforcers. You can count on them to monitor and help sustain the Tribes learning environment for the class.

Asking Reflection Questions

The activity alone is not enough! This phrase is the key to moving beyond just using small-group strategies and expecting them to make a difference in student learning. Cooperative learning strategies need to be followed with reflection (or process) questions so that students can focus on the interaction or learning that has happened. Research studies as well as the experience of hundreds of teachers verify that the time taken to ask reflection questions can double the retention of the facts and concepts learned in an academic lesson.[1] See Chapter 12 for an article on the exciting results of a cooperative learning study on the impact of "group processing," or reflection.

Reflection questions can double the retention of the facts and concepts learned in an academic lesson.

In Tribes TLC® we prefer to use the word "reflection" rather than "process" in order to

- Distinguish the after-strategy questions from the Tribes group development process

- Teach and emphasize that reflection is a skill critical to doing well in a complex world of information and relationships

---

Three Types of Reflection Questions

Content/Thinking questions are focused on the **content** of the lesson, and on the thinking skills that were used in order to work with the content. The content consists of facts, concepts, and information.

Collaborative/Social questions focus on the **interaction** that happens within a tribe or learning group and on the collaborative skills that were used.

Personal learning questions focus on what the **individual** has learned or felt.

Here are examples from two classes using the Tribes process. The first is a kindergarten and the second is a class of high school seniors.

The activity alone is not enough!

Bob Holloway's Kindergarten Class

The kindergarten tribes have been learning about cooperation by having each tribe prepare a fruit salad together.

1. **Content:** *"Which fruits did your tribe put into your salad? Tell me what they were."*

    Thinking: *"What did you have to do to get the different fruits ready for the salad?"*

2. **Collaborative:** *"What did your tribe do when some people started to eat the cherries instead of putting them into your tribe's salad?"*

3. **Personal:** *"What did you learn?" "Why did you like doing this?"*

Jill Langley's Senior Literature Class
The class has been reading a Dostoevsky short story, "A Gentle Creature."

1. **Content:** *"Why did the shopkeeper and the woman begin to quarrel?"*

    Thinking: *"What steps did your group take to analyze the main theme?"*

2. **Collaborative:** *"Looking back at how your group worked together, what did various people do to help the group complete the task?"*

3. **Personal:** *"What emotions did you feel?" "How do you feel about your participation in your group?"*

You need not ask all three types of reflection questions after a strategy, but do use at least two of the different types. Base your choice on what you believe will make the content memorable and the learning experience meaningful for the majority of students in the class.

Time out for reflection develops the capacity of introspection...to learn from experience and understand the working dynamics of groups and systems. It supports this definition of human development: to discover, sustain, and alter "situations"—to move into ever-widening realms of knowledge and experience.

The questions suggested for each strategy in this book may not be the best ones to ask your own class. There simply are no sure-fire questions that are appropriate for all cultural populations and age levels. Your own intuition, creativity, and judgment are needed to draw out the most important learning from the group strategies that you use.

Encouraging Appreciation
As pointed out earlier in this chapter, in our discussion of Tribes agreements, much of the power of the Tribes process comes from the practice of giving students opportunities to express appreciation to each other after working together. To be able to hear one's peers acknowledge special qualities, skills, and contributions to the group is much more meaningful to most students than periodic affirmation from a teacher.

Keep in mind that it's all about caring support, encouraging participation, and communicating positive expectations. **Trust the process— it works!**

MANAGING DISRUPTIVE BEHAVIOR

Teachers have learned that there are several good ways to manage energetic people who disrupt the community's time together.

1. Before students come to the community circle, give them a topic to think, write or draw something about at their desks.

2. If any students become extremely disruptive, call out "Freeze," and ask everyone to "run the movie backward, in your heads, and recall what you saw happening." Keep the descriptions as objective as possible by not using names. An alternative is to send people to their desks and have them write or draw what happened in the group. After discussing the disruptive behaviors, you can:

   - Ask the class to suggest one thing that they could work on the next time that they meet in a community circle

   - Have each person jot down in their journals or share with their tribe one thing that they will do to improve circle time

3. Use an I-Message: *"I feel sad when people are so noisy that we can't hear the person who is speaking."*

4. Give students time out: *"Juan and Leslie, I would like you to go to your desks and return to the circle just as soon as you can commit to listening to other people and taking your turn to talk."*

5. The key a successful community circle is to use more structure and less time if people are having difficulty. As students learn to respect the Tribes agreements and manage their own behavior, lessen the structure and increase the time.

People also need to be encouraged to appreciate themselves, to be proud of a job well done or a special contribution. It's OK to brag! Some strategies that you might try are

Boasters   I'm Proud   Personal Journal

To believe in oneself is to have high self-regard...to feel empowered, competent, and confident of doing well in tomorrow's world. It is an essential component of resiliency.

Using Temporary Small Groups to Build Community

If you look at the Tribes Trail Map again, you will notice that pairs, triads, and temporary groups are also used to build inclusion in the community before people become members in long-term tribes.

While your students are working together in these "trial tribes" you can observe how people get along with others. This serves as valuable information when you are ready to move students into long-term tribes.

The major disadvantage of the large community circle format is that each student must spend more time listening than talking, which leads to restlessness.

Building Community Creatively

Please do not feel limited to the strategies and energizers in this book in order to develop a sense of community among all your students. Use your teacher ingenuity to create whatever will best reach your students.

An abundance of good inclusion activities exists in other books, many of which are listed in Chapter 12. The criteria for a good community building activity are:

- It has a win-win rather than a win-lose outcome—cooperation rather than competition

- It provides inclusion for everyone—all can participate

- It draws upon and highlights the contributions that people make in the course of the activity

- It is fun!

In a safe place
I am wanted.
Me, all the edges
And the angles
And the hidden
parts that are me.

A
Safe
Place

by Gilbert Rees[2]

And no one says,
"You just won't do.
You'll never be
The things I want
You never will."
No one says that
In a safe place.

And no one comes
With sudden anger
Or a "What am I
going to do with you?"
Look...in hopeless eyes.
Not in a safe place.

For there
If I reach my hand out only a little,
If I gently touch someone,
Then someone reaches back
As gently,
As softly,

And no one breaks
apart our reaching
And no one tears
apart our silence
In the safe place—
We make together.

6

Building Tribes

6
Building Tribes

*People are fidgety in the community circle this morning. Renata Berger
smiles to herself, knowing that the excitement centers on one question in the
mind of each 3rd grader: Who's in my tribe? No use waiting. The big day
is here. "Are we ready to get into tribes?" she says. "Yes!"... "Sure!"... "Can
we do it now?"... "How do we know who's with us, Mrs. Berger?"*

*Renata explains that she has hidden the pieces of six puzzles around the
classroom and that each piece has someone's name on it. "Find your own
puzzle piece and then find the four or five other people whose pieces fit
together with yours to make a complete puzzle." Twenty-seven wide-eyed,
giggling kids scurry around the room. Within five minutes six groups are
huddled around completed puzzles. They're excited to belong to a group,
ready to be together in the fine Tribes tradition.*

Yes, after building community inclusion and getting your students
familiar with the agreements of the Tribes process, the time has come
for students to become members of long-term learning groups—tribes.
The material in this chapter will enable you to do just that. You will
learn how to

- Determine when your class is ready for tribes

- Introduce your class to the Tribes concept

- Balance members in tribes sociometrically

- Build tribal inclusion

- Lead strategies in tribes

- Teach I-Messages

- Facilitate the transfer of responsibility to the student groups

- Resolve group issues and conflicts that commonly occur

Is Your Class Ready for Tribes?

After several weeks of community strategies, you may start asking yourself in the wee hours of the night whether the time has come to take the next step. Your class is probably ready to be in tribes when you can say "Yes" to the following questions:

Readiness for Tribes

1. Do students understand and respect the agreements?

2. Do they know one another's names?

3. Can you identify the leaders, the less popular students, the particular friendships, the possible behavior problems?

4. Have the students had many successful experiences in various trial tribes, or practice groups?

5. Do you feel ready? (Of course you do, after getting this far!)

Introducing the Concept

One day when you are feeling good and things are going smoothly, take a few minutes to talk about everyone's experience of being together, not only in the large community circle but in many small groups. Tell your students that the class is ready to become members of long-term learning groups. Of course, they will all begin to wonder who will be in their tribe. State that each person will write the names of several people they would like to have in their group, and assure them that one or more of those named will be in their tribe. Explain that the purpose of being in an ongoing group is to help one another learn important skills and curricula together.

You may want to spend some time talking about what it is like to be a member of a group, club, family, or team; perhaps have your students discuss the purpose of various social systems:

"Why do you think people need to learn how to work together?"

"Why do people join different groups?"

"Have you ever been in a club or group with a few people who became very special to you?"

You don't need to "sell" the concept. It is your decision as their teacher to use cooperative learning groups this year. Tell your students what they can expect, and answer their questions. Your attentive listening skills will let them know you are hearing their concerns. Some may feel excitement at this point, others apprehension about a new way of learning together. Do what you can to help them become invested in the idea of belonging to a learning group and working together rather than on their own.

Sociometry Made Easy—How to Build Tribes

The guidelines for assigning people to tribes are important:

1. Assign four or five people to each tribe

    Preschools use groups of three

    Kindergarten: threes and fours

    Elementary and middle school or junior high: fours and fives

    High school and adult classes: groups of five and six

2. Balance the number of boys and girls in each learning group

3. Distribute leaders among all the tribes

4. Distribute the less popular (shy, less social, disruptive, etc.) among all groups

5. Be absolutely certain that each person has at least one chosen friend in his or her tribe

Here is a step-by-step process that you can use to achieve a sociometric balance in your classroom groups, without using any cumbersome instruments. Give yourself enough time to do this.

Seven Friends

1. Give each person a 5" x 8" index card. Have people print their names in the center of the card.
2. Ask each person to print the names of seven other people they would like to have in a tribe. Ask for at least 3 boys and 3 girls. (Kindergarten and 1st grade children will need help.)
3. Collect all the cards. Remind your students that they will each be in a tribe with at least one identified friend, but not with all of those listed.
4. Assuming that you will have six tribes, select the cards belonging to six leader types, those who have been named the most by others and who also enjoy learning. Spread these cards out on a table.
5. Select the cards of six students who exhibit quiet or less positive behavior. Place one of their cards next to each of the leader's cards.
6. Add the remaining cards to each group, making sure that each card has a name requested by someone in the group.
7. Make any adjustments necessary to achieve a balance of boys and girls.
8. Check once more to be sure that each card is still matched with a friend.
9. Congratulations! You have just formed your tribes!

The "Seven Friends" method of building tribes enables you to match or separate students to achieve the best mix of skills, cultures, and relationships. It has the added advantage of allowing your students some influence in determining who will be in their tribe.

Forming Tribes

Once you have determined the composition of the tribes, set a date when everyone will move into the groups. Advance notice builds great anticipation. When "T Day" arrives, choose an exciting way for people to discover who is in their tribe. Here are the directions for the strategy used by the teacher in the beginning of this chapter:

People Puzzles

1. Begin with sheets of posterboard, one for each tribe.
2. Sketch a design on each sheet so that you can cut as many puzzle pieces as the number of students you want in a particular tribe.
3. Print a student's name on each piece. Make sure that all the members of a tribe are included in the same People Puzzle.
4. Hide the pieces around the classroom before school, or during lunch or recess.
5. Tell the class to look for their own names and to find people with matching pieces.

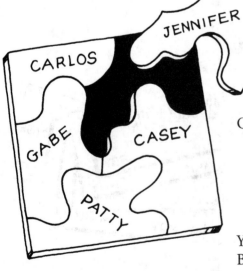

When everyone has found their tribe, assign the groups to different areas of the classroom. Desks and chairs need to be rearranged so that tribe members face one another. Tables may be used for high school and adult groups, and small rugs are great for preschool "tot tribes."

Once the tribes have settled down, ask reflection questions. Examples:

Personal: *What did you feel when you were trying to find other tribe members?*

Content/Thinking: *What made this strategy a good way to find your tribe?*

You can, of course, invent other ways to form tribes. "Barnyard Babble," in Chapter 11, has become quite popular even with adult groups. It provides a hilarious experience worth videotaping when teacher groups are doing it!

After the tribes have done some initial inclusion strategies, tell the class that people will remain in these groups for at least one month. Then the whole class will evaluate how their tribes are working and whether any changes need to be made. This defuses the inevitable remark, "I wanted to have someone else in my tribe!" Once we did a survey to learn how many new Tribes teachers actually had to alter the membership of the tribes. Those who had students stay in the same tribe for at least three weeks never felt the need to make any membership changes. The secret is that after that much time, the inclusion strategies, group process, and positive agreements have created a sense of belonging, caring, and trust. People have forgotten about wanting a particular friend—they have made several new close friends whom they like and do not want to leave.

Building Tribal Inclusion

Remember that Tribes Trail Map and discussion back in Chapter 4? Well, here is where your understanding of it really moves into application. Although you did many inclusion strategies with the whole class to build community before forming tribes, the need for inclusion continues. Each time a new group forms, people sense the same "stranger anxiety." If this issue is not addressed, it limits the ability of a group to work well together. Inclusion must happen all over again with the new tribes.

As a facilitator of this group process, you need to select a series of inclusion strategies that will help people present who they are, what they do well, and what their expectations, hopes, and needs might be. Taking the time to do this during the first days in tribes makes all the difference in managing the class and integrating other cooperative learning methods. People are not ready to work together on curricula unless inclusion and trust have been developed within their learning groups. Disruptive behavior in classrooms happens whenever students do not feel included and recognized. If you remember the discussion in Chapter 4, you'll recall that

> "A way to become included is to grab influence."

That's what plagues teachers throughout the day and school year. Anti-social behavior gains attention, meaning someone notices "me" and cares. It is a way to feel included and important in the midst of many others. The Tribes process decreases behavior problems in schools simply because everyone is included.

On the day before the new tribes are to be announced, invite people to bring something special from home to share at the first meeting of their new tribe. The item should have special meaning, perhaps an award, a gift, or something they have made. Sharing such treasures on the first day helps each person to talk about himself or herself and it develops positive energy in the group.

Strategies that Build Inclusion

Though we have said it before and will say it again, it is important that you select inclusion strategies geared to the interests, age level, and culture of your particular class. Do read the preface to Chapter 11 Strategies section before leaping into using them. Hopefully, you are involved in an in-service training conducted by one of CenterSource Systems' qualified Tribes TLC® District Trainers or Associates. If so, you will experience many good initial strategies that can be easily adapted to your class. Some of the favorites are

Name Game	Wishful Thinking
Spider Web	I'm Proud Circle
J.O.Y.	What's Your Bag
Kitchen Kaper	Campaign Manager
Interview Circle	

One teacher advises, "You need to be as flexible and creative as you are with all other curricula!"

The First Days of Using Tribes

1. Commit to begin and end each day with a community circle.
2. Ask students to review the class agreements.
3. Use an inclusion strategy for the whole community. Ask reflection questions. Give an overview of the day's schedule, work, and any announcements.
4. Have people move to their customary tribe's areas.
5. Explain the activity or task that the tribes will be working on and what skills and content people will be learning.
6. Give the directions one step at a time, using as few words as possible. Write the steps on the chalk board if there are several.
7. If clarification is needed on instructions, ask that the group confer among themselves before asking you.
8. State how much time there will be to complete the task or strategy. Ask each tribe to make sure that every member participates. If using group roles (to be discussed in Chapter 8), clarify the roles.
9. While the tribes are working together, observe their progress. Intervene only if absolutely necessary.
10. Signal when time is up, and have each tribe report progress by responding to appropriate reflection questions. Reflection questions can be handled either in community circle or in tribes.
11. Invite statements of appreciation.

Transferring Responsibility

One of the major objectives of tribes is to call forth positive leadership qualities and self-responsibility in children. This means that an intentional transfer of control needs to be made from the teacher to the tribe, and from the tribe to its members. As a sensitive teacher you can look for opportunities to have the tribes increase their capacity to function independently. Here are some of the ways in which responsibility can be transferred:

- Intervene only as necessary while the tribes are working together

- Encourage members to remind one another about the agreements

- When students ask you a question, refrain from answering immediately; turn it back to the class or tribe, asking "Who can help to clarify the instructions?" "What ideas do other people have?"

- Ask tribe members to assume helpful tasks and roles

- Have tribes keep attendance, make contact with people who are absent, and help returning members to catch up with the tribe and class

- Have the class make a list of classroom maintenance tasks, and have the tribes assume different ones for a period of time

- Have the tribes plan parties, field trips, parent involvement, and other class activities

- Ask tribes for suggestions to improve lesson plans, academic projects, and the learning environment

- Have them give feedback to you as the teacher

The process of transferring responsibility to students increases participation—and, if you recall, participation, caring, and high expectations contribute to the development of resiliency.

Observing the Process

Admittedly, it can feel strange to be in the background while your tribes tackle a challenging, engrossing task or strategy. This, however, is not a time to sit idly by, or to catch up on correcting those arithmetic papers! During these periods when your busy tribes cease to need you, you become the process observer, looking for the new skills and behaviors to be affirmed and noticing the dynamics within the tribes. Following is a list of some of the dynamics that you can observe while your tribes are working together.

Process Observation Checklist

1. **How are people sitting?**
   - Are they in a neat circle, or are some people sitting back?
   - Are they leaning forward attentively, or are they slouching, sprawling, or lying back?
2. **How are people participating?**
   - Are a few doing all the talking or work? Is participation balanced?
   - Are people lively and animated, or lethargic and tentative?
   - Is everyone focused on what is happening, or are side conversations taking place?
   - Are people passing?
3. **How are people taking care of one another?**
   - Are they listening to one another?
   - Are put-downs happening? (If so, are they being confronted by group members?)
   - Are disagreements being resolved in satisfying (win-win) ways?
   - Are kindness and cooperation being demonstrated?
   - Is appreciation being expressed?
   - Is the group drawing in the quieter people?
4. **How are people feeling and behaving?**
   - Are they smiling and/or laughing?
   - Is your intuitive response one of warmth and relaxation, or anxiety and tension?
5. **Are they working well on task or curricula?**
   - Who has assumed leadership?
   - Are the slower learners included?
   - Do they seem mindful of the goal to complete the task on time?
6. **What is happening for you?**
7. **Other**

Facilitating the Process

What happens when you observe breakdowns in the process? Let's use an example. You have given your 7th grade tribes the strategy "Brainstorming," so that they will learn the process and use it later in a history lesson. One recorder in each tribe is furiously attempting to write down all the ideas being voiced by tribe members. While observing the behaviors in each tribe, you notice that Tanya, one of the recorders, is really having a hard time getting all the information down on paper. People are saying things like, "Hey, you left out my idea!" "Slow poke!" Your impulse is to stride over to the group and take charge. Instead, you take a deep breath and reflect on all that is going on. You observe that only two students, Heidi and Jamal, are really "into" the strategy. They're leaning forward and putting forth many ideas. The other tribe members are sitting back rather apathetically, waiting for the time to run out.

What are your alternatives, other than intervening directively?

You could do nothing, in which case the situation would either

1. Stay the same.

2. Get better—someone might remind others of the agreements, or volunteer to help Tanya.

3. Get worse—an argument might erupt.

A better alternative is to stop the action anytime things seem strained or get a bit crazy. Simply call out, "Freeze," "Time out," or "Stop the action!" Wait patiently until order and silence fill the room. Then simply ask "What's happening?" First ask everyone to *look and listen* back to what was going on in the classroom or tribes. With young children, teachers can ask *"If you had been flies on the ceiling during the last few minutes and looked down, what would you have seen and heard?"* Or suggest that they *"run the movie backward"* in their heads, and describe what people were doing. You may want to list some reflection questions on the board, and give people thinking time. The first question for each person to answer should be *"I saw myself..."* (Describe your own behavior, not that of others.) *"I felt..."* (Describe your own feelings during the interaction.) Then ask for descriptions of specific sounds and actions. Following the Time Out Reflection Cycle below, help the class decide what everyone can do to improve things.

Time Out Reflection Cycle

- Stop the action—ask *"What's happening?"*

- Give everyone time to reflect—don't start diagnosing the situation yourself. Wait until people begin to speak up.

- Ask for descriptions of specific sounds and actions.

- Ask how people felt and how the behavior or situation affects the class as a whole.

- Invite or brainstorm ideas to change the situation.

- Have everyone decide what to do to improve things.

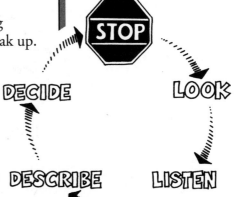

The repeated practice of reflecting on group and community interaction helps people to become aware of the impact of their behavior on others and the dynamics of groups. Reflection is emphasized in Tribes TLC® because it is essential for learning and development.

If you do not choose to take time out, be sure to have everyone reflect on the situation after the strategy or task is completed. You exclaim, "Why make all the tribes go through this when only one tribe had the problem?" Good question! In this case, the time out might accomplish the following:

- Tanya's tribe, in addition to exploring their own behaviors, would learn from the other tribes how they dealt with the same or similar issues

- The other tribes would benefit from discussing the same questions and reflecting on their own interaction

- In listening to the responses of Tanya's tribe, you would have additional data to use in deciding what specific work may need to happen with this tribe alone

Of course, if Tanya's tribe does not report on the behavior that you observed, you should comment on it. Not to do so would be interpreted as an indication that you were not paying attention, or that you did not think it was important.

Keeping Your Purpose and Role in Mind

The Tribes process, the positive environment, agreements, and all of the cooperative learning strategies have but one overall purpose:

to assure the healthy development of every child in the school community so that each has the knowledge, skills, and resilient strengths to be successful in a world of rapid change

The Tribes strategies are not time fillers for rainy days in the classroom, but are meaningful experiences to teach children how to reflect upon and learn to manage their own lives.

This interactive approach to human development and learning makes the "here and now" of each day a laboratory. Through group interaction, this generation of children will be able to move from a singular focus on "me" to "we"—and to a concern for our community, our nation, and the future of our world.

Your role is to make the cooperative learning process easy, exciting, and effective. You are the caretaker of the positive learning environment. The Tribes cooperative learning facilitator is more than a teacher. Now the profession can call forth the best within each and every child. Teachers need a new title—something like "learning and human development facilitators." Do send us your ideas on this!

Preventing Conflict Through Dialogues of Discovery

To create a classroom where students feel safe enough to challenge each other—and us—is to give them an enormous gift.

> —Alfie Kohn[1]

Have you noticed that every year conflict management programs are multiplying almost as fast as proverbial rabbits? The majority of approaches focus on managing rather than viewing conflict as a symptom in the school environment that can be prevented. Misunderstandings indeed are inevitable, whether in a classroom, school, district or parent organization. However, it became evident during my years of using the process of Tribes TLC® in preschool to university settings, that conflict need not undermine relationships or learning. We have only to shift our focus to creating a caring environment in which people feel safe enough to deal with misunderstandings before they become serious. For students, it means feeling safe enough to ask challenging questions, to learn and listen deeply, and to enter into genuine dialogue until they discover and understand the diverse perspectives, opinions and social values that in time could lead to conflict.

Our culture teaches us that listening is the mechanical act of using our auditory sense, listening to the words someone is saying without hearing the deeper messages under the words. Listening for "discovery" means listening with our hearts as well as our heads. The practice itself helps to create a safety in the environment. Moreover, it...

promotes openness, honesty and trust; clarifies thinking, feelings, perceptions, beliefs and assumptions; develops respect, acceptance and appreciation for individual gifts and resources

Listening, even in the midst of conflict, is the most important skill we can teach our students and children. If you think of a brick house, listening is like the mortar of that house. If the mortar erodes or is lost the building begins to crumble. Quality listening is the mortar of communication and learning. How else can we understand the needs, beliefs, values, hopes and dreams of another person?

Peter Senge, author of *The Fifth Discipline,* emphasizes the imperative of deep listening and thinking for learning organizations.[2] By now you are well aware that this is what the systems approach of Tribes TLC® is all about—transforming the whole school community into a caring learning community. It begins by teaching everyone to listen for discovery, which then creates genuine dialogue within a classroom, group or system. The big payoff is that dialogue allows a group to move beyond any one individual's perception, to build a collective understanding and to develop shared meaning and purpose.

Conflict management simply becomes an anachronism in safe and caring environments that involve students in heartfelt listening and meaningful dialogue. Alfie Kohn is wise when he says, "It is to give them an enormous gift." And I would add, *it's a gift for life.*

From a Teacher's View

• • • • • • • •

Ron Patrick

is the Director of Psychological and Student Services with the Mentor Exempted Village schools, Mentor, Ohio. He has used the process of Tribes TLC® from preschool to college classroom settings, and with a wide variety of school and community groups. Ron lives the caring philosophy of TLC® well wherever he goes as a District and Master Trainer.

One of the most important collaborative skills for today's students and teachers to learn is how to manage conflict—a dynamic that inevitably arises within any group of people working, playing, or living together. Denial or avoidance of a conflict ultimately undermines relationships, the group environment, and its ability to work well together. There's a saying, "There is no way around—only a way through."

Conflict is a natural part of life because as individuals we differ in what we want, need, and think. Conflicts occur over these differences. But conflict itself isn't the problem—it's *how we deal with it*. Most people have not learned how to manage conflict constructively. The adults in a child's world must learn to resolve conflict before they can teach the process to children.

Within each conflict there is an opportunity to gain new knowledge. If our intent is to learn, we will seek to understand why the conflict happened. In the process, each person discovers more about his or her own perceptions and unspoken assumptions, as well as those of other people. As a result, relationships will be more satisfying.

The capacity of teachers and students to work well together in cooperative learning groups is dependent upon how well they learn to solve problems and manage conflict. When a group has the commitment and skill to resolve all conflicts, individuals feel free to contribute ideas, explore one another's assumptions, and raise questions. This is essential in the process of becoming a learning community.

Resolving conflict needs to begin with the assumption that a "win-win" solution is possible. Strong feelings often make defining the problem difficult, and what appears to be the problem may be just a superficial issue. Once the real problem is identified and agreed upon, it becomes possible for people who have been in opposition to work out a solution that will be fair to both of them.

Gail Whang of Oakland Unified School District recalls how learning the Tribes process and a conflict resolution process affected their school staff at Hawthorne Elementary.

Conflict resolution brought people out of their classrooms and together. Tribes built on that power. Not only were we involved together in a schoolwide program, but because of the nature of both trainings, it brought the staff closer. We got beyond griping about students in the lunchroom and began talking to each other about what we valued and who we are. We began to change the culture of our school.

A Conflict Resolution Curriculum

The outstanding school curriculum *Conflict Resolution,* developed and published by the Community Board Program of San Francisco, recommends a set of "building blocks" for the effective resolution of conflict:[3]

- Awareness of conflict in our own lives and how we respond to it
- Appreciation for the differences between people
- Understanding of important feelings
- The ability to talk clearly to another person about a conflict
- The ability to listen to a person with whom we have a conflict

A specific sequence of steps is suggested for use whenever two students become involved in a conflict:

Step 1: Both students agree to the ground rules
"I agree not to interrupt, not to call a name, and I agree to work to solve the conflict."

Step 2: One person tells his/her side of the story using I-Messages, saying how s/he feels about what happened, and what s/he wants. The other person listens attentively and restates the problem.

Step 3: The second person restates what the problem is for the first person. Suggestion: begin with *"So the problem for you is..."*

Step 4: Steps 2 and 3 are repeated, with the 2nd student speaking.

Step 5: Both people suggest possible solutions.

Step 6: Both work to agree on a resolution that is:
- specific
- balanced—both people will be responsible for making it work
- realistic—and will solve the problem

Many Tribes schools not only use the Community Board Program within their elementary and secondary classrooms, but also train groups of students in the schools to be Conflict Managers who are available on the playground, and in classrooms, halls, and neighborhoods to help students resolve differences peaceably.

See Chapter 12 for information on contacting the Community Board Program and learning about materials and training.

Teaching I-Messages

An I-Message is a statement of the speaker's feelings in response to the behavior of others. Unlike a You-Message, an I-Message does not convey judgment, nor is it a put-down. Notice the difference between the following examples:

You-Message:

"Kim, you dummy, you ruined my chance to be the pitcher. You make me angry."

I-Message:

"Kim, I feel angry whenever a catcher isn't paying attention."

In the first example, Kim was rudely put down and blamed for the situation. In the second example, the speaker took responsibility for his feelings, stated them in strong terms...but did not put the blame on Kim. He defined the behavior that he perceived.

I-Messages	You-Messages
• State and own the speaker's feelings	• Hold another person responsible for the speaker's feelings
• Describe the perceived behavior or situation; not a personal judgment	• Blame others; judge and put people down

The purpose of an I-Message is to communicate feelings in such a way that the other person is not forced to defend herself or avoid the situation. The impact of the You-Message blames, shames, or intimidates the other person. It causes the other person to become resistant. The recipient of a You-Message hears the message as "you are bad or wrong," and is less likely to consider resolution of the difficulty. Worst of all, You-Messages escalate conflict.

You-Messages can also masquerade as I-Messages: *"I feel that you are always a nuisance"* is a disguised You-Message because

1. No feelings are stated or owned, even though the speaker says "I feel" (he really means "I think" or "I believe").

2. The phrase *"You are always a nuisance"* is a judgment, implying that the person is bad or incapable of being different.

In teaching people how to use I-Messages, it is helpful to write this formula on the board:

I feel_____(name the feeling)

when_____(describe the situation or behavior)

Give examples:

"I feel confused when people shout at me."

"I feel sad when I hear someone has hurt an animal."

"I feel scared when anyone threatens me."

I-Messages are also a good way to communicate positive feelings:

"I feel happy when I receive a compliment."

"I feel excited when we meet in tribes."

"I feel great when everyone participates."

The I-Message is a tricky concept to master, even though it seems quite simple at first. This is another instance in which you need to be an appropriate role model. It may take some time, but with daily practice your students will begin to use them.

Knowing When to Take Charge—Your Criteria

Yes, there are those crisis times when I-Messages just won't work—for instance, when you encounter one child hurting another.

"Stop that this instant!" is much more appropriate for the moment than "I feel unhappy when you hit Aaron."

Handling antisocial or inappropriate behavior depends upon thinking through in advance what your own criteria will be:

- When to use additional inclusion activities

- When to encourage students to use I-Messages with one another

- When to use an I-Message yourself

- When to use group problem solving (see the next chapter)

- When to be directive and take charge

Resolving Group Issues

The social climate in your classroom and your success with the Tribes process will be greatly influenced by the way in which conflicts and angry feelings are routinely expressed and resolved. As a Tribes teacher, your willingness to acknowledge, discuss, and resolve group issues in a caring, process-based manner will result in growth and learning for you and your students. All groups of people living, playing, or working together experience many predictable interpersonal issues. The chart on the following page gives an overview of typical questions that come up in a group's development, and it gives suggestions on how to resolve many situations.

Tribes Issue Chart

Issues	Questions/Feelings	You, the facilitator, need to
INCLUSION		
Presentation of Self	*"Will I like this group?"* *"How will they get to know me?"*	Be directive and provide structure; use many inclusion activities that permit each person to share who they are; what feelings, skills, qualities, and resources they have.
	"I feel nervous with these new people."	Have people work in pairs and triads; it feels less threatening.
	"Will they listen to me?" *"Will they put me down?"*	Teach listening skills. Make sure that people respect the Tribes agreements, especially "No put-downs."
Expectations and Needs	*"Will we finish by 3 o'clock?"* *"May we work outside today?"* *"Can you help me with a problem?"*	Provide opportunities for each member to state wants, needs, and expectations for the time the group is together.
Acknowledgment	*"Will they like me?"* *"Do I dare tell someone I think she is a nice person?"*	Be a good role model by giving and receiving appreciation easily. Provide opportunities for people to exchange statements of appreciation and good feelings.
	"Does anyone else feel the way I feel?"	Ask reflection questions that encourage people to share thoughts and feelings about coming together as a group.
INFLUENCE		
Me vs. the Group	*"Will my opinions be respected?"*	Provide activities that help people share individual differences and cultural strengths.
Goals	*"What are we to accomplish together?"*	Introduce techniques that elicit input from each member in defining group goals. Model and encourage acceptance of all ideas before choosing group goals.
Decision Making	*"How can we reach agreement?"*	Introduce techniques for consensus decision making.
Conflict	*"How can we work this out?"*	Introduce conflict resolution techniques, (active listening, I-Messages, role reversal). Assist group members in reaching win-win solutions. Teach collaborative skills.
Leadership & Authority	*"Do we need a leader?"*	Encourage rotation of roles. Urge natural leaders to draw out more passive members.
	"I resent it when someone tries to tell us what to do."	Ask reflection questions that help members discuss and resolve leadership problems. Use conflict resolution techniques as needed.
COMMUNITY		
Creativity	*"I feel good about my abilities."*	Recognize individuals for unique achievements and self-direction; encourage group members to do so with one another.
Cooperation	*"Our group really works well together."*	Assign group tasks that require innovation, cooperation, and creativity.
Achievement	*"We did a great job!"*	Assign projects: All group members receive the same grade or reward.
	"What shall we tackle next?"	Use groups for peer teaching, problem solving, planning, and fun! Be alert for inclusion/influence issues; support groups in resolving them.
Celebration	*"I really like our tribe and community."*	Take the time to celebrate—for whatever big or small reason!

As you begin to use the Tribes process you may hear statements that indicate group issues:

- "I pass!"
- "I don't like my tribe."
- "What about the new kid?"
- "Hey, that's a put-down!"
- "Let's form new tribes."

1. "I Pass!"

Early in the tribe-building process, some people may be passing all the time, and others may not be participating. This type of behavior is usually an indication that some people feel unsafe with their groups. Suggestions:

- Discuss the reasons why some people are not participating, and then have the small groups discuss what to do.

- Have people work in pairs. Match a shy person with a more confident, outgoing one.

- Make sure that you are using appropriate inclusion strategies. (Try "Interview Circle" in tribes.)

- Spend some time with the habitual passer. Learn his special interests and talents; encourage him to share them with the tribe.

- Assign the passer a role or task in the tribe.

- Make sure that the agreements are being honored so that the environment is safe.

2. "I don't like my tribe."

A person who feels uncomfortable in his group may say things like:

"I don't like the people in my tribe."

"I get bored in my tribe."

"People in my tribe are dumb."

"I want to be in Sarah's tribe."

Rather than trying to talk a student out of a complaint, use your listening skills to find out what is really going on. Suggestions:

- Enlist the help of the tribe to give the person more inclusion.

- Gear some activities to her learning style and interests.

- Ask the person to "hang in" with the tribe for two or three weeks; by this time things usually work themselves out.

- In some extreme cases, it may be advisable to transfer a student to another tribe, or to provide her with something to do alone while tribes are meeting. These are last-resort measures, only to be considered if all else fails.

3. "What about the new kid?"

When a new person enters your class after tribes have been formed, it is important to give her a special welcome.

A new girl named Robin shows up at school on Monday. She is given a short tour of the school; then she is introduced to her new teacher and classmates. The teacher may enlist the help of one or two students to explain to the newcomer what tribes are all about. Later in the morning, Robin experiences the Tribes Adoption Ceremony.

Adoption Ceremony

1. Introduce Robin and then ask the class how many people have ever moved to a new school, like Robin is doing.

2. In tribes, ask people to share their newcomer experiences. Transfer the time for sharing; five minutes is enough. Meanwhile, visit with Robin.

3. Then ask the question, "What ideas does your tribe have to help Robin feel welcome and included in our class?"

4. Ask each tribe to make Brainstorm lists of some positive, caring things its members could do. Allow five to ten minutes.

5. Have the tribes take turns reading their lists to Robin.

6. After all the tribes have done so, ask Robin to choose which tribe she would like to join.

During this activity, build inclusion with Robin by interviewing her, letting her know a bit about tribes and that it will be her choice as to which tribe she'll join. The choice may be limited to those tribes having fewer people. If you prefer to assign the newcomer to a tribe, you can still ask your tribes to come up with creative ideas for helping the person feel welcome and included. Hundreds of parents have expressed their great appreciation to tribes schools that use this ceremony. In a very transient society, it is wonderful to have your child come home the first day and say, *"I belong to a group already, and the kids were real nice to me!"*

4. **"Hey, that's a put-down!"**

If you find that in spite of your most heroic efforts, people are still using many put-down statements, you may need to take some remedial action. Suggestions:

- Have each student write on a card something someone said to them that really hurt. Put all cards in the center and have each draw one and read it without comment. Then discuss how it would feel to receive them.

- Initiate an "anti-put-down" campaign.

- Challenge the put-down experts to create statements of appreciation that they would like to receive.

- Provide lots of opportunities for statements of appreciation. Strategies like "Campaign Manager" and self-esteem cards are especially useful. With young children (K-3), you can use the "Warm Fuzzy" story and the related activity.

- Be a good role model, both in giving and accepting statements of appreciation. Just make sure you are honest at all times—kids can spot a "plastic fuzzy" a block away!

5. **"Let's form new tribes!"**

If your students begin agitating to change tribes, it is probably an indication that you need to do more full-group community inclusion and intergroup strategies. Suggestions:

- Remind your students that they will remain in the same tribes for at least three to four weeks before any changes are made.

- Combine two tribes for a strategy like "Interview Circle."

Membership in tribes needs to remain as constant as possible. The long-term membership factor develops cooperation and peer support for individual achievement.

There really is no way to anticipate and address all of the issues that may arise as you initiate cooperative learning groups in your classroom. The next chapter, "Calling Forth Power and Self-Worth," presents ways to handle issues of influence and problem solving. *Do* get together with other teachers who are using the Tribes process, so that you can share ideas, generate your own appropriate strategies, and enjoy ongoing membership in supportive tribes of your own. Chapter 10 contains ideas for staff support. After all—teachers are students too and, just like students, love school when in a tribe.

"

*They drew a circle
that shut me out,*

*Heretic, rebel,
a thing to flout,*

*But love and I
had wit to win,*

*We drew a circle
that took them in.*

—Edwin Markham

"

Burnt out

So what if he can't read

Teach him how to love

Himself? Me? Others?

Lost in a stack of paper

That good guy note he needed

I needed the look in the eyes

when you finally dig it out

The eyes say For me? From you?

A warm moment in a cold day

It passes math time

You forget—they remember.

Joe Rhodes—a teacher

7

Calling Forth Power and Self-Worth

7

Calling Forth
Power and Self-Worth

The meaning of the high cyclone fence around the inner-city school is two-fold. It keeps unwanted intruders out, and reminds everyone on the inside that they're a community of people who care for each other. The parents of the 1,446 middle school students speak 39 different languages and there is a 36 percent turnover within the transient student population each year.

"But we have to reach each and every one of them," teacher Joe Cimono says in the faculty planning session. "You're right," Principal Norma Terry says. "I'm certain that if we just keep using this Tribes cooperative learning process throughout the school, a sense of self-worth and mastery will happen for these kids."

Saul Bromberg adds, "We've done a lot of inclusion. Must be we need to recognize their need for influence, draw upon their diversity, and get them into decision making. They need to experience a sense of power over their lives."

"O.K., that's where we are! Let's get back to our faculty tribes and go to work. We just need to apply all we've been learning!"

This glimpse into one school staff meeting illustrates how a faculty is transforming its approach to teaching. The development of every student is their new focus. They are moving from the impersonal factory model of standardization to designing an approach that will reach all of the unique students in their school community. They're excited because they are learning to have the students help manage classroom behavior, to use the Tribes strategies for teaching academics, and to awaken self-worth within their students.

The material in this chapter will help you to

- Understand the dynamics and issues in the stage of influence

- Develop a sense of value and power for students through multicultural education, decision making, and problem solving

- Integrate academic content into the Tribes process

Acknowledging the Need for Influence

You thought you had it made. Your students had been in tribes for over a month and things were going great. No more agitating to change tribes. Almost no put-downs. And talk about working independently...one afternoon when they were working you realized that you could have gone home at one o'clock and nobody (except perhaps the principal) would have missed you!

Then one morning your lovely, smooth-running tribal classroom began to get a little out of hand. Some of the people you counted on as positive role models began acting up. During Tribes activities you noticed many subtle and not-so-subtle indicators that disagreements were happening. I-Messages and attentive listening were forgotten. It seemed like a terrible setback. You said to yourself, "Forget teaching with groups!"

Congratulations! Your class is now ready to really go to work! The inclusion, or "honeymoon," stage of the Tribes process has run its course, and the stage of influence has arrived! The new restlessness is a sign that your students are comfortable with the group process—they feel included and safe enough to speak out, even those shy ones.

The Stage of Influence

The stage of influence is not about fighting for control or power over others. It is an organizational stage in which people want to contribute value to their group or community. Take a few minutes before moving further into this chapter and review "The Stage of Influence" in Chapter 4.

It's important to remember that if groups ignore the underlying issues of the stage of influence rather than working through them, their capacity to work well together will suffer, and they will never come to appreciate the diversity of group members. There is no way around—only through! Your job as a process facilitator is to recognize the restlessness as a sign of progress, and use strategies that help people express their individuality. A sense of value and positive power then becomes a reality. As soon as that happens, your class (or staff or organization) will be a strong learning community in which everyone participates, shares leadership, and leaps ahead in learning.

There are five ways to empower people at this stage of group development. Indeed, they are the objectives for this stage:

> "
>
> *Cooperative structures create the conditions for reversing inequality, producing egalitarian social structures and caring relationships where diverse people can work together toward common goals.*[1]
>
> —Mara Sapon-Shevin and Nancy Schniedewind
>
> "

- Provide many opportunities for people to state their differing opinions, values, and beliefs openly

- Make multicultural education and cultural pluralism a focus in your classroom and school

- Teach strategies for individual and group decision making

- Teach strategies for individual and group problem solving

- Allow time for students to define individual and group goals

Learning to State Opinions

It takes courage and trust to take a stand in the midst of peers and say, "I feel differently about this than the rest of you do." The more that students are given opportunities to state diverse beliefs, the stronger they will be to do more than parrot back the words "Just say no."

Let's say you have a 9th grade history/civics class this year in which you've been using a theme such as "Self and Society" or "Contemporary Issues." You've been building class community and have seven classroom tribes, each composed of five students. Throughout the inclusion stage you also started to use some of the Tribes strategies as structures for lesson topics. You have yet to formalize all this into a lesson plan, but expect that will happen in time.

Today you have decided to tackle the first steps of the stage of influence. To do this we suggest that you begin with the four influence strategies listed below. Tailor the language and topics to fit the grade level and cultures of your students. The strategies are:

- Thumbs Up/Thumbs Down • Where Do I Stand

- One, Two, Three   • Put Yourself on the Line

Follow the directions as written, and remember: the strategy alone is not enough! Allow sufficient time for reflection questions so that in-depth learning happens. These four strategies could take several hours to do thoroughly. Work on them over several consecutive days. The first time that you use the strategies, use topics of personal interest.

Then use them again, but this time ask a controversial question from whatever material the class is studying.

Examples using the strategy "Put Yourself on the Line:"

"The only way to have a safe school is to have more rules, monitors and metal detectors."
Where do you stand?

"The age that you can vote and drive should be substantially lowered."
Where do you stand?

Ask several types of reflection questions. Although example questions are noted for the Tribes strategies in this book, craft your own special questions for the content of the lesson and your students.

The "Put Yourself on the Line" strategy can be followed up with many other learning opportunities.

Follow-up ideas:

1. People who agree on a position can form temporary new study groups to research and prepare a defense for their position.

2. The people on the extreme ends, who differ the most, can get together in debate and dialogue groups.

3. Students who learn through rhythm/music, visual/spatial, or body/kinesthetic intelligences may want to illustrate the various positions through role play, music, diagrams, or drawings. The next chapter discusses multiple learning styles and has many ideas to use.

The creative controversy that can evolve out of Tribes influence strategies can not only produce a wealth of learning in lesson content, but can also challenge students' critical thinking and collaborative skills. Best of all, different opinions are affirmed and valued.

Multicultural Education and Cultural Pluralism

Learning respect for different opinions during the stage of influence leads to the next important component, respect for multicultural diversity. Celebrate the fact that public schools are finally making a significant shift, from cultural assimilation to cultural pluralism.

Even though we're in the "How to Do It" section of this book, we would like you to keep reading back to the theory sections on the same topics. Take a few minutes now to look at

- Chapter 2, on "Multicultural Diversity"
- Chapter 3, "Creating Equal Opportunities for All Students"

Begin to plan with other teachers, parents, and administration how to initiate the five components considered essential to creating a culturally transformed school community. Again, they are:

1. Active involvement of the whole school community

2. A mission statement/policy centering on diversity

3. Redistribution of power and authority within school and classes

4. High expectations by teachers

5. Theme-focused multicultural curriculum, cooperative learning, a respect for individual learning styles, and well-trained multiethnic teachers

How can we make multicultural education effective when race relations are at an all-time low?

With the diversity among populations growing at unprecedented rates, cultural clashes and conflicts are inevitable. Often the conflicts become violent, as we saw in Los Angeles. It is essential that our schools and communities learn not only how to help children of different cultures, races, and ethnic groups get along with each other, but also how to create environments in which children of one culture can assert their pride in who they are and are excited to learn about the cultures of others.

The staff of our school realized a few years ago that Tribes provided an absolutely critical process to ensure the success of our multicultural efforts. While Tribes does not explicitly teach about stereotyping, or prejudice, the Tribes process should be in place before one attempts to teach this sensitive topic. By consistently implementing the agreements of Tribes and creating the caring, safe environment, the Tribes teacher can be assured that students will respect each other's cultures. Oftentimes when children talk about their culture, or a particular custom that is very different from those of the other students, a typical reaction is to laugh or make fun. With Tribes it not only is easy for the teacher to remind the class about "no put-downs" and the value of diversity, but it is easy for the students to share personal feelings. Teachers often need to stop teaching the

curriculum in order to deal with a conflict arising from a racist or sexist remark. Unless the teacher feels comfortable doing so, these remarks often go unnoticed or are handled only on an individual basis. In our Tribes classroom the environment is in place to resolve conflict as well as to seize the teachable moment and confront issues of racism or sexism.

Every morning we have a Tribes community circle. In one morning circle activity each person shares how he/she is feeling. Quite often during this sharing session feelings of anger come out as a result of a child being called a racial name. One time, some of the Asian students were angry because they were being called "Chino" by Latino students. Chino means Chinese in Spanish. "But," they protested, "we are not Chinese." At this time one Mexican student spoke up and said that maybe the Latino students were not putting the Asian students down. He went on to explain that in his culture, friends would sometimes call each other by names depicting a physical characteristic. "We call one friend 'Pansón' because he was a little fat." This was a wonderful opportunity to share differences within cultures.

Once I was having a disagreement with a Mien student about a conflict she had with another student. During this discussion, she never once looked at me. Instead, as she spoke, she looked down to

From a Teacher's View

• • • • • • •

Gail Whang

is the Health and Safety Program Manager for the Oakland Unified School District in California. As a long-time Tribes TLC® Master Trainer, she has used the Tribes process as a foundation for school-wide restructuring, district-wide conflict resolution and multicultural community development.

the side of me. I found myself feeling angry because I thought she was not listening to me. At this moment I realized we had two very different approaches to speaking and listening. Again, in the Tribes circle I raised this point for discussion. Many of the Laotian and Mien students shared that at home it is considered rude to look their parents in the eye when speaking to them. Looking down is a way of showing respect to their elders. As we discussed eye contact a Mien student shared that some teachers say, "Look me in the eye when I'm talking to you," and how it makes her uncomfortable. Through the discussion she realized how eye contact shows respect and that you are listening attentively in some cultures. With this knowledge Laotian and Mien students become aware of the differences as they go from one culture to another on a daily basis. The other students also learn that if a Laotian or Mien student isn't looking directly at them, it does not mean they are not listening.

With so many cultures living together in one school, it is inevitable that what is considered polite in one culture could be considered rude in another. It is impossible for teachers to know the characteristics and values of all the different cultures represented in her class. Inadvertently, children will offend others from a different culture. That's why a supportive Tribes environment facilitates learning about other cultures. Children feel free to express any emotion.

The Tribes classroom is **empowering for students**. Not only do students share how they are feeling, but we discuss what we can do to change a bad or difficult situation. An instance in which students were empowered occurred last year. Many students complained about a teacher in the school who they felt was being disrespectful to them. One student complained that the teacher called him a racial name. Another student said that the teacher made fun of how short he was. Again, in the Tribes community circle we discussed the problem openly. Going beyond how we felt about this, we brainstormed what we could do about changing the situation. Students suggested that a meeting be called with them and the teacher to express their concern. This was done while another teacher mediated. It became clear that the students had misinterpreted what the teacher had said. Positive suggestions were made by the students and the teacher on how to improve the situation and prevent future misunderstanding.

As you can see, Tribes doesn't explicitly teach about multicultural understanding, but without the Tribes process, multicultural understanding cannot take place. Tribes must be in place for rich lessons to be learned about other cultures.

6 Steps
Toward Cultural Pluralism

ESSENTIAL COMMITMENTS

1 Build Staff Awareness
- Examine the current curriculum
- Clarify misnomers and misinformation
- Examine racism/bias: what does it look like?

2 Develop Curriculum for Teaching Tolerance
- Conduct training in existing anti-bias curriculum
- Develop additional curriculum
- Identify levels of readiness

3 Celebrate Multicultural Diversity
- Use themes to integrate cultures rather than just studying one particular culture
- Utilize parent and community resources
- Include people with special needs
- Utilize staff's multicultural talents

4 Integrate Classes
- Define how to maintain integrity of bilingual program and integrate classes
- Pair up classes of different languages to work together
- Focus on inclusion of special needs students

5 Build Self-confidence and Self-worth
- Create and maintain a supportive and collaborative environment through the use of the Tribes process
- Teach and practice conflict-resolution skills
- Encourage student-initiated projects

6 Involve Parents
- Arrange cross-cultural workshops and support groups
- Sponsor family picnics, potlucks, and other events

Gail and her fellow staff have spent time defining what they believe are the essential components for multicultural education in their school, and they have made a commitment to focus on these areas for two years.

Admittedly, it will take time to do this, but you are already well on the way because the Tribes process helps to initiate all of the components.

Develop your own multicultural curriculum with the help of your students. Use some of the Tribes strategies to help people talk about their different countries, cultures, customs, languages, and uniqueness. Since space is limited in this book, we suggest you order a copy of *Open Minds to Equality: A Sourcebook of Learning Activities to Promote Race, Sex, Class and Age Equity* by Nancy Schniedewind and Ellen Davidson. (See Chapter 12.) No matter what strategies or activities you use, be sure to follow them up with Tribes reflection questions.

Create all-school activities, such as:

- Celebrating multicultural diversity
- Multiethnic fairs
- School family events
- Parent and grandparent story hours
- Multicultural movie night
- Staff awareness and training
- Parent involvement initiatives
- Classroom parent tribes

> "
>
> *In cooperative classrooms heterogeneity and diversity are not simply tolerated, they are nourished and valued.*[2]
>
> —Mara Sapon-Shevin and Nancy Schniedewind
>
> "

Help your students understand that each time the tribes reflect on their collaborative skills, the dynamics of their tribes, the resolving of conflict, and problem solving, they are learning the skills for living in a pluralistic world. Help them to become familiar with the concepts underlying intergroup education, and to generate their own activities based on these concepts.

1. Every person needs to have the sense of belonging to a group.

2. Ethnic groups have both similarities and differences.

3. Segregated people develop myths, prejudices, and stereotypes about other cultures.

This perspective on linkages between and among people, coupled with the harmonious networking of all groups, fosters unity out of diversity and promises the harmony so desperately needed throughout our communities and world.

Teaching Individual Decision Making and Problem Solving

Have you ever wondered why schools limit student choices to the extent that they do? Everything is so predictable for kids for twelve years—the classes one must take, the way the system works, the competition, the tests, the workbooks year after year. The opportunity to make choices is next to zero in traditional schools. If we truly want students to become self-directed and gain a sense of autonomy, learning how to make responsible decisions is essential.

The distinction between decisions and problems is an important one:

- Decisions are judgments made concerning information as perceived by an individual or a group.

- Problems are dilemmas, intricate issues, and predicaments that need to be analyzed in order to reach resolution.

The difference between the two defines the sequence that Tribes uses to teach decision making and problem solving.

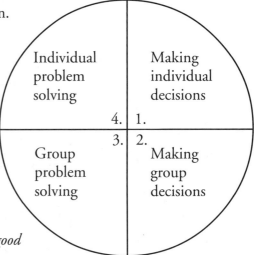

Individual problem solving 4.

Making individual decisions 1.

Group problem solving 3.

Making group decisions 2.

Making Individual Decisions

Three of the four strategies you used to help students express different opinions now can help them practice making individual decisions. Use topics appropriate for your class.

Thumbs Up/Thumbs Down

Your high school career tests suggest that you would be a good engineer. What decision would you make?

Someone tells you that you don't have to put on a seat belt in their car. What decision would you make?

One, Two, Three

If you were to take a vacation next week and money were no object, would you prefer to go to:

Disneyland

London for a week of theater

The World Series

Where Do I Stand?

Our class will be working on four issues about the Civil War during the next three weeks. Stand by the sign of the topic you want to work on.

1. Roles of European countries

2. The Emancipation Proclamation

3. Lincoln's personal and political dilemmas

4. Economics in the South and North

Individual decision making can be practiced throughout the teaching day by using many influence strategies and reflection questions. Reflection can happen in tribes or through writing in personal journals.

Individual decisions can also be made with the help of trusted tribe members, teachers, and parents through the Tribes strategy "Let's Talk."

> *Man ultimately decides for himself! And in the end, education must be education toward the ability to decide.*
>
> —Victor Frankl

LET'S TALK

1 Define the problem, situation, or concern
- Whenever I go over to my friend's house after school, his mother is not home and he wants me to drink beer. I don't want to say "No" because he won't like me if I do.

2 Repeat the problem back (if in a discussion)
- You mean that you think you have to drink with your friend or he won't be a friend anymore?
Repeating back the problem usually brings elaboration.

3 Think it through
- Would anybody lose respect for you if you did drink with your friend?

- Have you thought about the risks involved?

- Are you certain your friend will not see you anymore?

- Have you considered some alternatives?

4 Look at both sides
- What is the best thing that could happen if you said "No"?

- What is the worst?

5 Decide and act
- Having thought through the consequences, what is the most responsible choice you can make?

- Are you willing to accept the possible consequences by acting on your decision?

- If so, do it!

6 Evaluate the outcome
- What happened? What did you learn?

- Were you proud of your choice?

- Would you make the same one again?

Making Group Decisions and Action Plans

The stage of influence calls into question how tribes can make decisions together. Reaching agreement even on simple things (such as, Who will report for our tribe?) often proves to be difficult.

First, teach the tribes how to use the Brainstorming strategy in this book. Practice working on group decisions that are fun, such as Space Pioneers, or Family Camp Trek. Following these initial strategies, use Consensus Building and Goal Storming. Keep in mind that once your students are familiar with the strategies, the strategies can be used for lesson topics and real-time classroom decision making. For example:

- *We only have four kick balls to last us the year. How can we make sure that we don't lose any between now and June?*

- *How can we make sure that the plants get just the right amount of water each day?*

- *How can we share responsibility for feeding Benjamin Bunny and cleaning his cage?*

Practicing group decision making prepares young people to live in a democracy—to work responsibly with others. The more that we can give students the opportunity to reflect upon and analyze the dynamics that take place in their tribes, the better prepared they will be to "discover, sustain, and alter" the properties in their environments and systems (to quote the human development perspective of Tribes). This is the meaning of personal power.

If the tribes have made group decisions to work on something together, you may want to have them create "action plans" designating tasks to be done, persons responsible for each task, and expected times for completion. The action plan can be posted, reviewed daily, and revised if necessary. Action plans are "group contracts," which remind people of their accountability to one another.

TRIBAL ACTION PLAN Tribe Name:		
What	**Who**	**By When**

Group Problem Solving

The maxim is so simple, yet so difficult for adults to put into practice. Our immediate reaction is to suggest solutions, and then become aggravated when students care little about carrying them out. Our basic goal of preparing this generation to do well in today's world depends upon helping kids become responsible citizens. For this reason Tribes trains teachers to transfer responsibility to student groups as much as possible. Having tribes rather than adult personnel solve classroom or school problems is also the key to sustaining a mellow environment. Let's look at two problems in need of student solutions.

Problem #1:

A few 6th grade students of the school have been seen spraying graffiti designs on the outside wall of the gym on weekends. Some of the offenders may be in your 6th grade class.

Strategy: Tell the class about the problem. Then lead them through this Step-by-Step Process for Group Problem Solving.

STEP-BY-STEP PROCESS FOR GROUP PROBLEM SOLVING

1 Ask the tribes to discuss how they feel about people spraying paint on the wall of the school. Allow 3 to 5 minutes.

2 Pass out large sheets of paper and ask the tribes to brainstorm some ways that they could help solve the problem. Remind them of the rules for Tribes Brainstorming.

3 Ask each tribe to select their three best ideas or solutions to the problem. This can be done by consensus or by having each person write "1,2, or 3" after three items of their choice. Stickers of three different colors may also be used. In this case, each student selects his/her top choices by placing a blue sticker on the first choice, red on the second choice, and yellow on the third choice. The totals on each suggested solution are counted (blue stickers 15 points, red stickers 10 points, yellow stickers 5 points).

4 Have two people record the three ideas from each tribe on the blackboard as they are read to the class.

5 Combine any duplicate or similar solutions.

6 Have all of the students approach the board, tribe by tribe, and vote for one solution.

7 Ask for two volunteers to add up the sticker points for each item. The solution receiving the most votes will be the one that the class will carry out.

What is remarkable in this example is that the identity of the 6th graders causing the problem is never discussed. They may, in fact, have participated (somewhat silently) in the problem solving.

Behavior problems can easily be handled whenever peers are given the opportunity to express how they feel about a disagreeable behavior. Have your tribes brainstorm "behavior that bugs me." Count on the power of peer feedback! Just going through the process of identifying conduct that is not approved by peers can cause a behavior to disappear rather quickly.

Problem #2:

You notice that the tribes are having various interaction problems. You want them to learn how to resolve group problems or issues.

Strategy: Ask the class if they have noticed that people are having difficulties in working together. After hearing their replies, tell them that you also have observed some interaction problems, and that you would like them to figure out how to resolve them.

Then lead them through "Tribes Resolving Group Issues."

The more that students are involved in defining a solution to a problem, the more likely they are to accept the responsibility to make the solution work.

TRIBES RESOLVING GROUP ISSUES

1 Ask each person to reflect upon the group's interaction in recent work together, and using a 3" x 5" card jot down any difficulties that kept the tribe from working well together.

2 Have each tribe place its cards face down in a pile.

3 Collect the stacks and exchange them among the tribes so that no tribe has its own.

4 Give the tribes 10 minutes to identify one issue from the cards and make suggestions on what a tribe might do to resolve the problem.

5 Have each group share suggestions with the whole class. The tribe being discussed may remain anonymous.

Individual Problem Solving

There is an understandable concern about students sharing personal problems within groups in educational settings. We have always taken the position in Tribes that it is inappropriate for educational groups to deal with any personal problems that border on the psychological, and that only qualified professionals should do so. Tribes are educational, not therapy, groups!

It is inevitable, however, in these times of severe stress among children that family-oriented psychological problems become evident. The advice we give Tribes teachers is the same as that which their districts probably give. If you notice or hear anything that indicates a serious disturbance in a child, it is your responsibility to refer that student to the professional designated to handle such problems for the school.

Help your students understand that it is not the purpose of their tribes to deal with personal or family problems. Tribes may, however, help people think through concerns related to their school work, career questions, future goals, skill development, roles among peers, and friendships.

Here are three strategies you can use to help students sort out individual problems.

1. Practice the "Client Consultant" strategy, using educational, career, or personal interest topics.

2. Have people keep personal journals, sharing only what they would like peers to help them think through.

3. Use the strategy "Let's Talk."

If you do sense that an inappropriate personal problem is being discussed, intervene and determine the appropriate assistance for the student.

IMPORTANT! Should you ever hear anyone say that cooperative learning or Tribes TLC® groups are therapy groups, respond with vehemence—and share this material. *The purpose of all cooperative learning groups is the social and academic development of young people within school settings.* The benefits of cooperative group learning are too valuable for the process to be disparaged by unfounded assumptions.

Setting Goals and Making Individual Contracts

Social development also means helping students to become self-controlled and self-directed. Provide the time necessary for students to learn how to define positive goals—a key attribute of resiliency.

One way to start working on positive goals is to have students do the "Goal Storming" strategy independently. Ask people to choose something about themselves that they would like to improve (social or academic skills, attitudes, or behaviors) during the next weeks. Short time durations are better than long ones. As a way to model the activity, you might share your own list:

Teacher's List of Short-Term Goals

1. To exercise for ten minutes each morning this week.

2. To give up drinking coffee for at least one month.

3. To phone my friend tomorrow and apologize for forgetting her birthday.

Students may wish to share their goals with other Tribes members and write personal contracts, which can be signed by peers who agree to give encouragement and support. There is a form for the personal contract in Chapter 11 of this book. Positive peer support can work wonders!

Goals also can be recorded in personal journals, so that students can continue to reflect upon their experiences, document progress, and record changes. Personal journals are respected as private documents that are shared only if a student chooses to do so.

Influence is the sense that I am of value and have power over my life.

8

Designing and Implementing
Learning Experiences

8

Designing and Implementing Learning Experiences

The teachers of the Middletown Middle School now meet in grade level groups (their own tribes) for planning and to support each other. Like their students, they have also chosen names for their tribes, and they begin each meeting with inclusion. Margery Burnett of the Red Zingers has just facilitated the strategy J.O.Y.

After reflecting on their sharing, Jerry Carroll exclaims, "OK, let's go, Zingers. How do we keep reaching all of our 7th graders these next weeks? It's time to whip out another set of history-based learning experiences that reach them all."

"I've been thinking a lot about what we're doing," Joe Santini says. "Now that we're weaving themes and concepts into Tribes strategies and other interactive structures, even those apathetic kids are participating well. Learning is now more like a journey of meaningful discoveries that friends make together. And I've been meaning to tell you, I like teaching now and I'm not going to leave you guys at the end of the year."

Cheers go up! Then the Zingers gather around the table to continue their planning. Before leaving, Joe quietly tacks a colorful new sign up on the faculty room wall. Its message is heartening:

Teaching means reaching and Middletown is doing it!

Scenes like this one are taking place in schools throughout the country. **Teachers have become learners,** and the more that they learn about how kids learn, the more excited they become about designing learning experiences for their students.

What students understand does not correspond directly to what they have been told or read in authoritative texts.[1]

Teaching for Excellence

Now is the time to get the word around your school that the components and process of Tribes TLC® is a sound researched-based approach to improve student learning. Why? Hundreds of studies on cooperative group learning verify student academic success is increased more through properly facilitated small groups than whole class instruction relying on seat work. Shifting the responsibility and energy back to students for their own learning also is based on solid psychological theory and research. Moreover cognitive learning studies show that students working in small cooperative groups master material better and more quickly than students working individually.

How do we know the process of Tribes TLC® is promoting academic achievement? News like the following examples are coming back from schools throughout the country. Student scores on the SAT9 test at a school in Arizona were normally 15-25, and moved upward to the 40-50's in a bilingual class. The same district is heralding a teacher where the normally low scores became 60-70's in a regular class. An on-going study in a Wisconsin school reports that the consistent application of the Tribes process is resulting in significantly higher CTBS reading scores. We urge you to discuss the many benefits of cooperative learning with other educators and parents. It may be helpful for you to use the summarized list back in Chapter 2, page 49, of this book as a reference. The exciting benefits for teachers are on pages 55 and 57. Call CenterSource Systems for additional information on the results of using the process of Tribes TLC® .

Modifying the predominant practice of whole class teacher-centered instruction requires that teachers and parents, understand how human learning takes place. They need to decide whether they want students just to continue memorizing material for tests, or become constructive thinkers and problem-solvers for real life issues. More than 30 years ago respected educator Paulo Freire also pointed out the fallacy of didactic instruction as based on learning theory evidence. He became convinced that what students understand does not correspond directly to what they have been told or read in authoritative texts.[1]

Numerous cognitive learning research studies now affirm Freire's conclusion. Understanding incoming information, facts and concepts depends upon the meaning given to the information by the human brain.[2] The brain continually seeks to understand new information by linking it to previous patterns of knowledge in the mind. Each student's understanding depends upon a synthesis of what he or she has heard and read, as interpreted through previous experiences.

Familiar symbols, language and culture also affect individual understanding. Thus the term: "the brain is a meaning-maker." It is also known that meaningful knowledge is created and recreated between people as they explore, apply and do things together.[3] Group discourse and collaboration on conceptual problem-solving and the design of projects lead to greater academic achievement. It is time to dismiss the idea that a teacher's knowledge simply can be transferred into the minds of students. Some few determined students (probably those seeking all A's to get into prestigious universities) will take down lecture notes to memorize for a next test. Deep down most also know the facts and concepts heard or read will not be lasting. Knowing this aspect of cognition more than justifies moving from passive direct instruction to ways of active learning in cooperative small groups. Admittedly, we have a long way to go since it is estimated that 85% of teachers within 17,500 school districts in the U.S. use the traditional teacher-talk minimally effective approach.

Stages on the Continuum to Excellence Through Group Learning

The chart on the following page illustrates the continuum of change in teaching practices that thousands of teachers are making to reach and teach students more effectively. And to improve test scores! The continuum moves from traditional whole class instruction to active learning groups. Wherever you and your faculty are now on the continuum is truly o.k. What is important is that teachers support each other, coach each other and reflect upon their progress along the way. Change takes time, but once the direction is clarified, it builds the spirit of community, collegiality and excellence in learning throughout a school.

Oh, good, there's a chart on the next page!

Stages Towards Excellence Through Group Learning

Whole Class Instruction	Whole Class Tribes Community Circle	Cooperative Learning in Tribes	Discovery Learning in Tribes
teacher	**teacher**	**teacher**	**teacher:**
directs	directs	plans	selects topic/problem
lectures facts & concepts	initiates activity	initiates strategy	engages students thru inclusion
			makes connections to past + present learning experiences
			lays groundwork for group task
asks questions	asks questions	**tribes**	**student tribes:**
		discuss & work on task or problem	**1. engage**
seeks correct answers	affirms multiple answers	seek ideas and report solutions to class	define inquiry questions and process
assigns desk work			each tribe selects question to explore
manages behavior	manages behavior	manage task & interaction	(teacher acts as resource facilitator)
	builds inclusion	build inclusion and influence	**2. explore**
	students		implement activities to explore inquiry
	use agreements	monitor agreements	manage and assess group interaction
	learn collaborative skills	use appreciation	**3. explain**
			articulate observations and ideas
	work in collaboration		share and clarify terms/language with facilitator
tests for facts	reflect on interaction	reflect on learning and group interaction	(facilitator determines misconceptions & levels of understanding)
			present learning/project to whole class or parents
		assess for knowledge and learning	justify conclusion based on academic knowledge
			4. elaborate
			expand on concepts
			make connections to real world
			5. evaluate
students	learn together	learn together	reflect on performance outcomes
learn alone			share appreciation
			students (and teacher) assess learning

About the Stages

As pointed out in earlier chapters, as soon as teachers of a school have become trained in the basic Tribes Learning Community course, they are ready to implement the process by engaging students daily in a Tribes community circle. The objective of this first stage is to build inclusion, to learn to use the four Tribes agreements and to teach students to assess their participation and learning through group reflection. The community circle is teacher-centered - all eyes and ears on the teacher while he or she introduces topics, asks questions and controls behavior. Unfortunately some few teachers assume that they "are doing Tribes" because they have their class meet in the circle configuration. The community circle stage used consistently, does develop a caring community climate and social skills, but it is only the launching pad to the next stage, Tribes Cooperative Learning.

As soon as students are familiar with the Tribes community process and collaborative skills to work well together teacher and students organize tribes for cooperative learning.

The classroom becomes student-centered, filled with new energy, as the teacher's style changes from didactic instruction to facilitating active group learning. Gradually increased responsibility is transferred to students to learn academic material, to monitor the agreements and to manage the interaction of their tribes. The transfer from teacher to students not only is motivational but meets their development needs. This is especially true for middle level and high school adolescents. No longer do teachers spend 70% of their time lecturing, asking questions, giving instructions and disciplining. As facilitators of cooperative learning, teachers then have that much time to give support and encouragement to students. Best of all they have time to know their students and tailor learning experiences to their interests and needs.

Turn back to page 57 to recall the student-centered classroom study.

The move to Tribes Discovery Learning adds even a more significant dimension and promise for the education of today's children. The Tribes Discovery Learning process is based on decades of learning about teaching by such eminent leaders as John Dewey, John Piaget, Jerome Bruner, Howard Gardner and Lev Vygotsky, to name but a few. Even back to the 18th century a Neapolitan philosopher, Gambattista Vico, asserted that humans can only understand what they have themselves "constructed." Today the concept has become known as constructivism, and is gaining ever-increasing validity from recent evidence in the brain and biological sciences.[3] The approach engages students in social dialogue to define questions for inquiry, research, problem-solving, and to challenge hypotheses, design projects, test/defend solutions and evaluate their collaborative results. It transforms academic concepts for young learners into meaningful real-world possibilities.

Most teachers have learned the hard way that placing socially unskilled students in a learning group and expecting them to cooperate will not be successful. They must have learned essential social skills for collaboration. This is the reason many teachers give up cooperative learning—students do not know how to work well together.

"Sure, and that happens with adult groups too!"

Tribes is the glue that holds it all together...

...and makes group learning successful!

Tribes Discovery Learning is an integration of two frameworks: (1) the Tribes group development process of inclusion/influence/community, and the collaborative group skills and agreements;

(2) a constructivist instructional model, developed for the Biological Science Curriculum Study, Roger Bybee, Principal Investigator, Miami Museum of Science, and known as the "Five E's" standing for <u>E</u>ngage, <u>E</u>xplore, <u>E</u>xplain, <u>E</u>laborate, and <u>E</u>valuate.[4]

The complementary frameworks make planning easy for teachers who want students to gain meaningful real-life.

"This book got too heavy to add all of the how-to-do-it-well text and materials for Tribes Discovery Learning. Additional Materials are in the book, "Discovering Gifts in Middle School."

Connecting the Essential Elements of Cooperative Learning Through the Tribes Process

Among those who have done so much to advance the cooperative learning field are Drs. David and Roger Johnson of the University of Minnesota. In response to the inevitable question, "What is cooperative learning?" they have identified the following five basic elements considered essential to all cooperative learning groups:[5]

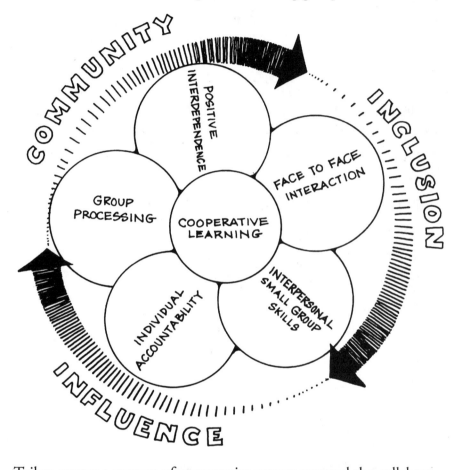

Positive interdependence
People undertake a group task with a feeling of mutuality, each person contributing, doing his or her own part, knowing "we sink or swim together."

Face-to-face interaction
People help each other to understand the task, check comprehension, and reflect on what was learned.

Interpersonal and small-group social skills
People learn interactive skills, manage conflict, develop trust and respect within a group.

Individual accountability
Group members take personal responsibility for learning the material, contributing to the group, and assessing both individual and group achievement.

Group processing
Members reflect upon and analyze group effectiveness, and define ways to improve group work together.

Tribes creates a context of community agreements and the collaborative skills students need to be successful in cooperative learning groups. If this foundation is simply taken for granted, teachers are often frustrated by their students' "inability to work together." Each student needs to feel a sense of inclusion, to feel of value to the group, in order to participate fully. Strategies and structures alone are not enough to assure the success of group learning.

We must shift from the traditional role of "knowledge dispenser" to that of model, mentor, and organizer of experiences that help students grow.

—Lynn Stoddard[6]

Designing Learning Experiences—The TLC® Plan

You may have noticed that instead of talking about designing curricula, we're talking about designing learning experiences. Of course, it's up to you which phrase you want to use. Most Tribes teachers agree that "learning experience" conveys a goal orientation, the intentional selection of strategies to achieve objectives, and real-time discovery for students.

The purpose of the Tribes TLC® form on the next page is to help you organize meaningful learning experiences for your students. You can use the form either for integrating academic content into a single Tribes strategy, or for writing a more comprehensive sequence of interactive strategies and cooperative learning structures. Two example plans are contained on the next two pages. A blank form that you can copy for your own use is contained in Chapter 12, Resources.

The **Tribes TLC® Plan** form is headed by five important sections that you need to think about before selecting any strategies:

1. Stages of group development—appropriate inclusion activity

2. Learning Objectives—Content and Collaborative/Social Skills

3. Sequence of Strategies and Structures

4. Reflection/Accountability

5. Appreciation

Stages of Group Development
What stage are the tribes in now?

- Has inclusion been developed sufficiently in the classroom?
- Do people know and honor the Tribes agreements?
- Do they all know each other?
- Have they gone through the issues of the stage of influence?
- Are they making decisions together? Voicing different opinions?
- Do they respect the diversity of their members?
- Are they working on tasks cooperatively?

| EXAMPLE | A Tribes TLC® Learning Experience | Grade: 4-8 |

1. Provide for **inclusion**—a question, activity, or energizer.

   Energizer: *Knots, page 387*

2. Identify the **content objective** to be learned and the **collaborative/social skill** objective to be practiced.

   Content Objective (write): *To learn and apply knowledge of geometric terms*

   Collaborative Skills: (check)
   - ☑ Participating fully
   - ❏ Listening attentively
   - ❏ Expressing appreciation
   - ❏ Reflecting on experience
   - ❏ Valuing diversity of culture/ideas
   - ☑ Thinking constructively
   - ❏ Making responsible decisions
   - ☑ Resolving conflict
   - ❏ Solving problems creatively
   - ❏ Working on tasks together
   - ❏ Assessing improvement
   - ❏ Celebrating achievement

   Social Skills:
   - ❏ Sharing
   - ☑ Listening
   - ☑ Respecting
   - ❏ No Put-Downs
   - ❏ Empathizing

   Other:

3. Identify the **strategy**(ies).

   Give Me a Clue, page 373: Have class in groups or tribes. Remind students of agreements. Clarify roles: facilitator, reporter, encourager. Follow directions in book.

4. Ask **reflection questions** about what was learned.

   Content: *What terms did you have to clarify to come to a solution? What comments from your tribe or group members helped to open up your thinking?*

   Collaborative: *What skills did you use?*

   Personal: *On a scale of 1-5 what was your level of participation? (Hold up fingers.)*

5. Provide an opportunity for **appreciation**.

   "It was helpful when (name) (behavior)"

   "I appreciated..."

Objectives

What academic content is to be learned? Of course, this depends on where your school is in preparing students for the 21st century, and what the district requirements are.

You may want to look back at Chapter 2, to review the list of learning experiences needed to prepare today's students for the 21st century. Because the list goes beyond the teaching of separate disciplines, it is important for school communities to generate a framework that integrates what they consider important for students as a meaningful whole. Marion Brady suggests four areas, based on their "probable contribution to human survival," and a synthesizing component to weld the four into a single discipline:[7]

- Learning about our physical environment

- Learning about the humans who occupy the environment

- Understanding states of mind that underlie human action

- Understanding how assumptions and beliefs manifest themselves in human behavior

- Synthesizing all these study areas into meaningful themes on national and global issues affecting humankind

Brady writes:

> If we are to survive as a society, we and our students need comprehensive answers to the question, What's going on here? We are not going to get those answers from the random, ethnocentric images of reality provided by the traditional disciplines. We need to look at reality freshly, and, if we are to put what we see in perspective, we need the means for seeing it as a whole...To send students out into the world without a conceptual framework for organizing experience is to fail them in the most fundamental sense possible.[8]

Which Thinking Skills?

The constructive thinking skills needed by young people in today's world may also be considered as *collaborative* skills in every sense of the word. The ability to contribute to a learning group or a work team depends upon clear thinking and expression. Academic content is the vehicle to develop higher order (constructive) thinking skills. Two challenges become evident: (1) Which thinking skills should be emphasized? (2) How do we help students learn about their own thinking processes?

"

It is time to think of curriculum as an integrated meaningful whole—to see subjects in terms of CONCEPTS, and to utilize all the basic skills to support and clarify those concepts, giving students a once-in-a-lifetime opportunity to develop their personal learning power.

—Susan Kovalik[9]

"

Students today need to know how to:

1. **Access information** from a wide array of resources

2. **Infer and interpret** its meaning

3. **Synthesize and link** it to existing knowledge

4. **Plan and apply** it to a real-life issue or problem

5. **Evaluate and refine** it for ongoing application or conclusion

The list is influenced by our belief that students need to be able to seek out and construct their own knowledge—not simply learn current knowledge, but know how to access relevant information at any time in life, whether from a data bank, a library, or any other source. It is startling to read that only one in five young adults (under 22 years old) can read and interpret a bus, train, or airline schedule. The capacity to plan and evaluate is essential for an era in which the rate of change is accelerated well beyond the stability of former decades.

Some Strategies to Develop Constructive Thinking Skills

Accessing Information
- Using group investigation and inquiry
- Learning to use the library, computers, data banks, and public records
- Conducting surveys and interviews
- Using the "Jigsaw" process

Inferring and Interpreting
- Using graphic organizers, displaying data on graphs or charts
- Debating; discussing; drawing; dancing
- Writing; using role play and music

Synthesizing and Linking
- Summarizing previous knowledge
- Comparing and integrating concepts and resources

Planning and Applying
- Analyzing relevance to a problem or situation
- Using problem-solving strategies
- Designing and creating applications
- Implementing action

Evaluating and Refining
- Reflecting
- Monitoring; measuring; interviewing
- Reporting; judging

Which Collaborative/Social Skills?

David and Roger Johnson emphasize that two types of instructional objectives need to be articulated in cooperative learning lessons: an academic objective and a collaborative skills objective. The latter designates the interpersonal and small-group skills that will be learned or practiced during a cooperative learning lesson. Each school community needs to choose the collaborative/social skills important to their own cultural population. Following are some of these skills inherent in the Tribes process. It is helpful to have people practice the same skill for many days at a time, or for the whole school to focus on one skill for a month.

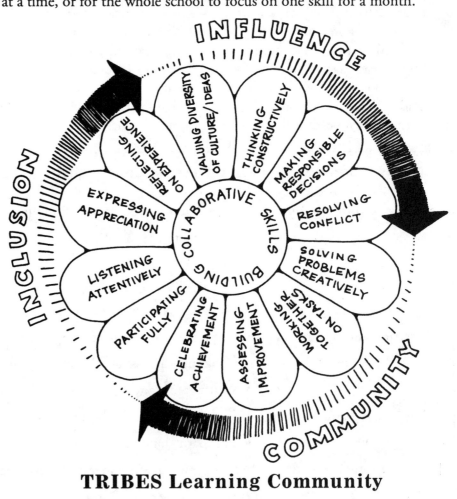

TRIBES Learning Community

Selecting Strategies and Structures

The Tribes strategies and/or cooperative learning structures that you select to carry the lesson content need to support the observed stage of group development. For instance, you would not want to use "Where Do I Stand," a strategy for the stage of influence, if tribes still need inclusion. Moreover, if they are to work on a task involving controversial issues, they should already have practiced a number of influence strategies. The exciting thing about the majority of the Tribes strategies is that they can be used over and over again as interactive formats for academic content.

Reaching Students of Multiple Learning Styles

Picture nine students sitting in a semicircle in front of you. They all have different learning styles because they all have different intelligences. Yet the traditional classroom reaches only two out of the nine, the 20 percent that learn through verbal/linguistic and logical/mathematical methods. National statistics tell us that at least three out of the other seven will become dropouts if not reached academically in the elementary and middle school years. One thing is for certain—they are not stupid kids! They simply have ways of knowing that differ from students with verbal/linguistic and logical/mathematical intelligences. They are not failing—their schools are failing to reach them.

I certainly can't create nine different lesson plans every day!

Of course not!

The Multiple Intelligences Idea Chart summarizes a wide range of ways to help you achieve that big goal of reaching each and every student.[11&12]

> 66
>
> *The good news about teaching with multiple intelligences is that it is not an "add on" to already overfilled curricula.*
>
> —David Lazear[10]
>
> 99

MULTIPLE INTELLIGENCES IDEA CHART

EXISTENTIAL

Engage in reflection
  and self-study
Read books on the
  meaning of life
Attend some form of worship
Watch films on big life questions
Record thoughts in a journal
Listen to inspirational music
Study literature, art, philosophy
Discuss life-human issues in a group
Record dreams and mystical events
Paint while listening to music
Create a private "centering" space

NATURALIST

Keep a journal of
  observations
Collect and categorize data
Make a taxonomy of plants or
  animals
Explain similarities among species
Study means of survival
Examine cellular structures
  with a microscope
Illustrate cellular material
Take out-of-door field trips
Visit an aquarium
Camp outside to identify stars

MULTIPLE INTELLIGENCES IDEA CHART

VERBAL LINGUISTIC

Write story problems
Create TV advertisements
Compile a notebook of jokes
Debate current/historical issues
Play "Trivial Pursuit"
Explain a situation/problem
Create poems
Impromptu speaking/writing
Create crossword puzzles
Teach "concept mapping"
Learn a foreign language
Write instructions
Read stories to others
Describe an object for
    another to draw
Make up a story about
    a piece of music
Describe the steps
    to a dance
Write a role play/drama
Keep a personal journal

LOGICAL MATHEMATICAL

Create a time line
Compare/contrast ideas
Predict the next events in a story
Define patterns in history
Follow a recipe/instructions
Rank-order factors
Analyze causes and effects
Learn patterns
Analyze similarities/differences
Classify biological specimens
Create outlines of stories
Create computer programs
Use a story grid/creative writing
Create a "paint-by-number" picture
Read/design maps
Solve math problems
Teach calculator/computer use
Decipher codes
Compose music from a matrix

VISUAL SPATIAL

Make visual diagrams/flow charts
Illustrate a story/historical event
Design/paint murals
Imagine the future/go back in time
Play "Pictionary"
Teach "mind mapping" for notetaking
Write/decipher codes
Graph results of a survey
Create posters/flyers
Create collages on topics
Draw maps
Study the arts of a culture
Make clay maps/buildings/figures
Create visual diagrams/machines
Illustrate dance steps/physical games
Teach Tribes energizers
Learn spatial games
Draw from different perspectives
Draw to music

MUSICAL RHYTHMIC

Create "raps" (key dates, math, poems)
Teach songs from different cultures and eras
Play musical instruments
Make simple musical instruments
Learn via songs and jingles
Learn through drum beats/rhythm
Make up sounds and sound effects
Practice impromptu music
Create interpretive dance to music
Lead singing (songs from different cultures)
Write to music
Reduce stress with music
Teach rhythm patterns/different cultures
Compose music for a dramatic production
Teach dance steps
Identify social issues through lyrics
Illustrate different moods through dance steps
Lead physical exercise to music
Clap a rhythm for the class to repeat

BODY KINESTHETIC

Lead Tribes energizers and
   cooperative games
Practice physical exercises
Lead students in stretching to music,
   deep breathing, tai chi, and yoga poses
Learn dances of different cultures
   and periods of history
Practice aerobic routines to fast music
Measure items or distances with thumbs,
   feet, or hands
Illustrate geometrical figures (parallel
   lines, triangles, rectangles, circles)
   with arms, legs and/or fingers
Conduct hands-on experiments
Act out scenes from stories or plays
Design role plays
Invent a new household tool
Prepare food or snacks
Simulate various situations
Learn alphabet through physical movement
Learn/teach sign language
Make up a cooperative playground game
Create human sculptures to illustrate situations

INTERPERSONAL

Role play a historical/literary or
   class situation
Analyze a story
Tell stories
Read poetry using different moods
Teach arithmetic, math, computer games
Review a book orally
Act out a different cultural perspective
Design and act out dramas/role play
Help tribe come to a consensus or
   resolve a problem
Facilitate participation in the tribe
Coach peers and/or younger children
Teach cooperative games
Help people deliver appreciation
   statements
Solve complex story problems
Discuss/debate controversial issues
Analyze group dynamics/relationships
Learn to sing and lead rounds
Plan and arrange social events
Find relationships between objects,
   cultures, situations

INTRAPERSONAL

Keep a personal journal or feelings diary
Analyze historical personalities
Write on personal learning experiences
Evaluate personal and group strengths/weaknesses
Analyze thinking patterns
Understand group dynamics
Use, design, or lead guided imagery
Write an autobiography
Analyze literary characters and historical
   personalities

Define personal reflection questions
Imagine and write about the future
Dance different stages in life
Lead Tribes personal inclusion activities
Practice relaxation techniques
Imagine self as character in history or story
Illustrate feelings/moods
Listen attentively
Draw self at different periods in life
Share how music affects feelings
Observe self (metacognition perspective)

Reflection Questions

The most important part of any TLC learning experience may be the reflection questions that you ask your students, because:

1. Asking good reflection questions within cooperative learning groups can double the rate of knowledge retention[9]

2. Students understand that they are not just learning information, but also higher-order thinking, social, and personal skills—competencies critical to their futures

3. Well-chosen reflection questions are an immediate way to assess how well your learning objectives were achieved

What questions will you ask so that your students realize what they have learned? If you check back to Chapter 5, you will recall that Tribes uses three types of reflection questions, Content/Thinking, Collaborative/Social, and Personal.

- **Content/Thinking** questions are focused on the content of the lesson and on the thinking skills that were used in order to work with the content. The content consists of the concepts learned.

- **Collaborative/Social** questions focus on the interaction that happens within a tribe or learning community, and on the interpersonal and collaborative group skills that were used.

- **Personal** questions focus on what the individual has learned.

Plan the questions you will use, and jot them down on the TLC Lesson Plan form. Of course, there will be times when you will want to change them due to events that happen during the class experience. Ask questions that will be most relevant and underline the key learning experiences.

Appreciation

Last but hardly least, opportunities need to be provided for people to express appreciation to those with whom they have worked. Never let a group finish work together without allowing time for statements of appreciation. It might be helpful to review "Encouraging Appreciation" in Chapter 5.

The more that appreciation happens, the more cohesive the tribes will be—the more comfortable they will be to keep working together, the better they will accomplish learning tasks, and the greater will be every student's sense of self-worth.

Lesson plans are not the whole answer, of course, to encouraging student learning. Your skills in presenting the learning experience are equally important. Reaching and teaching all students means personalizing the lesson, asking productive questions, and ensuring cooperation in learning groups.

Accountability: Individual and Group

The Tribes TLC teacher can use a variety of ways to determine the degree to which the three types of learning objectives are being achieved by tribes and individual members. The objectives are:

Collaborative skills—both thinking and social interaction

Content—curricular content and integrating themes

Collaborative skills

In Chapter 12 there are four forms that may be used to assess how well your students are learning and practicing collaborative skills. Form A is to be used by the teacher or an another observer (such as a parent volunteer) to assess attentive listening within tribes or as demonstrated by individual students. Each time that a behavior listed in the vertical columns is observed, place a check mark in the corresponding box. Totals may be added up at the end of the observation time. Be sure to tell the students beforehand what will be observed. Let them know their progress over time and make suggestions on how their tribe or the class can improve the ability to listen attentively. Other collaborative skills may be observed in the same way by listing the behaviors of a skill and keeping a tally.

The other three forms may be used by students to reflect upon and assess their own participation in their tribes, the quality of their working together, and their use of various constructive thinking skills.

Form B is used by individual students to reflect on their own participation in their tribe. They can monitor how well they are using certain skills, based on their personal observations over a period of time. The form can become part of their portfolios, recorded in personal journals, shared with their tribe, or shared with you.

Form C can be used either by individual group members or by the whole tribe to reflect on how well they worked together during a learning experience. If done by individual members, the tribe can total and average all of the ratings for a group score. In addition, the reflection questions that you ask throughout all learning experiences will indicate how well the collaborative objectives are being achieved by your class.

The first level of assessment on thinking skills is done through the reflection questions that you ask throughout the learning experience. Students can also help to evaluate the extent to which they used various thinking skills by using the fourth form, form D. This assessment can be used individually or by the tribe after the tribes have worked together to solve a problem or accomplish a difficult learning task. If the assessment is made by the whole tribe together, allow the students sufficient discussion time to cite specific examples of how various thinking skills were used. This can be a very rich learning experience.

Form A

Teacher Observation
Assessing Collaborative Skills—Listening

Form B

Student Assessment
Participation in My Group

Form C

Student Assessment
Our Tribe's Work Together

Form D

Student Assessment
My Thinking Skills

Content

You and your faculty need to determine and generate ways to evaluate the learning of academic content. The scope can vary and include:

- Reflection questions
- Project presentations (speeches; role play; video; oral reports)
- Portfolios
- Individual or group testing
- Written reports
- Video and audiotapes
- Teacher interviews with groups
- Student-to-student interviews

Assessment of the Tribes TLC® Process and Outcomes

All Tribes school communities will want to know the impact of the Tribes process on various outcomes such as a decrease in behavior problems, increase in academic achievement, attendance and other long term goals the school may have. Research on group learning indicates that the greater the extent that the process components of Tribes are used, the greater extent targeted outcomes will be realized. The Northwest Regional Education Laboratory designed an Assessment Kit to help your school strengthen its use of the process and assess outcomes. Check out page 428 for a description of the Kit or phone CenterSource Systems for information on the process and instruments.

Implementing a Tribe Learning Experience in Five Steps

1. Inclusion

Introduce the learning experience as people sit either in the community circle or in tribes, with an inclusion strategy (content linked to lesson topic) or a YOU question.

2. Objectives

Tell the students what content objective and what collaborative skills are to be learned or practiced.

3. Implementation of Strategies

Explain the task, group roles, and time available.

- Ask, "What questions do you have?"

- Observe and monitor the dynamics of the tribes working together, intervening only if they cannot resolve a situation or problem.

4. Reflection/Accountability

Ask reflection questions. Use written tests for individual and/or group accountability.

5. Appreciation

Invite statements of appreciation.

Personalizing the Learning Experience

Earlier we discussed how learning happens—how the human brain seeks out and catalogues patterns, linking new information to prior knowledge and experiences. Moreover, learning is accelerated when this happens. It becomes obvious that if we want students to learn new content, we need to connect it to previous experiences at the introduction of a lesson.

One way to do this is to initiate the lesson with personalized YOU questions, which also serve as inclusion activities for the class community or tribes.

Example: The lesson content is about the California Gold Rush. Begin the learning experience with a YOU question.

- Have YOU dreamed of finding a lost treasure? What was it?

- If YOU found a priceless treasure, what would you do?

- If YOU had to work out of doors in a remote place for a very long time alone, what would you take with you in order to survive?

The YOU question

- Is addressed directly to the student

- Is relevant to personal experiences, interests, feelings, or previous knowledge

- Evokes interest, recollection, opinions, and energy

- Appeals to the imagination

- Is shared prior to the introduction of lesson content

Responses to YOU questions are best shared in tribes, pairs, or triads. The questions can be used in a writing activity such as an imaginary letter to a friend, or recorded in the students' personal journals. YOU questions can be structured into these Tribes strategies or CL structures:

Think/Pair/Share	**One, Two, Three**
Think/Write or Draw/Pair/Share	**Community Circle**
Tribes/Brainstorm/Record/Report	**Open Forum**
Chain Reaction	**One-Minute Biography**

Asking Inviting Questions

Teachers ask questions! Yes, all kinds of questions. However, real learning depends upon the kinds of questions asked. Here's a short list of questions that are less than productive.[13]

Student: I want to study about the fish in the Great Barrier Reef.

Teacher: Do you have a library card? (Question is irrelevant and does not encourage student.)

Teacher: So how come the Pilgrims had to make friends with the Indians? (pause) No one knows? Well, it's because they needed their help in learning about the new land. (This is a teacher monologue question and gives students no thinking time or opportunity to answer.)

Teacher: What were the causes of World War II? (The question is too big and complex for a clear verbal response; may be intended only to showcase the brightest student.)

Teacher: Is the theme of the book "War and Peace" complicated? (The question calls for a "yes" or "no" answer, and closes off response.)

No doubt you can think of many others that keep classrooms from being student-centered and are unproductive. Step number one for teachers committed to moving to a new pattern of interaction with students is to ask open questions which invite richer responses.

This is the difference between open and closed questions:

Closed Questions	Open Questions
Have Yes or No Answers	*Invite More Complete Answers*
Did you...	How did you...
Would you...	Why would that...
Can you...	Tell me how...

Productive questions are open-ended and provocative, and challenge higher levels of thinking. They are clearly stated and focus on the big idea, the content issue of the lesson, or the thinking and interpersonal skills that were used.

Examples: What is your understanding of the events that led to the Vietnam War? (assessing/interpreting)

What's different about each of the three little pigs? (analyzing)

Which of the characters in the play *As You Like It* would you have wanted for a friend?

What data from the play supports your choice? (accessing, analyzing, relating, strategizing)

Questions that are Affirmative

Questions can be used to affirm positive behavior, constructive thinking skills, and multiple intelligences.

Examples:

- How did you ever guess that our class would have such a great time singing and beating out rhythm to your Brazilian tapes, Ricardo?

- Carly, what made you decide to invite your whole tribe?

- Andy, how did you manage to continue your sketching with all of the confusion going on around you?

- Tell us how your tribe decided to help the kindergarten children on the playground.

Extending Student Thinking

Teachers can help students to extend their thinking in a variety of ways when implementing Tribes learning experiences.

Practice "wait time:" Provide at least 3 seconds of thinking time after a question and after a response.

Use "think/pair/share:" Allow individual thinking time, and discussion with a partner, then open up for class discussion.

Ask follow-ups: Why? Do you agree? Can you elaborate? Tell me more. Can you give an example?

Withhold judgment: Respond to student answers in a nonevaluative fashion.

Ask for a summary: Could you please summarize John's point?

Survey the class: How many people agree with the author's point of view? (Thumbs up—Thumbs down)

Allow the student to call on someone: Jason, will you please call on someone else to respond?

Play the devil's advocate: Ask students to defend their reasoning against opposing points of view.

Ask students to "unpack their thinking:" Describe how you arrived at your answer. Think out loud.

Call on students randomly: Don't limit yourself just to those with raised hands.

Cue student responses: There is no single correct answer for this question. Please consider many alternatives.

From a Teacher's View

••••••

Nancy Lindhjem, Ed.S.

is a school psychologist and a Tribes TLC® Master Trainer who has worked for more than twelve years in public school settings in Indianapolis, Indiana, using the Tribes process as the foundation for a wide range of middle and high school peer programs. Her shift to private practice with Children's Resource Group allows her the flexibility to work as a CenterSource Systems Professional Development Consultant, sharing the Tribes philosophy and process with educators across the country.

Tribes is...an *Attitude*

As I travel around the country sharing the Tribes philosophy with educators, students, parents and community members, I feel compelled to make sure people understand that Tribes isn't "something else" they have to squeeze into their already-busy lives. I have come to the conclusion that the process of Tribes is more of an "attitude"—of respect, caring and acceptance. I have seen so many examples of positive change as the Tribes process begins to permeate the environment of a school community.

A few years ago, I had the opportunity to facilitate a Tribes training at an urban school in the East, one which had seen tremendous decline over the past several years. This school at one time had been seen as a "state of the art" facility but now was suffering from economic and demographic challenges as well as a downward shift in morale. The staff had experienced a significant number of administrative changes over the past several years. Although the current principal had expended great effort in providing numerous opportunities for staff development, she had expressed a great deal of frustration due to the lack of positive change resulting from the various learning experiences. Cynicism and a defeatist attitude greeted me as I entered the school environment, and I felt like I had my work cut out for me.

It was obvious within the first hours of the training that there was hope in this school for a new way of learning. There were, however, dynamics that needed to be addressed, openly and honestly. For example, as I began the first day of training, I was confronted by several seasoned teachers who had the "arms crossed," "what are you possibly going to tell me that I don't already know" attitude. Undaunted and convinced that the Tribes process can truly effect change, I began the process of building inclusion. By the end of the first hour, the transformation had begun. I heard comments such as, "Boy, I've taught next door to this person for the last 20 years never knew how special he is." Or, "We've had a lot of staff development in cooperative learning and team-building before, but now it's all starting to make sense!"

A highlight for me personally was seeing one particularly reluctant male participant (of the "folded arms" camp) demonstrate an incredible shift in attitude by bringing flowers to all of his female colleagues and food for the whole group on the final day of the training. He admitted that it is still difficult for him to communicate openly, but now he feels much more comfortable doing so in this more accepting environment. He also stated that he doesn't feel so isolated any more and can ask a colleague for help or ideas instead of doing everything "on his own."

It was truly inspiring and exciting

to witness the beginnings of growth in these dedicated professionals. It was especially moving to see how the once-disenchanted administrator had begun to understand that Tribes is a process and real change takes time. At a brief follow-up about six months later, I was elated to hear her say, "I never thought Tribes would be happening in my building, but it's happening all over this building!" The former discipline plan had been replaced by the Tribes agreements which were gradually embraced by the teachers, administrators, and initially-wary students. Referrals to the office were cut drastically as were suspensions and expulsions. After experiencing a year of the Tribes process in her building, this administrator has now expressed interest in becoming a Tribes trainer to continue to promote the process in her building and raise the level of awareness in her district.

When I returned to this school for the follow-up after six months of implementation, I felt an entirely different atmosphere than what I had experienced upon my initial arrival. People were more open, more relaxed. They laughed more and listened intently to one another. They were able to immediately work cooperatively to complete tasks. Their relationships to one another had obviously been heightened. There are still issues to be dealt with, to be sure, but it seems this staff has been able to develop the necessary climate of respect, caring and acceptance of one another which will allow the continuation of positive growth and change.

The Tribes process is a powerful tool to promote change and improve the climate, whether it be within the school, home, community, or within ourselves. I feel very fortunate to have these opportunities to spread the word about Tribes, and if one needs to cop an attitude, let it be a "Tribes" attitude. It works.

"

The more we help children to have their wonderful ideas and to feel good about themselves for having them, the more likely it is that they will some day happen upon wonderful ideas that no one else has happened upon before.[14]

Eleanor Duckworth
—*The Having of Wonderful Ideas*

"

Ensuring Interdependence

There are many ways to ensure cooperative interdependence in tribes or learning groups. Three important ones are to:

1. Develop bonding and group trust.

2. Use group roles.

3. Structure content areas.

Develop bonding and group trust

Teachers who use the Tribes process realize that the promotion of inclusion, safety, and trust produces close bonding after several weeks of inclusion strategies. This factor in itself develops the cooperation and interconnectedness among group members that all cooperative learning groups need in order to work well together on task. Groups that have experienced the Tribes process demonstrate thoughtfulness, and take care that everyone participates. The trust level also assures participation. Many teachers believe that the Tribes environment is an intrinsic rather than extrinsic way of assuring interdependence, and in time using group roles is optional.

Use group roles

Complementary group roles do help students learn to cooperate and count on each other's contribution and participation. Roles can be assigned by the teacher or selected by people within the tribes. It's important, of course, that roles are rotated, so that Dave isn't always the recorder, Heidi the encourager! Define roles that will be helpful to the completion of the task. Some of the roles used in cooperative learning groups are

Facilitator: Gets group started; makes sure directions are clear; encourages everyone to participate; calls the teacher if no one in the group can help

Recorder: Records group's work and shares with the community what the group has discovered

Encourager: Cheers people on; invites participation

Checker: Invites explanations from all members; checks materials

Accuracy coach: Checks for mistakes and the following of directions

Summarizer: Restates major conclusions; paraphrases agreements and disagreements

Elaboration seeker: Asks people to relate material to previous material

Time keeper: Helps group decide how much time will be needed; tells group how much time remains task completion; gives 5 to 10 minute wrap-up warning

The roles can be combined in any way to help the tribes work on tasks well. Make certain that the responsibilities of the roles are clear each time people begin to work together. You will notice that roles are not written into many of the Tribes strategies. Roles are probably more helpful when working with academic tasks than when learning social skills. We have left it up to each teacher to decide when to use roles.

Structuring content areas

The content can be divided into as many sections as there are members in the tribes, so that each student has part of what is needed to complete the task. "Cooperative Squares" is also a good strategy to use initially to teach the importance of interdependence and introduce the slogan "Together We Sink or Swim." The EQUALS Math Program of the Lawrence Hall of Science contains innumerable interdependent activities (see Suggested Resources, Chapter 12).

Research on the very popular "Jigsaw" process, designed by Elliot Aronson, has repeatedly proven that lower achieving students alter the academic image they have of themselves as they experience being "experts," teaching a part of the lesson to peers within their cooperative learning groups.

At the secondary or university level, the use of "Group Inquiry" (see Strategy section) is a great way to involve students in researching and studying part of an academic topic over a period of time, and then teaching the content to their learning group. The richness attained by many people collaborating can exceed the amount of data and information disseminated by any one instructor. Collaboration also prepares people for the workforce of today and tomorrow—to work cooperatively as team members.

If You Sense They Are Not With You

There are those inevitable times when you realize your students have tuned you out. They are no longer listening, have a glaze in their eyes, and are drifting—beyond caring about what is going on in the classroom. You may have been working hard in your move to have a more participatory classroom, and are baffled whenever things seem to slip back. Not to worry...it is a signal to take time out, diagnose what has happened, and take positive action. This checklist may help you to determine why your students' attention is waning.

1. Are you connecting the topic or lesson to their personal experience and previous learning?

2. Are you getting off the topic or talking too long?

3. How long have your students been sitting or working without much physical movement?

4. Have you identified their stage of development and group issues so that you select appropriate strategies?

5. Are you using enough group strategies to maximize participation?

6. Are you hovering over the tribes, rather than giving them responsibility to help each other with the task?

7. After an activity are you asking personal or social reflection questions before asking content questions?

8. Is there a disturbing event that needs to be aired or resolved before learning can be resumed?

9. Are you sensitive to the loss-of-energy dynamic when it begins to happen?

10. Do you "stop the action" and ask students what is going on?

9

Working With People Big and Small

9

Working with People Big and Small

There's no doubt about it! The Saturday flea market in our town is an important community meeting place. A few weeks ago, Barbara Marshall, Principal of our middle school, waved wildly across a pottery table to the author of this book. "Jeanne," she said, "do you have time for coffee? I have something to ask you about Tribes." We wandered over to the coffee stand, and after I set down the pink bird cage and old desk lamp I had found, we talked for an hour. Barbara asked a familiar question. "How can we help school board members, parents, and other district people understand what the Tribes process is all about in our school? It's hard to convey the big difference that it is making at all grade levels and with the staff."

"Aha," I thought to myself, "it's time for the Flatlands story again."

I asked Barbara if she knew the story. She said she would like to hear it.

The story begins just as most stories do. Once upon a time...there was a country that had just two dimensions, length and width, but it had no third dimension, height. The people of Flatlands had to inch their way through space...around corners, along streets, and into their flat houses. It was very frustrating. They had no perspective.

One day a Flatlander bumped into a strange object and then heard a voice say, "Come with me. Up here...come up here with me." "Up? What's up?" said the Flatlands man. Then he felt a tug on his arm and was pulled in a direction he had never before explored. Later he would learn the word "ladder." The friendly person at the top smiled and said, "Look at your country now."

The Flatlands man was amazed! Flatlands was beautiful from this new perspective. He could see an easier way to go from his house to his office, and wonderful undeveloped areas that people could live in and enjoy. He was so excited that he thanked his new friend and slid back down the ladder to tell people what he had seen. But no one could understand. "Up? Down? Height? Ladder?" they asked. At first they considered the Flatlands explorer a bit crazy, but then people began to wonder and even hope that the new perspective was real. Finally, the Flatlands man realized that his words alone would never be enough. He too could only say "Come with me—see and experience the difference yourself."[1]

The postscript to this story is that Barbara Marshall got the message and did the same. Her school is now a Tribes demonstration school with a welcome sign out to anyone who wants to see Tribes at work at different grade levels, with special education classes, with staff and parent groups. Understanding a new way means experiencing it a bit with those who set out earlier into a different dimension.

The purpose of this chapter is to provide a peek into some applications of the Tribes process with populations other than the elementary level. We asked some teachers, trainers, and principals to describe what the process looks like in their school communities. So put down your backpack...(or pink bird cage), and come along. You will learn how Tribes is used with the following groups:

- **Kindergarten and pre-school**
- **Special Education**
- **Middle school**
- **High school**

Kindergarten and Pre-School

The use of the Tribes process for little people began many years ago when some pre-school Montessori teachers at the Wallingford Daycare Center in Seattle wanted 3- to 5-year-olds to learn pro-social behaviors as well as the individual responsibility that Montessori emphasizes. There, as well as in other pre-schools and kindergartens, it was learned that:

- The community circle should be used many times during the day, that the tribes should consist of no more than three people for 3- to 4-year-olds and four people for 5-year-olds.

- Each tribe needs to have a space designated just for them...a small rug or table of their own is essential. Just doing that much within a kindergarten or pre-school provides security for each child. Much of the aimless energy (running about) is an effort to find a safe and familiar place in the midst of many people. The atmosphere changes when small children can relate more closely to two or three others, who become caring friends. They love to name their tribes and feel proud of their tribes' accomplishments.

- Young children enjoy helping each other and learn from one another. Those who can tie shoes can help others. Pro-social behaviors modeled and affirmed by teachers and aides are quickly learned.

- First teach the skill of listening. During community circle time, pass an object such as a feather, ball of yarn, stuffed animal, or puppet to help people focus on who is speaking. Teach children a signal such as hand cupped to ear or the thumbs-up sign, to let speakers know they are being heard. Provide a purpose for listening. Example: *We will be making clay animals today and there are three things you must remember.* Ask people to repeat the directions that you have given. Have the children identify sound effects (crinkling cellophane=a lively fire; shaking a cookie sheet= thunder). Have buddies take turns telling each other how to draw an object or animal. Use continuing stories, each person adding a sentence. Also have children in tribes tell each other stories and then relay the stories heard to other tribes. Above all, model attentive listening and affirm it in your students as it happens.

- Since young children love to enforce rules with each other, the Tribes agreements (once illustrated and practiced daily) easily become part of the classroom environment.

- Managing the kindergarten or pre-school is easier and behavior problems lessen as teachers (just as with older students) learn to involve the tribes in problem-solving. These little people love to give advice; they are creative and honest whenever suggesting how to improve the classroom or Tribes interactions.

From a Teacher's View

• • • • • •

Brian Jones

Creative Canadian kindergarten teacher/consultant/speaker for the Durham Board of Education, Ontario, is now a Course Director/Professor for the Faculty of Education at York University. We are certain that Brian's knowledgeable experiences with children in the formative years will be extremely helpful in his work with teachers of all grade levels.

How can we use Tribes in pre-school and kindergarten?

Brian Jones' eyes sparkled when he talked about using the Tribes process with the 3 to 5 year-olds. Laughing at himself, he said, Yes, I had to learn that what worked on Monday, might not work on Friday. But I do know what these little people are like:

> They love to talk
>
> They love to touch, feel and manipulate objects
>
> They are egocentric
>
> They play beside each other before playing with a partner
>
> They enjoy the element of fantasy
>
> They love praise, positive reinforcement
>
> They mimic and model behavior
>
> They talk spontaneously
>
> They want to be heard
>
> They like choices and situations they can control
>
> They want to share, and
>
> They are honest.

The Tribes process gave me the structure we needed. The biggest improvement has been having these very early learners reflect upon their experiences and feelings.

Each day I discuss the agenda in our community circle and share what will happen in various blocks of time known as morning circle, the 8 intelligence centers and "study-buddies," (tribes).

Community circle topics of interest promote participation... especially those that give advice to me, the teacher. We pass a teddy bear around the circle. Whoever has the bear is the speaker and the others are listeners. Some great topics have been:

- Today is going to be a good day because...

- I know someone loves me when...

- What's your favorite fairy tale? Why?

- If a hockey stick wasn't a hockey stick, what else could it be?

- What would be a good name for a new dinosaur? Donut-o-saurus? Sing-a-saurus?

- What do you think I should get my wife, Mrs. Jones, for her birthday?

Social skills are a vital part of every lesson. I constantly refer to Gonzo. This puppet oversees all social skill T-charts. Here are a few modifications to some of the Tribes strategies for 3-5 year-olds.

- **Two-on-a-Crayon:** (p. 223) becomes two-on-a-paper at first!

- **Jigsaw:** (p. 330) Tell a few (2-4) students how to complete a learning activity so that they become the "experts." Have small groups sit with these experts to learn the expectations.

- **Gallery Walk:** (p. 238) Have students stand beside their art masterpieces, and answer one question and acknowledge one appreciation statement that observers may ask.

- **People Hunt:** (p. 280) Use pictures.

- **Brainstorming:** (p. 259) Whole class brainstorming with teacher recording in words or images. Popular topics included:

  Build a super-duper sandwich

  Build a best dinner

  Build a better bedroom

  Build a better bathroom

- **Kitchen Kapers:** (p. 290) Give partners or tribes a bag of junk. They can make anything they want to as long as it is all attached.

- **Life Map:** (p. 291) Change this to "day map."

  Example: *Got up, had breakfast, brushed teeth, combed hair, etc.*

- **Barnyard Babble:** (p. 233) Give students a small plastic zoo or farm animal to hold while they move around the room making the animal sound.

- **Am I Napoleon?** (p. 263) Tape pictures and/ or an alphabet letter on the backs of people.

- **Where do I Stand?** (p. 323) Give small people only two choices.

  Examples: *Who is braver: Jack in the Beanstalk or Little Red Riding Hood?*

  Should the world have weapons? Yes/No?

- **Appreciating Others:** (p. 269) Have two hats available in the classroom; one labeled "Praiser" and the other labeled "Encourager." People who wear these hats have the job of circulating throughout the room, finding out what peers are doing and giving appreciation statements.

In preparing lessons I read an activity and then re-think it through the eyes of kindergarten students. I ask myself how can I modify it to meet the children's developmental level and at the same time use it as a vehicle to teach the Ontario Provincial Curriculum Expectations. The Tribes process has helped me to survive a full day program with 25 3-5 year-old students and no classroom assistant.

> "
> *My tribe are my friends— we work together and like us lots.*
>
> —Sarah, 4 years old
> "

> "
> *I know it's working when my students go to each other as a source of help and learning. It makes my class size almost manageable to be able to have them in small groups working together so that I can devote my focus to a few children at a time. But the overall message is that they can seek in each other the skills and know-how to accomplish wonderful things.*
>
> —Kindergarten teacher, San Francisco
> "

From a Teacher's View

● ● ● ● ● ●

Mary Palin, M.A.

*is a Master Tribes TLC®
Trainer and Professional
Development Consultant
for CenterSource Systems.
She teaches 6th grade
Challenge Class—"kids
who are a challenge or
need one"—in the Lake
Tahoe Unified School
District, California.
Mary says that she
enjoys working with
adolescents because of
their spirit, creativity,
and energy and because of
the challenge they provide
—which is well-matched
by the same qualities
in Mary.*

What happens when Tribes is used with middle school students?

After years of training staff in the Tribes process, and then watching a teacher's reaction when she bounces into a secondary school classroom and tries a strategy like "J.O.Y." and gets little or no response from her students—some tips for the process are important.

Typically, middle school adolescents are very egocentric. They love to talk about themselves, and their many opinions. However, respect for those outside their peer group or sharing the spotlight with peers is difficult. For the secondary student, a clear expectation of behavior and a "reason for doing this" should precede any activity.

Establishing trust in the classroom is essential and adolescents know enough about life to not give their trust easily. They have an uncanny sense of what is fair and what is not. The Tribes agreements are most important to the security of the classroom. The teacher/facilitator must be a positive and consistent model, establishing and modeling the agreements as a baseline for a positive classroom climate. When introducing or reviewing the agreements at the beginning of an activity, stress that the purpose of the "right to pass" is to assure people that it is their option to participate or not. I have found it effective to present the right to pass in terms of the right to participate. This gives middle school students a positive expectation for behavior without minimizing the importance of their right to pass. Tribes strategies and other

activities that are low risk and encourage all to participate will be most successful.

Most adolescents possess a sharp wit and tongue. Their brand of kidding more often than not can include many put-downs. Acknowledge their sense of humor, but raise their consciousness on how put-downs hurt people. Some ways to do this are:

- Have students view excerpts from a favorite television show, and count the put-downs. Reflect on how the characters must have felt receiving them.

- Have them do a survey for one week, tallying the put-downs that they receive and their reactions to them. Make a grand tally for the whole class. Repeat this several weeks later and compare results.

- Have students in tribes brainstorm how to eliminate put-downs in the class, among younger children— even on TV programs.

Attentive listening, a collaborative skill, should be taught as an objective right along with academic objectives. Once students know that they will grade each other or be graded on how well they listen, they begin to practice it to perfection. Do teach them the elements of good listening first. The agreement of mutual respect, which also assures students of confidentiality, is perhaps the most honored and accepted of the agreements among middle school students. They feel good about sharing when they can count on their group's trust and support.

In choosing strategies for secondary students, there are some definite criteria to consider:

1. **Secondary students need a mix of competitive and cooperative activities**...an interesting situation since, typically, adolescents are proficient at neither! On some days, one may focus on inclusion; on others, influence and more times than not the class will want both. Adolescents desperately need to feel valued (influence), but they lack the self-confidence and self-respect (inclusion) to properly seek recognition. The structure that the Tribes process provides allows for constant reuse, or repeating, of different strategies, integrating different learning content. Some favorites include: Put Yourself on the Line, Brainstorming, Tower Building, Outlines, Life Map, and What's My Bag.

2. **Reflect on the activity or strategy before, during, and at the end.** This keeps the limits and learning objectives well-defined, keeps communication flowing between the teacher and students, and provides ongoing assessment of what is happening. Remember the phrase "the activity alone is not enough?" With secondary students, the point is moot; their participation and ways of learning demand constant reinforcement and assessment.

3. **Facilitators must participate!** Your behavior and life experience are most interesting and secondary students will not perform without good reason and showmanship. Do not ask your class to do anything that you would not do first.

The path of the Tribes process through middle school may not always be predictable, but the returns are high and come in unexpected packages. After weeks of making small steps with a class or group, a strategy or reflection question will magically open new doors. However, prepare yourself for the day when those fun-loving sixth graders suddenly become shy and skeptical seventh graders—and a favorite energizer like "I love you, honey" gets a very different response. Trust the process... it works!

"

Middle grade schools—junior high, intermediate, and middle schools—are potentially society's most powerful force to recapture millions of youths adrift and help young people thrive during early adolescence. Yet all too often these schools exacerbate the problems of young adolescents.

**Turning Points:
Preparing American
Youth for the
21st Century
1989**

"

The Wider Challenge for Middle Schools

Middle schools across the country have been scrambling to initiate different ways "to recapture millions of youth adrift." They are introducing interdisciplinary teams, block schedules, advisory programs, exploratory subjects, integrated study themes, and curriculum focusing on problem-solving. Yet, the curriculum still may not be reflective of what is known about the needs of the early adolescence;[2] and the pattern of interaction has not been altered to meet the disparate needs of the population.

This time in a child's life is a dramatic one of personal and social change. It is a time of experimentation with new roles and values, and a time to discover identity. **Who one is** depends upon **who one is with.** A sense of acceptance and power among peers is central to young adolescents' sense of self-worth, thus central to their motivation and learning. Their major concerns seem to be more connected to coping, surviving and adjusting than to success. A recent survey of 9 to 16-year-olds found that:[3]

- 66% need guidance in understanding how to get along with others

- 42% want to know how to communicate with and relate to their parents and teachers

- 33% need help in dealing with loneliness or grief

- 25% want assistance in dealing with alcohol and/or other drug-addicted parents

James A. Beane, author of *A Middle School Curriculum: From Rhetoric to Reality*, makes the point that the developmental concerns of early adolescence must be addressed along with the social issues that these young people are facing. He writes:[4]

"The middle school ought to be a general education school, and its version of general education ought to be based upon personal and social concerns."

In recognition of the fact that the need for identity, belonging, and power among peers is not being met by the traditional middle school structure, especially in large middle schools, the 1989 Carnegie Council Task Force Report urged schools to provide membership structures, "communities of learning."[5] The committee envisioned that these communities could help students:

- gain the skills, knowledge, and attitudes necessary to create strong families, work groups, and communities;

- and acquire cognitive and relational skills.

The suggestion was heard, and since then many schools have created school-within-a-school, or "house," structures of teachers and students working together. The smaller units often consist of four teachers with 100 students. However, many are finding that students still have difficulty in relating to each other and developing close bonding with peers. Smaller groups are still needed. Ongoing membership in learning groups of four to six, and the use of the Tribes community building process are ways to structure the inclusion and identity that all students of this age group especially need. When teachers and students within the "house" learn and use the same collaborative skills, positive agreements, and caring process a new way of learning together can happen.

The Tribes Process with Special Education Students

The realization and legislation (Public Law 94-142) that students with mild disabilities should spend at least part of each school day in regular classrooms has been a challenge to many teachers. Teachers using the Tribes cooperative learning process report that the inclusive Tribes process is the best way they have found to mainstream these students because their regular students, so accept individual uniqueness and diversity that the special learners are simply considered part of "our community." Margery Hadden, in Park City, Utah, told us about a teacher with a student who was in a wheelchair. "Within a few weeks my fifth graders even seemed to forget about the chair and just took it for granted that John would be part of every activity."

Research has more than verified that all students achieve more in cooperative learning than in traditional (competitive or individualistic) classrooms, and that "this finding held for all age groups, ability levels, subject ages and learning tasks."[6] Studies just on the achievement of handicapped students verify that not only do they have higher achievement, but that individualistic instruction may be detrimental to their achievement.[7] This information alone provides special education teachers with sufficient rationale to implement cooperative learning classrooms. The Tribes process has been recognized as a particularly good way to teach special education students social skills since it assures the caring and accepting environment so essential to their relational needs.[8] Learning, whether within the realm of academic content or social skills, simply does not happen for them unless the classroom is inclusive, safe, and affectionate. Like all students, they need a place to share their feelings, concerns, and hopes. They need ongoing opportunities to make decisions, solve problems, assume leadership, and relate to peers in positive ways.

From a Teacher's View

• • • • • •

Michele Cahall, M.A.

has been a special education teacher of communicatively handicapped middle school students for more than 15 years for the El Dorado County Superintendent of Schools Office in California. She is a Tribes TLC® Master Trainer and Professional Development Consultant for CenterSource Systems. Michele has been deeply involved in the research and development of Tribes TLC® training and materials. In the midst of meetings, she can be counted on to remind everyone of her own primary purpose—"to improve the lives of kids and their families."

How does the Tribes process work with special ed students?

The Tribes process creates the positive social climate so critical to the needs of the special education student. Typically, special ed classrooms are populated by multiple age groups of multi-ability-level students. With some modifications, Tribes can be implemented with these classes as well as in regular classes that have mainstreamed special needs students. Here are some tips to special education teachers:

- Follow the same group development sequence as described in this book

- Introduce the Tribes agreements one by one; make sure that students understand the need for each agreement and how it will be helpful to the class and to themselves; post visuals (posters, pictures, and written instructions) of the agreements and refer to them often; practice each one in many ways (auditory, kinesthetic, musical) over an extensive number of days until they become "the way we are together"

The community circle is the most important strategy to develop in special education classrooms. It gives you the opportunity to gather everyone together; to practice the agreements; to experience inclusion strategies, address problems, and make group decisions. Be sure to give clear directions as well as visual cues for whatever topics are being talked about. Always model a response first yourself to be certain that directions for the strategy are clear. Trust built through regular use of a community circle enables reticent students to express themselves and to find commonalities with peers. Use many affirmative reflection questions, such as, "Terry, how did you decide that everyone would enjoy learning about fly fishing?"

Such reflection questions, repeatedly used, can help to move students to higher thinking skills and also build self-esteem. Just as in all classes using the Tribes process, an invitation to peers to give appreciation statements needs to follow every activity.

Most of the Tribes strategies can be used as written or with the modifications shared above. A valuable resource for implementing Tribes in special education classes is the book *In Their Own Way*, by Thomas Armstrong. Armstrong was a special education teacher who saw that the application of Howard Gardner's work on seven intelligences would be of immense value in working with students with special needs. The book helps teachers and parents to understand that students may be stronger in other intelligences than in those traditionally used in schools. Teachers having a clear understanding of the seven intelligences can provide their special students with choices on how they can share their knowledge of the material. The Multiple Intelligence Idea Chart in Chapter 8 and the description of the intelligences in Chapter 3 can help you to enrich the ways in which you work with your class.

Tribes energizers (contained in the Strategy section) are also a great way to involve special learners, especially the kinesthetic youngster who has a difficult time sitting for long periods of time doing tasks that do not require physical activity. In order for these children to reclaim their energy for learning, they need to be involved periodically in complex movements in the large muscles of the arms, legs, and torso.

Energizers lend themselves to classroom use with a minimal amount of preparation time.

A management technique that is very helpful is "Stop the Action." Whenever a lot of disruptions are happening, simply call out "freeze" or "stop the action." Then guide your students to identify whatever was happening, and the behaviors that would be more helpful. Ask them to share ways they can help the class accomplish the desired behaviors. This helps them to recognize their own responsibility and the positive contribution that each one can make to the community.

Do read about the Research Triangle Institute's identification of Tribes for teaching social skills to students with disabilities. A summary is in Chapter 12, "Resources."

The following strategies and energizers are easy to implement in special education classes because they require little or no modification:

Community Circle

Two on a Crayon

Fuzzyland Map

Creative Storytelling

Warm Fuzzies

Warm Fuzzybag

Five Tribles

Brainstorming

Sharing from a Sack

Bumper Sticker

Spider Web

Life Map

Kitchen Kapers

Cooperation Squares

One, Two, Three

Thumbs Up–Thumbs Down

Where Do I Stand?

Put Yourself on the Line

Peer Response Huddle

Love My Neighbor

I Love You, Honey

Zap!

Snowball

From the Teachers' View

• • • • • •

Gloria Woodside

is an experienced High School teacher having worked for 25 years with the Durham Board of Education in Ontario, Canada. As a Business and Information Technology Teacher, Gloria taught grades 9 to 13. She has also worked as a consultant developing curriculum and introducing teachers and administrators to Tribes.

Michele Cahall, M.A.

See her educator biography on page 184.

How Can the Process of Tribes be Used in High School and Beyond?

Over and over we hear the question, "Can the process of Tribes really be used in high school classes?"

Repeatedly we respond, "Yes, it certainly can!" Teenagers especially are seeking inclusion with peers and thrive when involved in learning that is meaningful to their interests and lives. The traditional whole class instruction/lecture approach is particularly frustrating for this age group, causing many to tune out or drop out. At the same time, high school teachers are concerned about the lack of time in each class period, the amount of curricula they are expected to cover, and the large number of students in their classes. These are legitimate concerns for discussion in all school districts.

What is known, both from research and from the experience of thousands of secondary and university teachers, is that learning in cooperative groups engages and motivates student learning. Organizing students into ongoing study or investigative groups is not only effective for classes of any length of time, but is a participatory management system that involves all students. Review the significant benefits of cooperative groups with your high school faculty (as discussed in Chapter Two): increased productivity and achievement, motivation, critical thinking, self-esteem, improved

intergroup relationships, psychological health, social support and social competency are immeasurable payoffs for the high school years. The U.S. Department of Labor has issued a report entitled, What Work Requires of Schools. The Tribes process teaches the skills identified in this report, the skills that young people entering the work force need: how to identify and organize information and resources, how to relate well with others in work teams, and how to understand social and organizational systems.

Implementing the Tribes process in high school and college classes should follow the same sequential steps of establishing agreements and building inclusion, influence and community. Initial inclusion strategies help students to learn the names of their classmates and the unique skills, interests and contributions that each can make to the learning community. Students need to be given a voice regarding who they would like to have in their ongoing study groups. Responsibility and decision making need to be transferred to student groups. Groupings of five to six people work well with older students and adults.

Academic content can be integrated well into study groups through Tribes strategies and cooperative learning structures. Controversial issues can be explored by using the strategy *Put Yourself on the Line.* Have students research and debate the opposite opinion from the one initially chosen. This opportunity develops a sensitivity, understanding and respect for different ideas and opinions. Concurrent with this strategy, understanding changes in legal, political or economic theory can be initiated by using *Our World is Changing.* Have each student draw a personal *Life Map* and have the tribe research and draw an economic or historical map of the same period. The two maps then can be examined side-by-side so that the relationship between their lives and the world (or country) can be studied.

Jig Saw is a great way to structure team learning for high school students because it mirrors the team approach now being widely used throughout business and other organizations. Inasmuch as each group has specific tasks and a limited amount of time for research, the strategy helps students cover a great deal of material in a thorough and efficient way. *Campaign Manager* is also an engaging way to review concepts. Instead of having each team member putting his or her name on the slip of paper, prepare slips ahead with a concept to be learned. After drawing the slips, the students outline, research or lead discussions within their tribes of the most important aspects of the concept.

A useful way to examine the effects of new law or policy is through the use of *Celebrity Sign-In.* For example, when a government presents a budget, its ramifications on the community can be examined. Assign each study group a population that will be affected by the issue and have the group research the changes that the budget will bring. At the conclusion of the research time have the whole classroom meet, and invite each team to speak for the population group that they represent.

Report back time to the whole class provides each study group the opportunity to summarize what they have learned together. After each interactive strategy, reflection questions are essential. The questions should help students identify the thinking skills used within their groups, and the group's effectiveness, as well as academic content learned. Reflection is critical to the retention of learning.

Since all groups inevitably must be able to make decisions and solve problems, they also need to learn and practice those skills. Check out Chapter Seven again so that you can move your students through a sequence of strategies. Keep in mind that learning decision-making and problem-solving techniques can be done using curricula issues.

The high school years and higher education give educational systems the final opportunity to develop the essential collaborative skills, constructive thinking and resiliency that young people need in order to do well in their lives. We need to clarify our priorities and ask what will most awaken and sustain life long learning within each young person who comes our way. That's what this process of Tribes is really all about.

I want to instill in them a hunger for knowledge, truth, and justice. I see teaching as the opportunity to light the fire that will send them on a quest for lifelong learning and for justice.[9]

—David Christiano, High School English Teacher

High School Groups

Investigative or inquiry groups are most helpful and stimulating for students at the upper grade levels, college and adult classes. There are several different effective models:

1. **Coop-Coop,** developed by Spencer Kagan,[10] calls for selecting a main topic of study and then sub-dividing it into mini-topics. Each student selects a mini-topic, studies it and then shares the information with his group. The group compiles all information and presents it to the class. Evaluation covers the student's work in the group and individual papers.

2. **Group Investigation or Group Inquiry,** developed by Shlomo Sharon and Rachel Hertz-Lazarowitz[11] emphasizes interdependence among groups. An area of study is selected by the teacher. Student groups then select a topic related to the area that interests them. The teacher and the groups decide how to investigate the topic. Each member carries out an individual investigation, the group then summarizes findings and prepares an interesting presentation for the class. With younger children, work-stations can be set up in the classroom where research is conducted.

3. **Jigsaw,** developed by Elliot Aronson,[12] works well for on-going tribe groups. Again the main topic of study and mini-topics are selected by the teacher. Students number off within the tribes and join mini-topic groups to research and become experts in one aspect of the topic. In time, they return to their tribes and teach their peers the content learned.

These methods are particularly helpful in practicing higher level thinking skills, such as analyzing, synthesizing and applying. The groups also learn that achievement depends upon their effective use of collaborative skills. The complete instructions for these strategies are contained in the Strategy Section of this book.

The high school years give educational systems the final opportunity to develop the essential resilient attributes young people need in order to do well in their lives. We need to ask what really are the priorities and what will most awaken the innate potentials within each young person who comes our way.

Just a Teacher

Today I was a nurse binding a hurt with the white bandage of compassion,
A doctor healing a small broken world,
A surgeon suturing a friendship together.

Today I was an alchemist seeking gold in base metals,
A scientist answering endless whys,
A philosopher pondering elusive truths.

Today, I was an entertainer, refreshing young minds with laughter,
A fisherman dangling learning as a bait,
A pilot guiding youth away from ignorance.

Today, I was a general campaigning against intolerance,
A lawyer speaking out for brotherhood,
A juror weighing right and wrong.

Today, I was a philanthropist sharing the might of the past,
A mother wholly giving love,
A humble follower of truth.

Mine are such varied occupations.
How can they know me?
Just a teacher.

—author unknown

10
Bringing It All Together

10

Bringing It All Together

Remember us? We're the people who were asking all the questions, back in Chapter 1 of this book, on how to improve the quality of education for all of the kids in our school. We've been looking forward to this last chapter because it describes how to involve the whole school community in collaborative action to achieve the developmental goals that we have for students. Participation just doesn't happen—it must be structured so that everyone feels included, acknowledged, and valued. That's what it takes to create a learning community.

- *Now every person belongs to a tribe (a small group of peers)—students with students, teachers with teachers, parents with parents, community resource people and administrators with one another.*

- *Every person understands and uses the same inclusive Tribes process, positive agreements, and collaborative skills as taught to our students.*

- *Every person is involved in strategizing how to bring about the healthy development and resiliency of all students and quite possibly ourselves! The "new way of learning together" within our many peer groups has given us an authentic sense of community, which makes collaboration possible.*

Innovation Happens Through Peer Learning Communities

The Tribes process is an innovation that, like any other, challenges people to adopt new ways of perceiving, relating, and acting. Invariably, new methods are met with varying degrees of enthusiasm and persistence. Here at Tribes headquarters, we are sometimes asked how long it takes for a majority of teachers in a school to make the TLC process their own, or how long will it take to develop a TLC school community. Our reply is that it depends upon the rate of movement through the following stages:

> *Most people evaluate an innovation not on the basis of scientific research by experts, but on the subjective evaluations of near peers who have already adopted the innovation.*
>
> —Everett Rogers

1. **Knowledge:** Some decision makers or leaders gain an understanding and perceive the benefits of the new process or method.

2. **Persuasion:** The early adopters (peers) tell others.

3. **Decision:** People agree to participate in an activity that leads to making a choice (that is, hear a presentation, discuss with peers, watch a video, visit demonstration classrooms).

4. **Implementation:** People take steps to learn (training, support, and peer coaching).

5. **Confirmation:** People give each other support and reinforcement.

Everett Rogers, who has written extensively about the adoption of innovations and defined the stages above, emphasizes that it is the activation of peer networks that leads to "take off."[1] This is why school restructuring efforts need to begin with the formation of small membership groups of peers: students, teachers, parents, administrators, and community resource people. Peter Senge, author of *The Fifth Discipline, The Art and Practice of the Learning Organization*, says:

> *"Virtually all important decisions occur in groups. The learning units of organizations are 'teams,' groups of people who need one another to act."*

Although the concept of school "learning communities" is blanketing educational journals and conference speeches these days, how to structure such communities and how to create a collaborative environment within them has remained vague. In other words, most people agree on the vision but are searching for a way to make it happen. Once a staff learns how to use the Tribes group development process in classrooms, they also can organize the faculty, parents, and resource people into learning groups (tribes), and plan across groups for network action. This makes the school learning community a reality.

Then all of the peer groups can discuss common issues, solve problems, and make collaborative decisions. They can investigate and design supportive strategies for the school community. Their new collegial structure supports learning just as it does for students in classrooms. The integrated school community can acquire knowledge, collaborative skills, and resources.

Parents and teacher tribes can learn about the protective factors that build resiliency, and they can implement a wide range of activities for students of different grade levels. The essence of the protective factors (caring and sharing, participation, and positive expectations) catalyze action throughout the school community system. Integrated through the Tribes group process of inclusion, influence, and community, the school learning community not only has a new way of learning together but a new way of being together.

Successful Implementation

Successful implementation of the Tribes cooperative learning process, whether in classrooms or the whole school community, depends upon the following:

Steps for the Successful Implementation of Tribes TLC®

1. Recognition that the Tribes approach is a beneficial innovation

2. Commitment for implementation from teachers who have explored the Tribes process, concepts, and methods

3. Strong, continuing administrative support

4. Sufficient time for training, peer coaching, curriculum planning, and classroom observations

5. A widely held desire for school community

6. Quality training for teachers conducted by qualified Tribes TLC district trainers and/or CenterSource Systems trainers using the most recent materials and methods

7. Formation of classroom parent groups, structured and facilitated by parents

8. Assessments designed and data collected, to check progress

9. Celebrations that happen regularly

> *It is social support from and accountability to valued peers that motivates committed efforts to succeed.*
>
> —David and Roger Johnson

From an Administrator's View

• • • • • •

Marilyn Sumner, M.Ed., has been the Executive Director for Instructional Support Services for the Spring Branch Independent School District in Houston, Texas and has recently retired to become a private consultant.
Annette Griffith, M.A., is the Director of Guidance and Health Services as well as the Spring Branch ISD coordinator for Tribes.
Linda Reed, M.A., is the Area Superintendent for 10 Schools: Elementary, Middle and High School. All three are highly skilled administrators, Tribes Trainers and professional leaders in their communities and nationwide.

A District Story—Creating a Caring Community

We often hear the question: "Why have schools of your district chosen to use Tribes?" Our response is very clear. First, we wanted to transform classrooms into interdependent learning environments that increased success for all students. Secondly, we recognized that the Tribes process provides a framework to actively link other instructional initiatives and align them through strategies and a common language across grade levels and subjects.

In less than two years from the first Tribes 24-hour training classes, we realized that the impact of Tribes would be bigger, more systematic and more powerful than we predicted. As teachers and other staff began to use the strategies and process, vivid success stories literally telegraphed from teacher to teacher and school to school. Without a district mandate and with limited district funding, Tribes grew from two schools to implementation in all twenty-six elementary schools and a quarter of the middle schools.

Campus commitment was critical to the implementation at each school. Administrators, teaching staff, and the Campus Advisory Team showed commitment by participating in and writing follow-up support and resources into their campus plans. Initial training was offered first to educators and schools who were ready to use Tribes.

The district allocated resources for training and materials. CenterSource Systems trained a cadre of 44 Tribes district facilitators with the goal of having two per campus. A collaborative district network supports and sustains implementation. It addresses the needs of the trainers, including everything from training materials to study group meetings, to discuss progress of campus implementation and future needs.

Campus and district administrators were offered courses and urged to involve the entire community of students, parents, and staff in learning and using the process. Principal commitment was a key component to the implementation process. Principals and campus facilitators modeled the use of Tribes in faculty meetings, served as trainers and supported the development of trainers for their campus. Opportunities were created for staff to share successes, ask hard questions and reflect about their learning. Throughout the district, various departments began to voluntarily identify ways that Tribes related to their work. Assessments, formal and informal, have helped each campus and the district to improve its support of Tribes implementation each year. As a result, demand for Tribes classes is still greater than the number of classes that can be provided.

As greater proportions of the staff are trained, there is more and more observable evidence that behaviors and attitudes are changing among staff, students and parents. For example, we realized that many classroom discipline approaches adopted in the past endeavored to teach students responsibility, but did not transfer responsibility, nor the monitoring and modeling of responsibility to students themselves. In district evaluation teachers who have implemented Tribes indicated that they spent less time managing student behavior. Students in those classes reported that they got along better with others. By far the most exciting stories profile youngsters who change from "dropped out but present" in class to full participation. Group behaviors changed even at bus stops because students are accepting more responsibility for their behavior.

Our schools face daunting challenges that require new solutions, new ways to reach and teach all students. Evaluations of initiatives are critical to maintain community and administrative support. In the spring of 1999, 55 classroom teachers and their students, grades three through five responded to an evaluation survey. In Tribes classrooms mutual respect was consistently evidenced through behaviors. Students and teachers consciously were not a part of rumors or gossip. New people and visitors felt welcomed. Teachers indicated that they had more time for creative teaching, and students saw new learning as "fun." This Tribes evaluation process substantiated the many stories about teaching being more fun, students more focused.

Our most effective meetings look similar to the Tribes TLC® lesson components. Meeting plans incorporate time for inclusion, clear statements of purpose and objective, strategies to accomplish tasks, reflection and appreciation. And yes, as educators we do need to refine our collaborative skills in order to work well together in different contexts. Even the routine of brief energizers enables adults to maintain focus longer. Work teams often comment on the emerging sense of community and positive energy as they produce results! It is no coincidence that the business world is engaged in a similar journey of organizational learning to meet the myriad of external forces of change. (Brown and Isaacs, 1996).[2]

Our schools' journey with Tribes is indeed weaving an amazing, stronger human fiber to improve the way we "do school." Talk about Tribes permeates through and around the system. The process not only develops a caring community but supports and aligns our work with powerful tools and a common language. Of course, Spring Branch schools are still in the midst of their Tribes journey heralded by celebrations all along the way. Wouldn't you also celebrate the day when the middle school teachers started asking each other why their sixth graders were acting kinder and more cooperative? No need to answer! Just accept our invitation to join us in this journey that truly brings joy to learning and relationships.

> "
> *A sense of community is a perception that members have of belonging and being important to each other.*[3]
> —Florin and Chavis
> "

"

You can't improve schools
without good teachers, but
you can't get good teach-
ers unless you treat them
as professionals.

—Marc Tucker[4]

"

What Administrators Can Do

As an administrator, you need to be clear about the potential payoffs of working in a new pattern of interaction throughout the school community. If you have some questions about what the Tribes process can do for your students and school, give us a call at CenterSource Systems so that we can put you in touch with other principals and administrators who have been using the process for some time. There are benefits not only for classroom management, but for the school as a whole. Once a faculty becomes familiar with using the Tribes process in grade or departmental level small groups, shared decision making and school site planning become collaborative and satisfying.

Just as with other new programs, you need to identify the following resources that will be needed over time:

- Experienced and qualified trainers
- Initial training and release time
- Materials
- Coaching and follow-up time for the faculty
- Assessment tools

The full implementation of the school community Tribes process takes time. A staff will go through predictable stages as they increase their skill and confidence in using the Tribes process and integrating it with curriculum in a variety of ways. Progress takes a big leap whenever a principal uses the decentralized process (teacher tribes) for staff meetings or school improvement planning. Whether solving a parking problem, establishing a new grading policy, or revising curriculum, the collaborative "people skills" and caring environment make management and change easier. Nothing makes collaboration clearer than the principal's willingness to become a learner too.

Staff Development and Ongoing Support

Time out for a question. How many times have you participated in "staff development, in-service, or an educational course" that sent you back to your classroom with some great activities that you whipped through, and then said to yourself, "Now what?" Effective training provides the WHY, the WHAT, and the HOW. The WHY is the theoretical basis for the teaching approach or method. Unless we understand the rationale, some of the research, and why a process or method is appropriate for a population or the times, WHAT to do and HOW to do it are limited.

Quality in-service training and ongoing support are essential. Research (also common sense) tells us that teachers not only need to have knowledge of the theoretical basis or rationale for the teaching method, but they need to be able to:

- Observe demonstrations by persons who are well versed in the TLC classroom process

- Practice and be given feedback under controlled conditions (such as trying out the strategy with one another before using it with students)

- Coach one another as they begin to implement the process, and to

- Reflect upon and evaluate their progress.[5]

Demonstrations can happen any of these ways. You can:

- Visit some Tribes classrooms in your area

- Invite a qualified Tribes TLC® District Trainer to do demonstrations in classrooms of your school

- Or you can encourage any of your own teachers who may have been using the process for a period of time have others observe their students working in tribes.

Be sure to take the time to reflect with those demonstration teachers on what you observed.

We urge all Tribes schools to arrange for ongoing meeting time so that teachers' grade level and planning groups can meet regularly. Teacher tribes need to:

- Support and coach each other

- Design integrated learning experiences (lesson plans)

- Identify appropriate materials and resources

- Assess progress toward learning objectives, and

- Plan training for the parent facilitators of classroom parent groups

It takes the realization at the district level that teachers as learners and planners are a school's best bet toward improving education for students. Some schools add days to the teaching year so that their teachers have two hours every week to work together. Others add monthly in-service days, and even paid meeting and sabbatical time. As helpful as periodic in-service days may be, ongoing learning/planning/coaching groups are the most effective way to assure year-long support.

A Principal's Perspective

• • • • • •

Carole Freehan, M.Ed.

is the Principal of Pearl Harbor Kai Elementary School in Honolulu, Hawaii. She has also been a vice principal, general education teacher and special education teacher in various elementary schools on Oahu. Since becoming a Tribes trainer, she has trained both in-service and pre-service teachers. Using the Tribes process, Carole has immersed the staff at Pearl Harbor Kai Elementary in creating a community that supports increased student learning.

Transforming a School

Transforming any school into an excellent school involves everyone working hard. It takes the commitment of parents, teaching staff, paraprofessionals, clerical, cafeteria and custodial staff to create an exceptional learning environment for children. As educators, we need to continually find ways to improve and strengthen our teaching strategies while school is in session. We are under unbelievable pressure from a multitude of constituencies: parents, boards of education, community, and society. The stakes are constantly being raised.

How can the transformation of a school take place? I believe it comes when everyone knows what excellence looks like, feels like and sounds like. It comes when we can collaborate to seek out the hard issues of what is important for children to learn. It happens when the re-culturing of the school ensures that all the constituents' voices are heard and included.

Historically, Pearl Harbor Kai Elementary has regularly scored in the average or slightly above average on standardized tests. As a staff we were struggling with making changes by implementing programs. We were hoping that the next *program* would be the one to help us rise above mediocrity and transport us to a higher level of excellence. As part of the change process, I put teachers into groups and asked them to work together on school-wide professional issues.

While some groups functioned very well, others were less successful. I arranged and rearranged groups of teachers by interest and expertise. The end result was a scattering of many good ideas that did not lead to a coherent workable structure for school improvement. Individually the teachers were excellent teachers, but working collaboratively as a group was a very different and underdeveloped skill.

As much as I rationalized this whole process, I knew that I was missing something–a something that could really affect change in the staff. The lightning bolt of discovery hit me when I went through my first four-day Tribes TLC® training with half of my staff. I realized that my teachers and other staff members were not a learning community or *any* type of community, even though many of them had worked together for over a decade! Just as a teacher has a classroom of children who come with diverse talents and gifts, I had the same situation, although my *students* were adults in the school. A few months after I completed the Tribes TLC® training, I was able to provide another four-day training for the rest of my staff and a two-day program for my classified staff and parent leaders in the school. Training everyone at the school was the first and the easiest step we needed to take.

Tribes TLC® is not that *next*

program; rather it is a philosophy and process that is critical to creating an environment in which everyone is both a teacher and a learner. One of my roles as the principal is to model the process for the teachers. Teachers need support when they are trying something new or different. They too need to be supported to use the caring Tribes agreements, to experience strategies and take time for reflection questions that are critical to learning. We all know that experience is the best teacher!

So how has the process of Tribes helped us? Well, as we continue to work to become an excellent school, we find that our efforts are not as frustrating as before. All of the teachers, paraprofessionals, classified staff, and students speak the same language. We have a common understanding of the Community Agreements. This understanding is extending to our parents. We are traveling the journey to transform ourselves. Along the way we are creating a community, a community that is caring and supportive and learning. Pedagogical differences among the teaching staff are to be expected. Immersion in the process of Tribes has helped us to deal with the differences and see them as opportunities for professional growth. Now that we include everyone in a respectful and supportive environment, the teachers are more willing to take risks. I see a staff that works daily with the process of Tribes with their classrooms of students and with their colleagues. I hear student and teachers speak respect-

fully with each other reducing conflicts. I feel the support that radiates from students, teachers and staff to each other.

Tribes TLC® is not the panacea to a school's problems. Just spending four days going through the training will not, by itself, change anything. We have to live the process every day. As the Principal, I know that I am responsible for carrying the torch for the school. Are we at the top level of excellence yet? Of course not! Have our standardized test scores improved? Yes, they have! As the school travels the Tribes trail together, I see the synergy of the teachers learning from each other and creating exciting opportunities for our students. There are still areas of instruction and assessment we need to define, study, align, update and improve so that we increase student achievement. Knowing how to work and learn together, we are able to pass over any barriers that block our way towards consistent success. Now that we are a community, I find there are many hands carrying that torch now.

Building a Parent Network

Although studies have more than proven that there is a direct correlation between family/school collaboration and gains in student achievement,[6] how to involve a majority of parents has been an ongoing puzzle. Getting out to evening meetings at the school after a long day of work needs to be something more than an obligation. Parents are people too! They have the same human need for attentive listening, appreciation, and a sense of community.

Unfortunately, typical school meetings follow a traditional "we'll-tell-you-what-you-need-to-know" format, and are not structured for inclusion and active participation. Tribes schools have a big advantage! Knowing the TLC process, their teachers can facilitate a school-wide support system for hundreds of parents. The system is based on *parents reaching parents rather than teachers reaching parents*. Here's how it works! Have each teacher identify two parents of students in his or her class. The two parents identified from all of the classrooms are invited to become facilitators of parent groups (tribes) in their child's classroom. The parent volunteers participate in an initial two hours of training to learn and practice how they will lead the first classroom meeting. Back-to-School-Night is a good time to have parents begin meeting in their own small groups. The two parents in each classroom who have been trained to facilitate the parent tribes invite, by phone or letter, the other parents in the class. A phone call from another classroom parent is more effective in terms of getting a response than a notice or letter from the school. The first class meeting is one hour long. The teacher introduces the parents and shares the purpose of the hour: to have parents meet each other and experience some of the process being used in classrooms. The teacher states that he or she will talk about current curricula and the cooperative learning process during the last 10 or 15 minutes of the meeting.

The parent facilitators lead the meeting as detailed in the plan contained in Resources section of this book. At the end of the hour, reflection questions are used within the groups and a feedback card is filled out. The important question asked by the facilitators at the end of the meeting is, "How many of you enjoyed having time to talk with other parents?" And, "How many would like to meet again using this process to define ways we can support learning for our students?" Names and phone numbers are jotted down within each tribe, and given to the parent facilitators for duplication and mailing back to the members of each parent tribe. People in each tribe can make phone calls to invite their parent tribe members to learning events and celebrations throughout the year. The gatherings during the year continue to use the TLC process with parents staying in the same groups to build a sense of community.

We sent invitations to all of the parents of our 948 kids to come to the meeting, and 23 came.

—A teacher

We had to create a school where people understood the developmental needs of the children and could establish a relationship between home and school that would enhance them.[7]

—James Comer

Learning groups throughout the year can help parents to

- understand their children's current stage of development;

- learn about resiliency and protective factors; discuss how to strengthen protective strategies within their families;

- learn and practice the same collaborative skills in their homes that are being taught in the classroom;

- and support the learning goals and objectives of the class and school.

Why is this an effective way to get parent involvement? Come on, we bet that you know by now. Inclusion, caring, and participation happen just as in classroom tribes. Influence is invited, and commonalities experienced, building a sense of community throughout the year. The approach gives the parent learning community its own support system to help make real the beautiful perspective expressed in the African motto "It takes a whole village to raise a child."

The system is based on parents reaching parents rather than teachers reaching parents.

More Ways to Engage Parents

There are a variety of ways to share the Tribes process with parents. Michele Cahall suggests that on Back-to-School Night teachers have an hour or more to involve the parents in several inclusion strategies. They discuss how the Tribes agreements establish a positive classroom environment to improve academic learning.

Even though intermediate and high school teachers often have as little as ten minutes to present information to parents, many share the important Tribes agreements, and invite parents to share their names and a positive characteristic of their teenager. Regardless of the time available, parents gain an appreciation of how the Tribes process is being used in the classroom.

Celebrations of Learning, short presentations of student learning, are scheduled throughout the school year. This gives students an opportunity to demonstrate their newly acquired knowledge and skills. Celebrations can be scheduled during the school day or in the evening. The format is flexible and is best chosen and planned by students themselves. It can be a play, literature reading, inclusion strategies, cooperative learning structures, or hands-on activities in which the parents participate. Celebrations of Learning are a wonderful way for parents to experience first hand the benefits of the Tribes process for their children. The TLC process is also used within parenting classes and parent support groups. Classes emphasize family meetings, agreements, effective communication techniques, decision-making strategies, problem solving, and win/win conflict resolution. The intent is to transfer the same supportive process to families so that a deeper level of caring and sharing touches them too.

From a Teacher's View

• • • • • •

Betty White

Betty White used Tribes in her own 6th grade class for 3 years before taking a two year leave to train whole school staffs throughout the country in Success for All, *the John Hopkins University reading curriculum. She continues training as a Tribes TLC® Master Trainer, and shares her expertise as a Professional Development Consultant for CenterSource Systems. Betty quite naturally is a reading facilitator for the schoolwide reading program of the Central Canyon Elementary School in Caldwell, Idaho.*

How to transform at-risk environments rather than kids

For two consecutive years, I had the opportunity to travel across the United States as an instructional facilitator for a well-known educational research project. The majority of the numerous schools that I worked with were in very impoverished neighborhoods with populations of "at risk" children. While most of the teachers at these schools had never heard of what we call the caring Tribes process, they too believed in the importance of enhancing human development through kinder school environments. All were convinced that their children needed to learn the social and collaborative skills that not only would help them survive, but move beyond the difficult environments in which they were growing up. It comes at no surprise that daily interaction with these needy children drains the energy and enthusiasm from too many good teachers. Though they give their all, they simply burn out.

I came to realize that even in this world of constant transition, challenge and despair, education is a tough profession. Yet teachers are a resilient group! By training teachers in Tribes, no matter where they teach, we give them the bolster, on-going support and ability to "hang in there." Once they have the tools to achieve the goals that called them into the teaching profession...they can help their students become healthy well-adjusted beings in an ever changing world.

A Tribes training is the license for a staff to laugh and learn together, to compliment each other, to share concerns and to care for each other. It transforms the teaching experience knowing there is an opportunity to share ideas and ask for suggestions. In my own district, teachers who have been through the Tribes training enroll to take the course again and again. When asked why, they most assuredly reply that it is their "shot in the arm." After the first day of a training, one teacher told me, "I always knew how I wanted my classroom to be. I just didn't know how to get there. Now I do!"

Schools committed to lasting change or reform provide on-going Tribes training and support to teachers by establishing "teacher tribes," and allocating regular weekly time for the staff support system to work together. Once this staff restructuring happens, a noticeable climate of enthusiasm, togetherness and high energy changes the school community. In such schools you will find staff, students, and parents all working together with the same common goal of creating a safe and caring learning community...

a place where everyone looks forward to coming to school each day!

This is my message and dream for all those schools exhausted with trying to fix, control and teach children "at risk." It's not the children, it's the "at risk" environments that must be transformed.

The Tribes TLC® process over time can indeed transform the culture of a school system, and quality training for staff is the way to bring it about. Unlike many training approaches which become dependent upon "outside consultants and trainers," CenterSource Systems has defined a capacity building model of professional development which prepares teachers and administrators themselves to conduct training in their own schools. Check out the page on CenterSource System's Professional Development opportunities in the Resource section. It's step one in starting your school on a whole new way of being and learning together.

The Tribes School

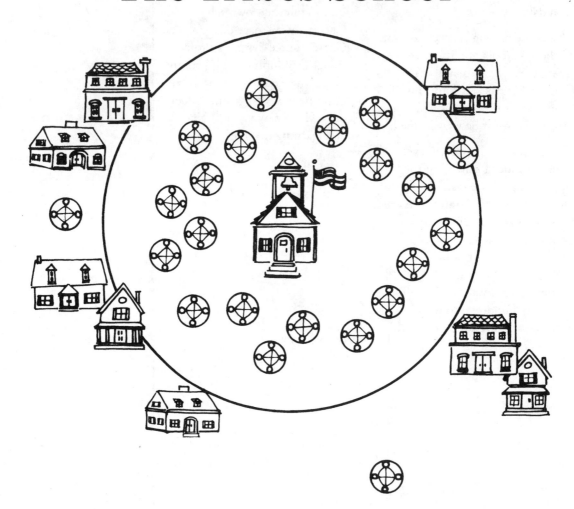

- is student-centered
- actively involves the staff in participative management
- welcomes parents and community involvement in the same process of learning
- everyone has a tribe of their own—students, staff, even parents and community
- at home, families learn to use the same communication skills to strengthen family bonds

Where students, staff and families work together to create a learning environment for healthy human development

11
Strategies and Energizers

11

Strategies and Energizers

Strategies

Old friends will notice that this section is no longer referred to as "Tribes Activities," as it was in our earlier edition. Strategies are ways to achieve learning objectives, whereas activities too often are considered time-fillers. The majority of Tribes strategies are formats for subject content. They can be used in combination with the many Spencer Kagan cooperative learning structures.

The Strategy Index Grid that follows these introductory pages is alphabetized and coded so that you can select appropriate strategies and energizers. Each strategy contains the following notations:

1. Objectives

2. Suggested grade levels

3. Grouping: community circle, tribes, sub groups

4. Approximate time required

5. Materials needed

Following the instructions are three kinds of suggested reflection questions: content/thinking, collaborative/social skills, and personal learning. Last, but every bit as important, are invitations for appreciation. As you know, the follow-up reflection questions and statements of appreciation not only enhance learning for students, but sustain the positive environment.

Many of the strategies have been adapted from other sources, some familiar to you. The Resource section following this chapter contains listings of many collections. Some of the best, however, have been contributed by creative Tribes teachers.

Strategies need to be selected carefully, and tailored to fit the ethnicity, culture, age level, interests, language, and socio-economic status of the students in your class. A strategy that is not sensitive to community culture undermines the teaching process. Following are some examples of this:

- Using the names of Christian holidays but not those of other religions.

- Urging Native Americans, Latinos, and indigenous populations to make personal statements during the inclusion stage. The opportunity first to share about their culture, family, or group is traditional for them, and therefore more comfortable and inclusive.

- Ignoring the economic realities of a community (i.e.: using examples of luxury items in a low-income area).

- Urging Cambodian and Thai students to demonstrate eye contact during attentive listening (when in their own culture averting one's eyes denotes respect).

It also is very important to plan and implement strategies well. The chart on the next page will give you a quick summary for implementing Tribes strategies.

Energizers

In the midst of any time together groups of people will periodically experience lower energy within their environments. Concentration becomes more difficult; boredom and sleepiness can set in and will be counterproductive to accomplishing the task at hand. Students, especially, become restless. They are likely to withdraw or even create a disturbance. The remedy? A quick five-minute physical activity to revitalize the group with an "energizer."

Energizers are satisfying because they engage many of the multiple intelligences primarily: body/kinesthetic, musical/rhythmic, interpersonal and visual/spatial.

Six outcomes can be achieved through the use of energizers:

1. The energy of the classroom or group is revitalized.
2. People's attention can be drawn back to the classroom after a time away (recess, lunch break, or some other interruption).
3. Different types of academic learning activities can be bridged, renewing energy and concentration.
4. People can feel connected again with one another and the whole community.
5. Multiple intelligences can be reached and are engaged.
6. They add to the fun of learning and being together!

The pages that follow contain a collection of some favorite Tribes energizers. Some are more physical than others, and as with other activities in this book it is up to you to select the most appropriate ones for your students. Much depends upon the level of trust within the class at any one time, and the age level of your students.

Summary: Facilitating Tribes Strategies

1. Remind students about the Tribes agreements:
   - Whenever appropriate, ask the class or tribe to review the agreements.
   - Have the agreements posted at all times.
   - Respect and model the agreements congruently yourself.
2. Give the instructions:
   - Select and tailor an appropriate strategy or series of them to achieve your learning objectives.
   - Tell your students what the objectives are (what they will learn).
   - Give instructions simply and concisely; do not get off the track or use too many words.
   - Tell students how much time they will have to complete the task.
3. If students are in a community circle:
   - Initiate the sharing yourself.
   - Let the students know who will be next—which way you'll go around the circle.
   - Ask people to speak directly to one another.
   - Withhold your own comments on what students share.
   - Encourage people to use first names.
   - Make it okay to pass.
   - Deal with put-downs or a lack of attentive listening.
   - Give people a second opportunity to share if they pass the first time.
   - Ask appropriate content, social, and/or personal reflection questions.
   - Wind things up when people feel bored or restless.

4. If students are working in tribes or small groups:
   - Follow suggestions noted above in sections two and three.
   - If using roles, discuss them, assign them, or have students choose them.
   - Describe the task to be accomplished (materials, resources, and time for completion).
   - Ask students to clarify the task to you or each other.
   - Observe their interaction and assist only as needed.
   - Ask reflection questions.
   - Assess (or have students assess) and evaluate outcomes.
5. Invite statements of appreciation:
   - Suggest sentence starters.
   - Be a good role model.
6. Celebrate class, tribe, or individual contributions and achievements.

STRATEGY TITLE	Page	INCLUSION	Presenting Self	Social Skills	Agreements	INFLUENCE	Decisions/Problem Solving	Resolving Conflict	Goal Setting	COMMUNITY	Energizer	Celebration	ACADEMICS
Abstract Painting Of Feelings	227	●	●	●		●	●						
All In The Family	275	●	●	●									
Alligator Attack	388									●	●		
Alligators	388									●	●		
Am I Napoleon?	263	●	●			●				●			●
Animal Triads	331				●		●	●					●
Appreciating Others	269	●		●						●		●	
Barnyard Babble	233	●											
Boasters	271	●	●	●	●								
Brainstorming	259	●	●			●	●	●		●		●	●
Bubble Gum	388									●	●		
Building A Time Machine	350	●		●		●	●	●					
Bumper Sticker	268	●	●	●						●		●	
Bumpety-Bump-Bump	395									●	●		
Campaign Manager	301	●	●							●		●	●
Career Choices	351	●	●			●	●						●
Celebrity Sign-In	335		●			●	●						●
Chain Reaction	260	●	●	●						●		●	●
Changes	387									●	●		
Clap-Slap	391									●	●		
Client-Consultants	306	●		●		●	●						●
Community Circle	219	●	●	●	●					●		●	●
Community Circle Metaphor	352	●	●	●						●		●	
Confrontation	316	●		●		●		●	●				
Consensus-Building	327	●		●		●	●	●	●				
Cooperation Squares	307	●		●		●	●	●					
Creative Storytelling	239	●	●							●			●
Current Events Debate	334	●			●	●	●						●
Dear Abby	309	●	●			●	●	●					

STRATEGY TITLE	Page	INCLUSION	Presenting Self	Social Skills	Agreements	INFLUENCE	Decisions/Problem Solving	Resolving Conflict	Goal Setting	COMMUNITY	Energizer	Celebration	ACADEMICS
Interview Circle	258	•	•	•		•	•						
Jigsaw	330	•		•		•	•						•
Joy	234	•	•	•									
Kitchen Kapers	290	•	•			•	•	•					
Knots	387									•	•		
The Lap Game	392									•	•		
Life Map	291	•	•	•									
Line-up	390									•	•		
Live Wire	305	•	•	•									
Look At Me!	295	•	•	•									
Making a Choice	361			•		•	•						•
Me Book	222	•	•	•									
Meet Someone Special	252	•	•	•									
Milling To Music	267	•	•	•									•
Mirror...Mirror	229	•	•										
Mirrors	387									•	•		
Monkey, Elephant, Palm Tree	394									•	•		
My Favorite People & Things	231	•	•	•									
My Name In Print	257	•	•	•									
Name Game	248	•	•	•									
Name Wave	395									•	•		
Newspaper Scavenger Hunt	363	•		•		•	•						•
Novel in an Hour	297						•			•			•
Now I Am	224	•		•									
On My Back	279	•	•										•
One Special Thing About Me	365	•	•	•									•
One, Two, Three	324	•		•		•	•						
One-Minute History	299	•	•	•									
Open Forum	286	•	•	•		•	•						

STRATEGIES MATRIX

STRATEGY TITLE	Page	INCLUSION	Presenting Self	Social Skills	Agreements	INFLUENCE	Decisions/Problem Solving	Resolving Conflict	Goal Setting	COMMUNITY	Energizer	Celebration	ACADEMICS
Singing The Blues	256	•	•	•									
Skin The Snake	394									•	•		
Slip Game	293	•	•	•									
Snowball I-Messages	371	•		•									•
Something Good	255	•	•	•									
Something I Cherish	273	•	•	•									
Space Pioneers	312	•		•		•	•						
Special Friend I Know	345	•	•	•									
Spider Web	246	•	•	•						•		•	•
Stand Off	387									•	•		
Stand Up	387									•	•		
Student-Developed Lesson	372	•		•		•	•						•
Suggestion Circle	375	•		•		•	•	•					
Taking A Closer Look	235	•		•		•	•						
Teaching Agreements	378	•		•	•	•	•						
Teaching I-Messages	376	•		•		•		•					
Teaching Listening	251	•		•									
Teaching Paraph/Ref Feelings	377	•		•									•
That's Me—That's Us!	379	•	•							•		•	
Third-Party Mediation	320	•		•		•	•	•					
This Is Me	287	•	•	•									
Three Ball Pass	389									•	•		
Thumbs Up, Thumbs Down	321					•	•						
Tower-Building	314	•		•		•	•						
Tribal Peer Coaching	329	•		•		•	•						•
Tribe Graffiti	300	•		•									
Tribe Mimes/Role-Play	303	•	•			•		•					•
Tribe Portrait	338	•	•	•									
Trust Circle	387									•	•		

STRATEGY TITLE	Page	INCLUSION	Presenting Self	Social Skills	Agreements	INFLUENCE	Decisions/Problem Solving	Resolving Conflict	Goal Setting	COMMUNITY	Energizer	Celebration	ACADEMICS
Trust Walk	387									•	•		
Two On A Crayon	223	•		•		•	•						
Two Truths and a Lie	389									•	•		
Unfinished Fantasies	310	•	•			•		•	•				
Urgent!	298	•		•		•	•						
Warm Fuzzies	243	•			•								
Warm Fuzzy Bag	245	•			•								
Week In Perspective	304	•	•	•									
What Feelings Do You Have?	226	•	•										
What Will Happen Next?	340	•		•		•	•						•
What's In A Name?	341	•		•									
What's In My Name?	276	•	•	•									
What's In Your Wallet?	344	•	•	•									
What's The Tint...Glasses?	349	•		•		•		•					
What's Your Bag?	292	•	•	•									
Where Do I Stand?	323	•	•	•		•	•						
Why Is This Word Important?	343	•	•			•	•						
Wink	387									•	•		
Wishful Thinking	254	•	•	•									
Zap	390									•	•		
Zoo Stories	225	•	•	•									
Zoom, Zoom, Brake!	389									•	•		

Community Circle

Grades:	K-adult
Time:	20 minutes
Grouping:	community
Materials:	none

Objectives

1. To build inclusion and community
2. To teach social skills

Instructions

1. Have the community sit in a large circle.
2. Review the Tribes agreements.
3. Ask a "Question-of-the-Day."
   Example: "I feel happy when..."
   See more suggested questions on the next page.
4. Have everyone respond in turn to the question. Allow time at the end for those who passed to respond if they desire.

Suggested Reflection Questions

Content/Thinking

- What's one new thing you learned in the community?
- Why is it sometimes difficult to find something to say in a large group?

Social

- How does sharing this way help our class?
- How well did the community listen when you shared?

Personal

- How did you feel about sharing with the community today?

Appreciation

Invite statements of appreciation:

- "I liked it when..."
- "I feel like you when..."

Suggested Questions-of-the-Day

1. I feel happy when...
2. I feel sad when...
3. I feel angry when...
4. I feel scared when...
5. The scariest thing is...
6. The biggest thing in the world is...
7. I'm bigger than...
8. I'm smaller than...
9. The smallest thing is...
10. My favorite toy is...
11. My favorite pet is...
12. My favorite food is...
13. My favorite T.V. show is...
14. My favorite song is...
15. My favorite story is...
16. My favorite color is...
17. My favorite weather is...
18. Rain makes me feel...
19. Wind makes me feel...
20. Sunshine makes me feel...
21. Snow makes me feel...
22. Fog makes me feel...
23. When I think of blue, I think of...
24. When I think of red, I think of...
25. When I think of green, I think of...
26. When I think of yellow, I think of...
27. When I think of orange, I think of...
28. When I think of black, I think of...
29. When I think of brown, I think of...
30. Today I feel...
31. What is something scratchy?
32. What is something soft?
33. What is something sharp?
34. What is something smooth?
35. What is something sour?
36. What is something sweet?
37. What is something cold?
38. What is something cool?
39. What is something warm?
40. What is something hot?
41. If I were an animal, I would be...
42. If I were a building, I would be a...
43. The first thing I want to do when I grow up is...
44. When I grow up, I want to be...
45. When I daydream, I usually think about...
46. Someday I want to...
47. Friends are...
48. Put downs make me feel...
49. When I am doing math I am most like what animal?
50. Relate to the curriculum:
    - The best/worst thing about this science project is...
    - The main character in the book we are reading is like/not like me when...
    - These math problems make me feel...

Note: The best questions are those most relevant to the participants' experiences, interests and cultures.

The Ideal Classroom

Grades:	K-adult
Time:	40 minutes
Grouping:	tribes, pairs
Materials:	paper, pencils

Objectives

1. To involve students in defining class agreements
2. To alter the climate from negative to positive
3. To transfer responsibility to students
4. To experience influence

Instructions

1. Draw a large circle on the board and label it "The Ideal Classroom."
2. Ask the students to think about the following question: How would people act and interact in an ideal classroom?
3. Have student divide up into pairs.
4. Ask the partners to discuss and make a list of what an ideal classroom would be like. After ten minutes have them share their ideas with their tribe.
5. Have the tribes save the lists. Ask everyone to think about the question until the next day.
6. On the following day, use the strategy "One, Two, Three" or "Group Problem-Solving" to have the community select one to three ideas that they consider most important for their classroom.
7. Post the ideas in a prominent place.
8. Ask, "How many of you want to make these agreements that the whole community respects for the next [week, month or year]?" Invite students to stand and say, "That's me!"
9. Ask, "Who will help to remind others to respect our agreements?"

Suggested Reflection Questions:

Content/Thinking

- What is the ideal classroom like?
- What would have to change to make this classroom an ideal classroom?

Social

- What social skills would be needed in your ideal classroom?
- Why is working together in pairs a good idea?

Personal

- How can you make our classroom better?
- How can these rules apply to other areas of your life?

Appreciation

Invite statements of appreciation:
- "It felt good when..."
- "One thing I liked about what you said was..."

Me Book

Grades: K-3
Time: 20 minutes per day, 11 consecutive days
Grouping: community, tribes
Materials: paper, pencils, felt pens, crayons

Objectives

1. To build inclusion
2. To build self-esteem and self-awareness
3. To reinforce the relationship between oral and written language
4. To experience working on a long-range project

Instructions

1. Explain to the community that each student will be making a "Me Book" during the next ten days. Tell them they will work on one statement each day.

   Examples:
   - I feel great when...
   - I feel angry when...
   - I feel sleepy when...
   - My mom thinks I'm...
   - My dad thinks I'm...
   - I feel my brother is...
   - I feel my sister is...
   - My favorite toy is...
   - My favorite food is...
   - The place I like best to be is...

2. Have the students form tribes.
3. Have each tribe member draw a picture that illustrates the statement and then describe or write an explanation of his or her drawing.
4. Form the completed drawings into books.
5. Have students share completed books in tribes.

Note: For very young children, have them dictate statements and explanations to an aide or an older student.

Suggested Reflection Questions

Content/Thinking
- What is your favorite food, toy, etc.?
- What did you learn about a tribe member?

Social
- Who would like to share his or her "Me Book?"
- How did this activity help you get to know your classmates?

Personal
- Why is it difficult to think of things to draw?
- Did you discover anything new about yourself?

Appreciation

Invite statements of appreciation:
- "What I like about your 'Me Book' is..."
- "I liked it when..."

Two On A Crayon

Grades:	K-6
Time:	20 minutes
Grouping:	pairs
Materials:	paper, crayons, music

Objectives

1. To demonstrate the power of nonverbal communication
2. To promote cooperation and fun
3. To build inclusion and influence

Instructions

1. Have the community form pairs.
2. Give each pair one crayon and one piece of construction paper.
3. Explain that both partners will hold the crayon simultaneously and draw a picture together while a three- or four-minute song is played in the background. Tell the students that partners may not decide before the activity what kind of picture they will draw together, and that they may not talk to each other while they are drawing.

Suggested Reflection Questions

Content/Thinking
- What did you draw?
- What does it represent?

Social
- Was it difficult to not talk to your partner?
- How did this activity help you get to know your partner?
- How did you decide who would lead and who would follow?

Personal
- Did you discover anything new about yourself?

Appreciation

Invite statements of appreciation to partners:
- "I liked it when..."
- "I felt good when..."
- "I like your picture because..."

Now I Am

Grades: K-5
Time: 20 minutes
Grouping: community
Materials: none

Objectives

1. To recognize and identify feelings
2. To introduce the relationship between oral and written language
3. To develop observation skills
4. To build inclusion

Instructions

1. Have the community sit in a circle; review the agreements.
2. Whisper a different feeling or emotion in each student's ear one at a time.

   Examples:

fear	frustration	surprise	rage
nervousness	hope	soreness	love
dreaminess	anger	uncomfortable	wild
unhappiness	tired	embarrassed	weird
itchiness	stubborn	excitement	sleepy

3. Ask the students to act out their words nonverbally.
4. Have the community guess what each student is acting out.

Suggested Reflection Questions

Content/Thinking
- Which feelings were the easiest/most difficult to act out?
- How did you figure out what feeling was being represented?

Social
- How can you help each other discover the feelings you have at different times?

Personal
- When did you have one of the feelings that was represented?
- How difficult was it for you to act out your word?

Appreciation

Invite statements of appreciation:
- "I liked the way you acted it out because..."
- "I feel a lot like you when..."

Follow-Up Activities:

Have each student:

1. Draw feelings using colors that match the feelings.
2. Make a face of how you feel this minute.
3. Write a story about a person who always acts the same.
4. Print feeling words on cards, and have people act them out.
5. Follow with the strategy "Five Tribles."

Zoo Stories

Grades:	K-3
Time:	20 minutes
Grouping:	community, tribes
Materials:	none

Objectives

1. To build inclusion
2. To encourage sharing

Instructions

1. Have the community or tribe sit in a circle.
2. Each person takes a turn at answering the question: "What kind of animal do you feel like today?"

Suggested Reflection Questions

Content/Thinking

- What animals were in your tribe today?
- What were the similarities/differences between the animals?

Social

- How well did your tribe members participate in this activity?
- How did this activity help you get to know each other better?

Personal

- What was difficult about this activity for you?
- When was the last time you felt like this animal?
- What animal did someone else think of that you also liked?

Appreciation

Invite statements of appreciation:

- "I liked your animal because..."
- "I'm like your animal when..."

What Feelings Do You Have?

Grades: K-3
Time: 30 minutes
Grouping: community
Materials: chalkboard, chalk, chart, paper, pens

Objectives
1. To build inclusion
2. To encourage the expression of feelings

Instructions
1. Begin by discussing the importance of being aware of our feelings.
2. List some feelings and expressive colors.
   Examples:

Feeling	Three colors that seem to fit the feeling
Happy	Yellow, Pink, Orange
Angry	Black, Red, Brown
Sad	Blue, White, Black

3. Ask reflection questions (use think/pair/share structure with grades 2 and 3).

Suggested Reflection Questions
Content/Thinking
- Which colors represent happy/angry/sad?
- Why do colors seem like feelings?

Social
- How can a friend's choice of colors tell you how he or she feels?
- How well did we listen to each other?

Personal
- How did you feel when you chose your colors?

Appreciation
Invite statements of appreciation:
- "I liked it when you..."
- "I appreciated..."

Note: You can follow up this activity with "Abstract Painting of Feelings."

Abstract Painting Of Feelings

Grades:	K-3
Time:	30 minutes
Grouping:	tribes, subgroups
Materials:	12 x 18-inch paper, paints, and brushes

Objectives

1. To build inclusion
2. To express feelings by using colors

Instructions

1. Ask the students to meet in tribes or form groups of three to five.
2. Give each tribe member a sheet of paper and a brush.
3. Have each tribe choose three colors.
4. Ask each tribe member to paint a picture using the color that represents how he or she is feeling (refer to the chart made in the previous activity, "What Feelings Do You Have?").
5. Invite the students to share the feelings they painted.

Suggested Reflection Questions

Content/Thinking

- What were the different feelings painted by your tribe members?
- How did you know what colors to use?

Social

- How did this activity help you get to know your tribe members?

Personal

- Did you discover anything new about yourself?

Appreciation

Invite statements of appreciation:

- "I'm a lot like you when..."
- "I admired your honesty about..."
- "I liked it when you..."

Silhouettes

Grades: K-4
Time: 60 minutes or more
Grouping: pairs
Materials: paper, pencils, scissors, glue, magazines, envelopes

Objectives

1. To build self-esteem
2. To promote inclusion
3. To encourage positive statements towards one another

Instructions

1. Have the community form pairs.
2. Have the pairs place construction paper on the wall. Darken the room and place a bright light close to the wall.
3. Have one partner sit between the light and wall, making a profile shadow on the paper.
4. Tell the other partner to outline the shadow with a pencil.
5. Have the partners switch roles and repeat the activity.
6. After both silhouettes have been traced, the partners cut out and mount the silhouette.
7. Have each partner clip out magazine pictures that represent how he or she sees himself or herself, and glue a collage on his or her silhouette.
8. Display the silhouettes. Under each, attach an envelope with the name of the student drawn in big letters.
9. Explain that the envelopes are for appreciation statements that will be written during the year.
10. Ask the students to draw names and have them place written appreciation statements in the appropriate envelopes. Writers are to remain anonymous.

Suggested Reflection Questions

Content/Thinking

- How do the magazine pictures represent you?
- What did you learn?

Social

- How does this activity help you get to know other students?
- How well did you work with your partner?

Personal

- How did you feel when you finished your silhouette?
- What is one thing you can do to work better with a partner?

Appreciation

Invite statements of appreciation:

- "I liked it when..."
- "I am a lot like you because..."

Mirror...Mirror

Grade: K-4
Time: 45 minutes
Grouping: community, tribes
Materials: hand mirror, "Hand Mirror" worksheets, crayons

Objectives
1. To build inclusion
2. To facilitate sharing feelings
3. To build respect for diversity

Instructions
1. Have the community stand in one large circle and pass around a hand mirror.
2. Point out that mirrors reflect how people all look different in special ways (color of hair, eyes, skin, smiles, etc.) but that mirrors do not show what people think and feel, which is also very important.
3. Pass out "Hand Mirror" worksheets and ask the students to divide into tribes. Ask the students to write "I think" and "I feel" statements on their "Hand Mirror" worksheets. Have aides or older students help the nonreaders if necessary.
4. Have the students share their "Hand Mirror" worksheets in either tribes or the community.

Suggested Reflection Questions
Content/Thinking
- What do mirrors reflect to us?
- What do mirrors not reflect?
- Why is it important to know the difference between what mirrors reflect/don't reflect?

Social
- How can sharing your mirrors help you get along better?
- What social skills were used when mirrors were shared? (Remind the students of skills: listening, sharing, appreciation)
- Why is it important to use good listening skills when others share?

Personal
- What did you do to make others feel OK when they shared their mirrors? Why is that important?
- What is one thing you can do to listen better?

Appreciation
Invite statements of appreciation:
- "I liked it when..."
- "I liked Joel's mirror because..."
- "I think you are neat because..."

Mirror...Mirror

My Favorite People And Things

Grades:	K-3
Time:	30 minutes
Grouping:	triads
Materials:	circle/triangle worksheets, pencils, crayons

Objectives
1. To build inclusion
2. To encourage verbal ability, especially with ESL (English as a second language) students
3. To express likes and dislikes, and promote respect for diversity
4. To learn shapes (circle and triangle)

Instructions
1. Have the community stand in a large circle and have the students take turns stating their favorite colors.
2. Tell the students to form triads, and have the triad members tell each other what their favorite toys may be. Then have the students form new triads, and have the triad members tell each other what their favorite foods are. For grades 2 and 3, have the students form triads one more time, and have triad members share something they dislike.
3. Then have the community form a circle and join hands. Have the students sing or recite the rhyme below:
   "I like you, I like me
   Special people one, two, three,
   Different colors, different eyes
   Each of us is quite a prize!"
   (Lead a big cheer after this.)
4. Have the students again form triads.
5. Pass out "Circle/Triangle" worksheets; tell each student to draw in the spaces around the triangle:
   • his or her favorite color
   • his or her favorite toy
   • his or her favorite food
6. Have students draw a picture (in the middle of the triangle) of a person they really admire or like. (Vary the content so that it is appropriate for the age level and culture of your class.)
7. Have the students share one or all sections of their circle/triangles with their triads or the community.

Suggested Reflection Questions
Content/Thinking
   • What new things did you learn about your classmates?
Social
   • Why is sharing what we like with others important?
   • How well did we do at taking turns?
   • What can be done to help everyone take a turn?
Personal
   • How did you feel sharing your likes with others?

Appreciation
Invite statements of appreciation (to triad members):
   • "I like you because..."
   • "I liked it when..."

My Favorite People and Things

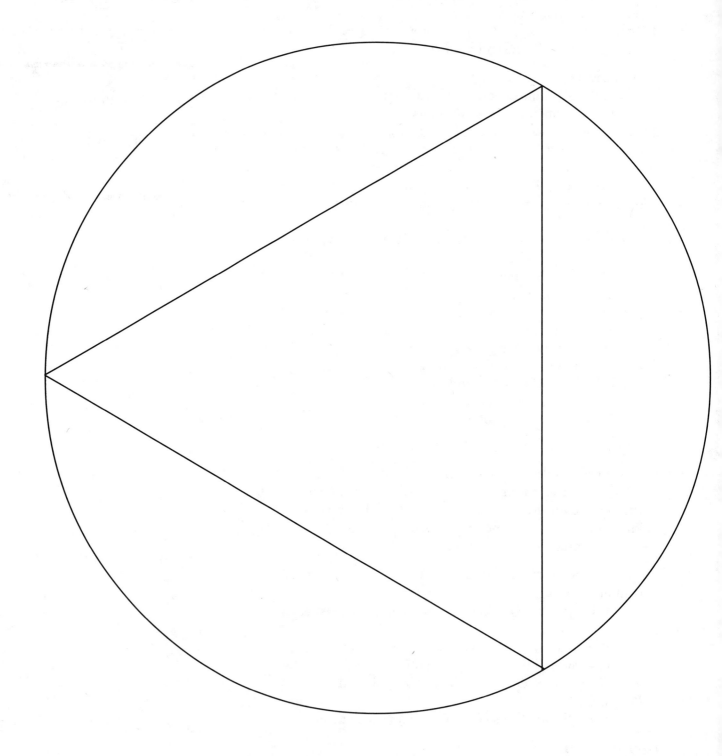

Barnyard Babble

Grades:	K-adult
Time:	15 minutes
Grouping:	community
Materials:	name slips

Objectives

1. To build community inclusion
2. To divide people into tribes or random groups
3. To have a hilarious time

Instructions

1. Prepare a small slip of paper for each student. Depending on the number of tribes that the community will divide into, select names of that many noisy animals. Examples: horse, cow, chicken, pig, sheep, donkey, mouse, rooster, dog, cat.
2. Write the name of an animal (or use a picture) on each slip so that the students in the "horse" tribe all have slips labeled "horse" and the students in the "chicken" tribe all have slips marked "chicken."
3. If you are assigning students to specific tribes, write the name of the student on one side of the slip and the name of the animal on the other side.
4. Before distributing the slips, tell the students that they are not to let anyone else know what animal names are on their slips.
5. Have the community circulate with eyes closed, making the noises of their animals.
6. When all the students with the same animal names find each other, have the "animal tribes" sit together and discuss and reflect.

Suggested Reflection Questions

Content/Thinking
- What do you think of this way of finding tribe members?
- What made this an exciting way to divide into tribes?

Social
- How did it feel when you found each other?

Personal
- How did you end up finding your tribe?
- How do you feel now?

Appreciation

Invite statements of appreciation:
- "I was [*feeling*] when..."
- "Thank you, [*name*] for..."
- "I liked it when..."

Option: Have the community divide into tribes by humming, or singing nursery rhymes or familiar tunes. Multi-cultural and adult groups (teachers and parents) may enjoy using different dance steps.

Joy

Grades: 2-adult
Time: 20 minutes
Grouping: community or tribes
Materials: none

Objectives

1. To give each person an opportunity to share something special with others
2. To practice listening skills
3. To build inclusion

Instruction

1. Ask each student to think of three things that he or she would like to share. Use the letters of the word "joy" to structure what is to be shared:

    J: something in your life that *just* happened
    O: *one* thing you would like to do for yourself
    Y: a part of *you* that makes you a very special person

    Point out that the key words say, "just one you!"

2. Urge the students to listen attentively as each student takes a turn sharing.

Suggested Reflection Questions

Content/Thinking
- Why is it helpful to share information about yourself?

Social
- How well were people listening?
- What can we do to help each other to be better listeners?

Personal
- How did this activity make you feel?
- What did you find out about yourself?

Appreciation

Invite statements of appreciation:
- "It helped me when..."
- "I appreciated..."
- "Thank you for..."

Taking A Closer Look

Grades:	5-adult
Time:	30 minutes
Grouping:	tribes, pairs
Materials:	question slips

Objectives

1. To explore individual attitudes about the use of alcohol or other drugs
2. To practice attentive listening skills
3. To build peer support and influence

Instructions

1. Have the community divide up into pairs, and have each partner decide whether he or she will be an "A" or a "B." Pass out pre-prepared question slips (see following page), or generate your own questions appropriate for the culture and age level of your students.
2. Suggest that the partners move to a comfortable place where they can hear each other well. Explain that partner A will begin by answering the questions while B listens, and that at the end of five minutes, the partners will switch roles.
3. Review the agreements, particularly attentive listening.
4. Give the signal to switch after five minutes, and call the partners back to the community circle after the additional five minutes.
5. Have the community discuss and reflect on the experience.

Suggested Reflection Questions

Content/Thinking
- What kind of messages did you get about using substances?
- How did this activity stretch your own thinking about drugs?

Social
- Why did we work in pairs rather than as a community?

Personal
- Did you make any new decisions as a result of this experience? What were they?

Appreciation

Invite statements of appreciation
- "I really appreciated it when..."
- "[*name*], you are special because..."
- Thank you, [*name*] for..."

Question Slip

Taking A Closer Look

1. What kind of messages did you get about cigarettes, alcohol, or drugs when you were younger (right or wrong to use/OK for men, but not for women/beer and wine don't hurt you)?

2. Where did these messages come from (school/family/media/church/ friends)?

3. What was the first decision you ever made about choosing to use or not use cigarettes, alcohol or drugs? How old were you? What happened? What process did you use to make a decision?

4. Describe what your life would be like if you did not use any of these substances. **Option:** What might it be like if you did use? Ask people to think about over-the-counter or prescription drugs they may use. Coffee?

5. What have you learned about chemical substances that you would want your brother, sister or child to know?

6. Would you feel comfortable with your child using cigarettes, drugs, or alcohol as much as you do?

Pantomime

Grades:	K-3
Time:	20 minutes
Grouping:	community
Materials:	none

Objectives

1. To build self-esteem
2. To build inclusion
3. To experience communication without words

Instructions

1. Have the students form two groups. Have each group take a turn doing expressions and movements.
2. There is no discussion until both groups have finished.
3. The following are suggestions of expressions and movement:
   - facial expressions: funny, scared, sad
   - feeling walks: walk angrily, walk sadly
   - weather walks: walk in the rain
   - people walks: robber, clown
   - animal walks: dog, cat, duck
   - characters and situations: an acrobat on a tightrope
   - exploring senses: taste a lemon, smell a skunk
   - handling imaginary objects: play with a yo-yo
   - experiencing different environments: you are on the moon

Suggested Reflection Questions

Content/Thinking
- Why was it easy/difficult to demonstrate your feelings?
- What did you find out about yourself and others?

Social
- What did we have to do to make this activity successful?
- How could you tell that others were being good watchers and listeners?

Personal
- How did you feel while you were participating in the activity?

Appreciation

Invite statements of appreciation:
- "I liked it when..."
- "I'm like you when..."
- "I felt good when..."

Gallery Walks

Grades: K-adult
Time: 30 minutes
Grouping: community and triads
Materials: student art work or lesson topic

Objectives
1. To build communication skills
2. To build self-esteem and pride in work
3. To build inclusion and influence

Instructions
1. Invite several students to stand next to projects on which they have been working. Refer to them as "Artists of the Day."
2. Have the remaining students form triads.
3. Invite the triads to take a "gallery walk" around the room to view articles on display, projects-in-making, etc.
4. Have each student artist stand by his or her work and share the origin of his or her ideas, materials used, personal objectives, feelings about finished work, etc.

Suggested Reflection Questions
Content/Thinking
- What kind of things did the artists mention?
- What different talents do people have?
- How did the artists seem to feel about their work?

Social
- What social skills did "gallery walkers" and artists need to use to make this activity successful?

Personal
- How did you feel when you shared your work?
- What did you do best when you presented your work?
- What did you do to keep the focus on the artist?

Appreciation
Invite statements of appreciation:
- "I liked it when you said..."
- "Some of your talents are..."
- "I like your masterpiece because..."

Creative Storytelling

Grades:	K-6
Time:	15-30 minutes
Grouping:	community
Materials:	none

Objectives

1. To encourage listening
2. To promote the expression of fantasy
3. To develop inclusion and influence

Instructions

1. Tell the community, "We are going to make up a group story."
2. Give instructions as follows: "The leader will start by saying a few sentences, then we'll choose someone to continue the story where the first person left off. That person will do the same until the story goes around the circle two or three times."
3. Choose a setting for the story that involves the students themselves yet leaves lots of room for fantasizing.
   Example: "Once there was a group of kids named [*name*], [*name*], [*name*] and [*name*] who wanted to find a place to go swimming together. They came upon a big water hole that looked very inviting. But as soon as one person jumped in, a funny animal reared its head out of the water and…"
4. Encourage the students to listen to each other, and have them continue the story however they want to.
5. Review the "right to pass" and other agreements.

Suggested Reflection Questions

Content/Thinking

- Why is creating a group story fun?
- How is it different if just one person creates a story for everyone to hear?

Social

- How can you improve the way you worked together on your story?

Personal

- How did you feel as a storyteller/listener?

Appreciation

Invite statements of appreciation:
- "I like your part of the story because…"
- "I felt good when…"

Fuzzyland Map

Grades: K-3
Time: 40 minutes
Grouping: tribes, subgroups
Materials: 24 x 36-inch paper, markers, crayons

Objectives

1. To build tribe inclusion
2. To understand the importance of kindness to others
3. To learn to work cooperatively on tasks

Instructions

1. Ask the community to meet in tribes.
2. Read, or preferably tell, the story "Fuzzyland."
3. Discuss and clarify the meaning of the story. Ask questions such as:
   - What is a warm fuzzy? A cold prickly?
   - Why did people in the story need warm fuzzies?
   - Why did people stop giving warm fuzzies freely after the witch cast her spell?
4. Give each tribe a large sheet of paper and colored markers or crayons.
5. Review the agreements. Ask each tribe to create a map of Fuzzyland, with each tribe member drawing some part of the map.
6. Visit each tribe to make sure the instructions are clear.
7. Ask each tribe to share its map with the community. Encourage each student to share what he or she has contributed.

Suggested Reflection Questions

Content/Thinking
   - What did you learn from the story of Fuzzyland?
   - Why did I have you create maps?

Social
   - Name two things your tribe did well while working together.
   - How well did you share ideas, materials, etc.?
   - Did everyone participate?

Personal
   - Would you like to give something nice to someone in your family? To whom? What would it be?

Appreciation

Invite tribe members to give each other warm fuzzies, such as:
   - "I liked it when you said..."
   - "You're neat because..."
   - "I'm like you when..."

Fuzzyland

Once upon a time, a long time ago and far from here, there was a place called Fuzzyland. People were very happy in Fuzzyland because in those happy times everyone at birth was given a small, soft, fuzzy bag. Any time a person reached into this bag he was able to pull out a warm fuzzy. Warm fuzzies were very much in demand because whenever somebody was given a warm fuzzy, it made him feel warm and good all over. People who didn't get warm fuzzies regularly were in danger of developing a sickness called "Fuzzy Deficiency Anemia." Their backs would shrivel up, and they would shrink up so much in size that they would hide from people.

In those days it was very easy to get warm fuzzies. Anytime you wanted a warm fuzzy, all you had to do was walk up to someone and say, "I'd like a warm fuzzy, please." The person would then reach into his bag and pull out a fuzzy the size of a little girl's hand. As soon as the fuzzy saw the light of day, it would smile and blossom into a large, shaggy warm fuzzy. The person would then lay it on your shoulder or head or lap and it would snuggle up and make you feel good all over. Fuzzies were always given freely, and getting enough of them was never a problem. Fuzzyland was a happy place because everyone felt so friendly and kind to each other.

One day, a bad witch came to Fuzzyland and tried to sell people her strange potions and salves. When no one wanted to buy them, she became very angry and cast an evil magic spell on the people of Fuzzyland. The spell made the people believe that warm fuzzies were getting scarce and that eventually the supply would run out. So people reached less and less into their fuzzy bags and became very stingy. Everyone began to notice the lack of warm fuzzies, and newspapers carried stories about the "great fuzzy shortage." People started to feel that they were shrinking, so they went to the witch to buy her potions and salves, even though they didn't seem to work at all.

The bad witch didn't really want people to shrink and hide. Who then would buy things from her? So she devised a new scheme. She gave everyone bags that were very similar to fuzzy bags, except these were cold instead of warm. Inside the bags were cold pricklies. These cold pricklies did not make people feel warm and fuzzy but made them feel cold, prickly, and crabby. From then on, people who would not share warm fuzzies would give away cold pricklies.

A lot of people were unhappy, feeling very cold, prickly, and crabby. Remember, it really all began with the coming of the bad witch, who made people believe that there was beginning to be a shortage of warm fuzzies in their land.

Finally, on one sunny day, a good witch arrived in Fuzzyland. She had not heard about the bad witch and wasn't worried about running out of warm fuzzies at all. She gave them freely to everyone. The kind witch knew that cold pricklies were bad for people. She never ever would give anyone a cold prickly. Many people disapproved of her because she was giving children the idea that they really should never worry about running out of warm fuzzies. And then a new wonderful magic began to happen! Each time the good witch gave a child one of her warm fuzzies, the bad witch's evil spell was broken, and that child could break the evil spell again by giving someone else a warm fuzzy. Many people, children and grown-ups alike, were so used to exchanging cold pricklies that at first they refused to accept warm fuzzies. But the children whom the good witch had befriended kept giving warm fuzzies freely until everyone in Fuzzyland was once again feeling good and warm and fuzzy all over—everyone, that is, except the bad witch. They say that she just sneaked out of Fuzzyland one dark night, hoping to peddle her potions and crabbiness elsewhere.

This story was adapted from *A Fairy Tale* by Claude Steiner, Sacramento, CA: JALMAR Press, Inc. 1977. Mr. Steiner gave permission for the adaptation and its use.

Warm Fuzzies

Grades:	K-3
Time:	30 minutes
Grouping:	tribes
Materials:	leftover yardage of yarn, felt, pipe cleaners, glue, scissors, pencils, cardboard

Objectives

1. To build inclusion
2. To express positive feelings towards others

Instructions

1. Ask the community to meet in tribes.
2. Demonstrate how to create a warm fuzzy. (Instructions are on the next page.)

Suggested Reflection Questions

Content/Thinking

* What is a warm fuzzy?
* What did you learn in the story about warm fuzzies?
* What can you do with the warm fuzzies you made?

Social

* How did you help each other make your warm fuzzies?
* How can your tribe work together better?

Personal

* How did you feel while making your warm fuzzy?

Appreciation

Invite statements of appreciation:

* "I like the warm fuzzy you made because..."
* "I feel good when..."

INSTRUCTIONS FOR MAKING A WARM FUZZY

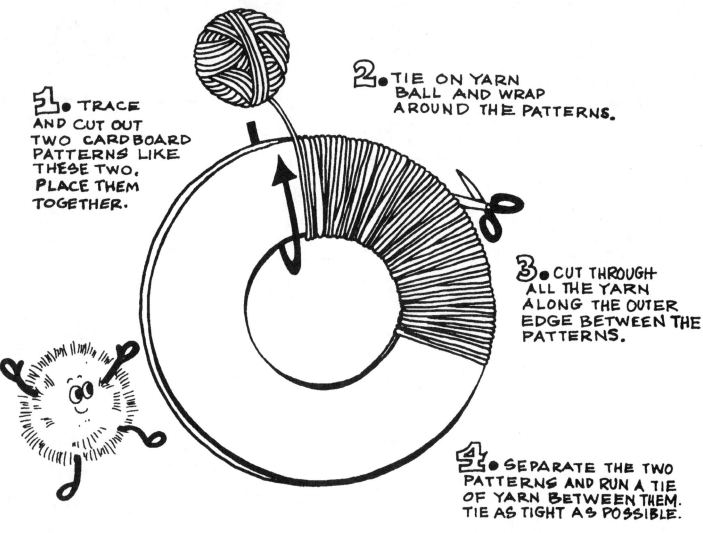

1. TRACE AND CUT OUT TWO CARDBOARD PATTERNS LIKE THESE TWO. PLACE THEM TOGETHER.

2. TIE ON YARN BALL AND WRAP AROUND THE PATTERNS.

3. CUT THROUGH ALL THE YARN ALONG THE OUTER EDGE BETWEEN THE PATTERNS.

4. SEPARATE THE TWO PATTERNS AND RUN A TIE OF YARN BETWEEN THEM. TIE AS TIGHT AS POSSIBLE.

5. PULL OUT PATTERNS, AND GIVE YOUR WARM FUZZY A "HAIRCUT" TO EVEN THE FUZZ.

6. DECORATE WITH FELT EYES, MOUTH AND PIPE CLEANER ARMS AND LEGS.

Warm Fuzzy Bag

Grades:	2-4
Time:	two 20-minute periods
Grouping:	tribes
Materials:	felt bags or envelopes, pencils, pens, paper

Objectives
1. To build group inclusion
2. To reinforce the concept of appreciation
3. To build self-esteem

Instructions
1. Have each person make a small bag out of poster paper, and print his or her name on it.
2. Have the students hang their bags around the room.
3. Ask each student to write a warm fuzzy statement for each member of his or her tribe or one for each member of the class, and place them in the warm fuzzy bags.
4. Tell the students that they can place additional warm fuzzies in the bags anytime throughout the month (or school year). Set aside time once a week for students to open their bags and read the messages they have received.

Suggested Reflection Questions
Content/Thinking
- What did we learn during this activity?
- Why is it important to know how to give warm fuzzies?
- How might your our world be a better place if people gave away more warm fuzzies?

Social
- How has the class climate changed as a result of this activity?

Personal
- How did you feel about receiving such nice messages?

Appreciation
Invite statements of appreciation:
- "I liked it when..."

Spider Web

Grades: K-adult
Time: varies depending on group size
Grouping: community
Materials: ball of colored yarn

Objectives
1. To build inclusion and a sense of community
2. To practice attentive listening

Instructions
1. Ask the community to sit in one large circle.
2. Explain that during this activity each student will have an opportunity to share his or her name and something special about himself or herself. Give the students a minute to think of something special.
3. Have one student begin the activity by stating his or her name and something about himself or herself.
   Example: "My name is Sue, and I am wonderful at organizing things." Then, have the student hold onto the end of the yarn and roll the yarn ball to someone across from him or her in the circle. Have the students continue this process until everyone has either shared or passed and a "spider web" pattern has been created.
4. It is fun to "play" with the web before rolling it up. Have everyone pick up the web, stand, hold it up overhead. Have them hold it waist high and shake it.
5. If time permits, have the students reroll the web one by one in reverse order. (Students below fifth grade have a hard time rerolling a ball of yarn.)

Suggested Reflection Questions
Content/Thinking
- How can you symbolically interpret this "spider web?" Note symbolism, design, community involvement, etc.
- Why is this a good community-building activity?
- What did you learn as a result of this activity?

Social
- How does "Spider Web" bring you closer together as a community?

Personal
- How did you feel before it was your turn/right after your turn?
- How do you feel right now?

Appreciation

Invite statements of appreciation:
- "I liked it when you said..."
- "I'm a lot like you when..."
- "I admire you for..."

Other Ways To Do Spider Web

- Make a statement of appreciation to someone in the circle; continue until each student has received a statement.
- Toss the yarn up and into the center, see where it goes, and then give that person a statement of appreciation.
- Paraphrase what the previous person said before giving his or her statement of appreciation.
- Answer a question asked of the community.

Name Game

Grades:	K-adult
Time:	varies
Grouping:	tribe or community
Materials:	none

Objectives
1. To help learn first names
2. To build inclusion

Instructions
1. Have the community sit in one large circle.
2. Have one student begin the activity by stating his or her name.
3. Have a second student repeat the first student's name and then state his or her own.
4. Have the third student repeat the first two names and then state his or her own.
   Example:
   "I'm Todd."
   "You're Todd, I'm Scott."
   "You're Todd, you're Scott, and I'm Karen."
5. Have the students continue the sequence around the circle until everyone has participated. The last student says everyone's name. Do give the community permission to help the students at the end of the circle. Everyone is not good at memorization.

Variation: Use alliterative adjectives ("Terrific Todd"), favorite foods ("Ice Cream Todd"), activities ("Football Todd"), etc.

Suggested Reflection Questions
Content/Thinking
- Why do you like being called by your first name?
- Why is this a good way to learn people's names?
Social
- Which social skills did we use in this activity?
- How did you help each other during this activity?
Personal
- How did you feel as your turn came closer?
- What's the mood of the community now compared to before starting this activity?

Appreciation
Invite statements of appreciation:
- "I felt good when..."
- "I like the way..."

Options
- With more than eight to ten students, have the community chant the names together so that pressure is not put on the last participants.
- Have each student say the names of the previous three to five people and then have the community chant the earlier names.

Objectives

1. To build inclusion
2. To share current feelings
3. To help build a feeling vocabulary

Instructions

1. To prepare for this strategy, duplicate the "Five Tribles" worksheet, one for each student.
2. Have community sit in a circle.
3. Talk about how they all arrived today with different feelings: some of them are happy and excited; some of them are feeling sad, tired, or angry; and some of them feel kind of in between in their own emotions: not happy, not sad, just here.
4. Pass out the "Five Tribles" worksheet.
5. Ask people to look at the five Tribles and decide which face looks most like they feel right now.
6. Review the Tribe agreements.
7. As the teacher, share first to model the activity. Be honest. Share which face you feel like and why.
8. Go around the circle, giving each student an opportunity to share or pass. If many pass, go around again until you feel that all who wish to share have done so.

Suggested Reflection Questions

Content/Thinking
- Why is it important to share how you are feeling with others?
- What were some of the feelings you shared?

Social
- How does sharing our feelings help us to know each other better?
- What's the mood of the community now?

Personal
- How did you feel as your turn came closer?
- What did you learn as a result of this activity?

Appreciation

Invite statements of appreciation:
- "I felt like you when…"
- "I liked it when…"

Option

- Use to show feelings on a particular idea, lesson, etc.

Five Tribles

Grades:	K-adult
Time:	15 minutes
Grouping:	community, tribes
Materials:	"Five Tribles" worksheet

A Trible is a warm, fuzzy, loving creature that first appeared from outer space in the television program "Star Trek."

Five Tribles

Objectives

1. To practice components of attentive listening:
   - Attending
   - Paraphrasing
   - Reflecting feelings
2. To share ideas and feelings about any given topic
3. To build inclusion

Teaching Listening

Grades:	2-adult
Time:	30 minutes
Grouping:	tribe
Materials:	none

Instructions

1. Discuss and demonstrate attentive listening skills (refer to chapter 5). Write components on chalkboard.
2. Ask the students to form triads, and designate each triad member as an A, B, or C. Ask for a show of hands of all A's, all B's and all C's to avoid confusion.
3. Explain that each triad member will have an opportunity to play each role; in round 1, A will observe, B will be the speaker, and C will be the listener. Post this chart:

	A	B	C
Round 1	Observer	Speaker	Listener
Round 2	Speaker	Listener	Observer
Round 3	Listener	Observer	Speaker

4. Give the speakers a topic of your choice (depending on age) to speak on for two to five minutes.
   Example: "Should students be allowed to vote?"
5. Ask the listeners to practice one or two components of attentive listening.
6. Ask the observers to pay attention to the interaction and after two to five minutes give feedback to the listeners. Ask them to include what they saw the listener doing both verbally and nonverbally, and their observations of how the speakers responded.
7. Have the triads repeat the process until all three members have had an opportunity to be observers, speakers, and listeners.

Suggested Reflection Questions

Content/Thinking
- Why was it important to have an observer?
- How can you be a good listener, speaker, or observer?

Social
- How can you tell if someone is being a good listener?
- Why is listening such an important social skill?

Personal
- How did it feel to be listened to in that way?
- How well did you attend, paraphrase, and reflect feelings?

Appreciation

Invite statements of appreciation:
- "I felt good when..."
- "I liked it when..."

Meet Someone Special

Grades:	K-adult
Time:	20-30 minutes
Grouping:	community, pairs
Materials:	none

Objectives

1. To introduce individuals to a community
2. To build community inclusion
3. To build self-esteem and appreciation for uniqueness

Instructions

1. This is a good activity to help new students introduce themselves to each other. Have the community sit in a circle while you give directions.
2. Review the Tribe agreements.
3. Ask each student to stand up, look about for someone he or she does not know well, invite that person to be his or her partner.
4. Have one partner interview the other one for three to ten minutes (depending on age), listening attentively so he or she will remember important unique qualities and details about the person; at the end of three to ten minutes, have the partners switch roles.
5. After the stated time, call the pairs back to the community circle and ask each student to introduce his or her partner and share the special things he or she learned.

Suggested Reflection Questions

Content/Thinking

- What new things did you learn from your partner?
- Why did you do this activity?

Social

- Why don't people take this type of time to get to know each other in other settings? In business and social organizations? In community meetings?
- What important social skills did you use during this activity?

Personal

- How well did you listen to your partner?
- How did you feel to have this much time to share about yourself?
- What did you learn about yourself that surprised you?

Appreciation

Invite statements of appreciation:
- "I appreciated it when..."
- "I liked it when..."

Objectives

1. To build inclusion
2. To form or assign membership in tribes

People Puzzles

Grades:	K-adult
Time:	20 minutes
Grouping:	tribes
Materials:	picture, puzzles

Instructions

1. Pre-prepare one puzzle for each group or tribe. Cut each puzzle so that the number of pieces matches the number of people in each group or tribe.
2. To build random groups, put all the pieces of all the puzzles in a box and have each person take a piece. To assign tribes put the name of one person on each piece of puzzle.
3. Before having the students form their tribes, have a discussion about what possible put-downs could occur and how to avoid them.
4. Ask the students to circulate and find the puzzle pieces that match the ones they are carrying. Tell them they are not to talk while doing this. Tell them they may talk when their group's puzzle has been completed.
5. Once all of the puzzles have been completed, you may choose to have each tribe make up a story relating to the picture its puzzle has formed. Have each tribe select one member to be a storyteller and tell the tribe's story to the community.

Suggested Reflection Questions

Content/Thinking

- What made this task difficult/easy?
- Was this a fun way to find students who would be in your tribe?

Social

- How did you react to students whose puzzle pieces didn't fit yours?
- What did you talk about when your puzzle was completed?
- How did you help each other during this activity?

Personal

- How did you feel when you first started this activity?
- How did you feel at the end?

Appreciation

Invite statements of appreciation:
- "I liked it when..."
- "I'm a lot like you when..."
- "I admire you for..."

Wishful Thinking

Grades:	K-adult
Time:	varies
Grouping:	tribes, community
Materials:	none

Objectives

1. To provide the opportunity to express a wish
2. To build inclusion

Instructions

1. Have the students sit or stand in a community circle or in tribes. Instruct them that no discussion is allowed during this activity.
2. Ask each student in turn to make a brief statement beginning with "I wish..." related to personal life, feelings about politics, school, the community, etc.
3. If possible, take turns around the circle more than once.

Suggested Reflection Questions

Content/Thinking

- How easy/difficult was it for you to think of wishes to share?
- Why are wishes important?
- What wishes do you have in common?

Social

- How well did your tribe members listen to each other's wishes?
- How do you know they listened?
- How did tribe members help each other share?

Personal

- How did you feel while you were sharing your wish/listening to others share?

Appreciation

Invite statements of appreciation:

- "I liked it when..."
- "I felt good when..."
- "I admired your honesty when..."

Something Good

Grades:	K-adult
Time:	varies
Grouping:	community
Materials:	none

Objectives
1. To build inclusion
2. To encourage sharing of positive feelings

Instructions
1. Have the community sit in a large circle.
2. Ask each student to share one positive experience that happened during the previous week or recent past. Say that there will be no discussion until all have shared.

Suggested Reflection Questions

Content/Thinking
- Were there any similarities about the "good things" you shared?
- When was the last time you told someone about a positive experience?

Social
- How can you tell if others are using good listening skills?
- Did you share more freely as the activity progressed? Why?
- How did this activity help the community?

Personal
- How did you feel while sharing with the community?

Appreciation
Invite statements of appreciation:
- "I liked it when..."
- "I'm like you when..."
- "I felt good when..."

Singing The Blues

Grades: K-3
Time: 20-30 minutes
Grouping: full group
Materials: none or a guitar

Objectives

1. To promote commonality and inclusion
2. To introduce sharing of concerns in a nonthreatening, enjoyable way
3. To channel community energy

Instructions

1. Ask the community if they know what "the blues" are. State that in this activity, having "the blues" means feeling badly about something.
2. Ask if anyone has the blues and why.
3. Sing or strum a melody that is simple and fun.
   Example: A seven-year-old boy says his dog was hurt. Words could be: "I've got the blues, I've got the blues, I've got the my-dog-was-hurt-blues."
4. Ask everyone to join in singing.
5. Share one of your own blues first. Lead the singing on it.
6. Invite the students to tell their blues and lead the singing.
7. Discourage the students from making fun of another's blues. Help them to understand it's a put-down to do so.

Suggested Reflection Questions

Content/Thinking

- What did you learn about "the blues" today?
- How were your "blues" similar?

Social

- How did the singing make it easier to share?

Personal

- How did you feel when you first started "singing the blues?"
- Do you feel different after "singing the blues?"
- How would you feel to sing about "good times?"

Appreciation

Invite statements of appreciation:

- "I enjoyed singing because..."
- "I feel like you do when..."

Objectives

1. To promote appreciation of personal qualities
2. To encourage respect for others
3. To build inclusion

Instructions

1. Have the community meet in tribes.
2. Distribute the materials.
3. Have each student write his or her first name in big colorful letters going down the left side of the paper.
4. Then have each student draw or cut out adjectives (words or phrases that describe special qualities) that begin with the letters of his or her first name.
   Example:

P	playful, powerful
A	active
T	talkative, tidy
T	terrific
I	interesting

5. Ask each student to share their "Names in Print" with the rest of the tribe or community.
6. Remind listeners to give full attention to the speaker. Say that questions or comments may be posed at the end of each presentation.
7. After asking reflection questions point out how well everyone listened. Give examples.

Suggested Reflection Questions

Content/Thinking

- How difficult/easy was it to find adjectives to describe yourself?
- Why is it important to use positive adjectives to describe yourself?
- Which adjectives did you like the best? Why?

Social

- How did this activity help you learn more about each other?
- How well did your tribe members listen to each other?

Personal

- How did you feel when you shared your adjectives?
- What did you do to make others comfortable when they shared?

Appreciation

Invite statements of appreciation:

- "[name], I liked it when you said..."
- "[name], I learned that you are..."
- "[name], I'm glad that we both have [quality] in common."

My Name In Print

Grades:	2-6
Time:	30-60 minutes
Grouping:	community, tribes
Materials:	9 x 12-inch paper, magazines, scissors, glue, markers

Interview Circle

Grades:	K-adult
Time:	15-30 minutes
Grouping:	community, tribes
Materials:	none

Objectives

1. To build inclusion and influence
2. To enhance communication skills
3. To share personal beliefs, feelings, and interests

Instructions

1. Ask the community to sit in a large circle.
2. Explain that we will interview one student who will sit in the center of the circle and answer three questions. The person will choose the questions from people who raise their hands. He or she has the right to "pass" on any questions that she or he chooses not to answer.
3. Model the activity first by being in the center and responding to three questions yourself.
4. Suggest that questions may be autobiographical or may relate to issues, curriculum, politics, hobbies, friendship, sports, etc.
5. Have the community interview a few students each day until everyone has had a turn.

Suggested Reflection Questions

Content/Thinking

- What did you discover about a community member?
- Why is it difficult to answer some of the questions?

Social

- Which social skills did community members use to make this activity successful?
- Did the community use good listening skills? How could you tell?

Personal

- How did you feel about being interviewed?
- What did you learn about yourself from this activity?

Appreciation

Invite statements of appreciation:

- "I liked it when..."
- "I admired your honesty when..."

Brainstorming

Grades:	K-adult
Time:	20 minutes
Grouping:	tribes
Materials:	markers, large paper

Objectives

1. To energize a tribe
2. To promote inclusion and influence
3. To experience the fun and creative power of brainstorming as a decision-making or problem-solving technique

Instructions

1. Ask each tribe to appoint a recorder to jot down all the ideas on paper, chalkboard, or newsprint as fast as ideas are called out. (With very young students use an aide or older student.)
2. Instruct the tribes on the "DOVE" rules that they need to follow in order to "brainstorm."

> D defer judgment
> O off beat, original
> V vast number
> E expand, elaborate

3. Have the community meet in tribes. Explain that each tribe will have five minutes to call out and write down as many ideas as possible on a subject.
   Examples:
   • "How could we design a better bathtub—one for more enjoyment, efficiency, and comfort than ordinary tubs?"
   • Other possible subjects: better bicycle, bedroom, car, school cafeteria, school
4. Stop the brainstorming after five minutes. Ask each recorder to read his or her tribe's list. Lead applause after each tribe's creativity.
5. If time allows, have the tribes draw their creations. Find a way to include everyone in the tribe.

Suggested Reflection Questions

Content/Thinking
• Why is brainstorming fun?
• How do the "DOVE" rules help you to brainstorm?

Social
• What would have happened if we had judged, commented, or discussed ideas as they were offered?
• How could you tell that your tribe members were enjoying themselves?
• How well did your tribe members follow the "DOVE" rules?

Personal
• How much did you participate?

Appreciation

Invite statements of appreciation:
• "I liked it when you said..."
• "I felt good when..."
• "Your suggestions helped me to..."

Chain Reaction

Grades: K-adult
Time: 15-30 minutes
Grouping: community, tribes
Materials: none

Objectives

1. To build inclusion and influence
2. To increase communication skills
3. To share personal interests, opinions and ideas
4. To ask each other questions about subject matter

Instructions

1. Have the community meet in tribes.
2. Remind the students of their right to pass and to honor the other agreements. Remind tribe members to give full, caring attention.
3. Have one tribe member begin by asking a question of a second tribe member. Have the second tribe member answer the question and then ask another question of a third tribe member. Instruct the tribes to continue the chain until each tribe member has answered and then asked a question. In large tribes have students ask the persons directly across from them. This helps the students to speak loudly enough.
4. Explain that questions may be autobiographical or deal with curriculum or a number of issues (politics, hobbies, education, friendship, family interests). (This is a good activity for students to help each other prepare for a test.)

Suggested Reflection Questions

Content/Thinking

- What did you learn about your tribe members?
- Why is this a good way to find out information about each other?

Social

- How could you tell whether your tribe was honoring the tribal agreements?
- How do the agreements protect you?
- How well did you give full, caring attention?

Personal

- How did you feel when it was your turn?
- What do you feel about your tribe members now?

Appreciation

Invite statements of appreciation:

- "I liked it when..."
- "I admired your honesty when..."

Objectives

1. To give each student an opportunity to share something special or meaningful about herself or himself
2. To build inclusion
3. To practice active listening

Instructions

1. Several days before this activity, ask each student to choose a special object to bring from home. The object may represent a hobby, interests, award, or symbol of a personal quality. Tell the students to bring the objects concealed in paper sacks.
2. Have community form one large circle or meet in tribes.
3. Going around the circle, ask each student to share his or her object by removing it from the sack and talking about it, telling why the object is important or symbolic.

Suggested Reflection Questions

Content/Thinking

- How did you choose what object you would bring?
- What did you learn about others?
- How did having your object in a sack before sharing make this activity more enjoyable?

Social

- Why did this activity help you get to know one another better?
- How well did you listen?

Personal

- How did you feel when you shared your object?
- How did you feel as you listened to others?

Appreciation

Invite statements of appreciation:

- "[name], you seem to love your hobby. May I do it with you sometime?"
- "[name], I liked it when you said…"
- "[name], thank you for listening…"

Sharing From A Sack

Grades:	K-adult
Time:	20-50 minutes
Grouping:	community, tribes
Materials:	each student brings an object in a paper sack

Shoe 'n Tell:

Grades: K-6
Time: 50 minutes
Grouping: community, tribes
Materials: each student brings a pair of shoes in a paper sack

Objectives

1. To build inclusion
2. To practice active listening
3. To have fun

Instructions

1. Ask each student to bring a pair of his or her shoes from home in a paper sack. (Allow a few days.)
2. Have full group or tribe sit in circle(s).
3. Explain that sharing from the sack could take on any of these forms:
   - how these shoes help me to do things that I like to do
   - sharing from the point of view of the shoe (what it's like being the shoe that belongs to the person sharing)
   - sharing from the point of view of the shoe (how I'd like to be taken care of if I could have it my way)

Suggested Reflection Questions

Content/Thinking
   - How did the shoes tell you about the students who shared?
   - How did you go about choosing the shoes you shared?

Social
   - How did tribe members show they were interested?

Personal
   - How did you feel sharing your shoes?

Appreciation

Invite statements of appreciation:
   - Going around the circle, ask each student to give a statement of appreciation to the student on left.
      - "[*name*], I liked it when..."

Objectives

1. To build inclusion
2. To identify and learn about famous people in history, politics, science, or some other academic content

Instructions

1. Give each person a 3 x 5-inch index card, a pin, and a pencil.
2. Ask each student to print on the card in large block letters the name of some famous person, living or dead. (With young students, use pictures of animals, plants, or fruits.)
3. Ask each student to pin his or her "famous person" card onto the back of another student, without letting that student know the name on the card.
4. Tell the students to find out who they are by milling around and asking other students questions that can be answered "yes" or "no." Students may ask only one question each time they talk to another student. Continue the process until everyone has identified his or her famous name. Simple hints from other students or the teacher may be given to help those having a difficult time.

Suggested Reflection Questions

Content/Thinking

- Who were some of the famous people?
- What kind of questions did you ask?
- What do you know about the person whose name was pinned onto your back?

Social

- How did you help each other successfully identify your famous people?

Personal

- Do you identify with your famous person in any way?
- What kind of questions will you ask next time?

Appreciation

Invite statements of appreciation:

- "I liked it when..."
- "I'm a lot like you when..."

"Am I Napoleon?"

Grades:	K-adult
Time:	20 minutes
Grouping:	community
Materials:	3 x 5-inch cards, pins, crayons or felt pens

Outlines

Grades: 3-adult
Time: 30-40 minutes
Grouping: community, tribes
Materials: "T-Shirt Outline" worksheet, colored pens or pencils

Objectives

1. To build inclusion
2. To practice communication and listening skills
3. To discuss academic topics

Instructions

1. Have the students meet either in their tribes or the community circle.
2. Explain the objectives, and pass out "T-shirt Outline" worksheets.
3. Tell students how to fill in the outline:
   - in area #1 write an alliterative adjective that goes with your first name. (Example: "Vivacious Vicki")
   - in area #2 write or draw two to three things you enjoy doing
   - in area #3 name a real or pretend place you would like to visit
   - in area #4 write a word you'd like people to say when they describe you
   - in area #5 write a wish you have for yourself
4. Sharing: First review the Tribes agreements, and ask the students to share the time equally so that each student has an opportunity to speak during each round.

   Round 1: each student shares his or her name and alliterative adjective with another student, telling why he or she chose the adjective (three minutes).

   Round 2: each student finds two other people and shares the information he or she wrote in area #2 (four minutes).

   Round 3: each student finds two other people and shares the information of area #3 (four minutes).

   Round 4: each finds three to four others and shares area #4 (four minutes).

   Round 5: each Round 4 group combines with another Round 4 group. Names and alliterative adjectives are shared again with students telling why they chose their particular adjectives.

Suggested Reflection Questions

Content/Thinking

- What did you learn about your tribe members?
- What were the similarities among your tribe members' wishes?

Social

- How well did you listen to each other? How could you tell?
- How many students do you feel you know better now?

Personal

- What was the best/most difficult thing for you about this activity?
- What did you learn about yourself?

Appreciation

Invite statements of appreciation:

- "I like it when..."
- "I'm glad you're..."

Note: There are endless other fine questions for this activity: someone you admire, a quality you like in a friend, something you want to learn, favorite subject or book, academic material. Select those most appropriate for group's age and culture.

T-Shirt Outline

Milling To Music

Grades:	3-adult
Time:	15-25 minutes
Grouping:	community
Materials:	slips with numbered topics, cassette tape player & lively music

Objectives

1. To build community inclusion
2. To review a curriculum topic

Instructions

1. Pre-prepare for each student a slip on which there are four numbered questions.
   Example:
   - Describe three cities or towns in which you have lived.
   - Share your favorite way to relax or spend vacation time.
   - Describe what your house, apartment, or living space is like.
   - If you were given $100,000 tomorrow, what would you do with it?
2. Give the students their slips with the four topics and ask them to stand up.
3. Explain that when the music starts they are to begin milling around silently but greeting each other as they pass by.
4. Explain that when the music stops (or when you give the hand signal), each student is to stop and discuss question #1 with a student standing close by for 1 minute. Explain that when the music begins again, they are to repeat the process until they have discussed all four questions.

Suggested Reflection Questions

Content/Thinking
- What kind of greetings did you use?
- What similar things did you share?

Social
- What skills did you have to use in this activity? (Suggest some: listening, speaking clearly, sharing time, respecting differences.)

Personal
- What do you feel now?
- How has the atmosphere changed in the room?

Appreciation

Invite statements of appreciation:
- "I liked it when..."
- "I appreciated the sharing that [*name*] did.

Bumper Sticker

Grades:	2-adult
Time:	30 minutes
Grouping:	community, tribes
Materials:	colored paper strips, crayons or markers

Objectives
1. To present something special about oneself
2. To build inclusion
3. To encourage attentive listening

Instructions
1. Review agreements.
2. Give each student a long strip of paper and a marker or crayon with which to create a "bumper sticker" that he or she would enjoy displaying on his or her automobile bumper (wagon, bicycle. etc.).
3. Have each student in turn share his or her bumper sticker with the community. Remind everyone to give their full attention to the speaker.
4. Tell the students they may ask questions, and express mutual feelings and concerns after everyone has shared.

Suggested Reflection Questions
Content/Thinking
- What similar kinds of things did you put on your bumper stickers?
- What's one special thing you learned about another student?
Social
- How well did everyone listen when you shared your bumper sticker?
Personal
- How did you feel as you shared?
- What can you do in the future to help others feel more comfortable when they share?
- Would you really want to put your sticker on your car or bicycle? Why or why not?

Appreciation
Invite statements of appreciation:
- "I liked it when..."
- "I admired you for..."

Appreciating Others

Grades:	2-adult
Time:	45 minutes
Grouping:	community, tribes
Materials:	"Appreciating Others" worksheets, pencils, large paper, felt pens

Objectives

1. To increase awareness of importance of stating appreciation
2. To practice the norms
3. To provide for initial inclusion

Instructions

1. Pass out "Appreciating Others" worksheet to all class members.
2. In the front of the room post a large visual of the worksheet from which you can work as a model.
3. Ask each student to fill in the boxes with positive statements, one to self, best friend, Mom and/or Dad, and a classmate. Suggest that they use some of the positive statement forms noted on the bottom of the worksheet, if they need to.
4. Ask the students to meet in tribes to share their positive statements.
5. Have one member of each tribe record all the core ideas that are included on the tribe members' worksheets.
6. Ask the recorder from each tribe to report the summaries to the community.
7. Suggest that students tell one of their statements to the person it was written to.

Suggested Reflection Questions

Content/Thinking

- Why did you learn to give statements of appreciation?
- What were three statements shared by your tribe members?

Social

- How can making statements of appreciation help a tribe work together better?
- Why is it important to make statements of appreciation to friends, family, and others?

Personal

- How do you feel when you receive a statement of appreciation from someone else?
- Which of the statements you wrote would make you feel good?

Appreciation

Invite statements of appreciation:
- "I liked it when..."
- "Thank you for..."

Option

Ask how many students would commit to using at least one appreciation statement every day. Have tribes write contracts to do so. Post the contracts and review them regularly.

Appreciating Others

Self	Best Friend
Mom/Dad	Classmate

Suggested positive statements forms:

_____, I liked it when you...

_____, I appreciate it when...

_____, I'm glad you...

_____, I want to give you a warm fuzzy for...

_____, thanks for...

Boasters

Grades:	2-adult
Time:	30-45 minutes
Grouping:	tribes, subgroups,
Materials:	12-inch-high cutouts of student profiles

Objectives

1. To make statements of appreciation to self and others
2. To build self-esteem
3. To build inclusion

Instructions

1. Prepare posterboard or construction paper cutouts similar to the one on the next page for each student, or have each student prepare one for himself or herself.
2. Ask the community to meet in tribes.
3. Have each student write his or her name in large, colorful letters on the head area of his or her cut-out.
4. Instruct the tribe members to pass the cutouts around the tribe so that each tribe member can write a positive statement on each other tribe member's cutout.
5. Have a discussion about complimenting yourself and how it is different than bragging. Then ask each student to write a positive statement about himself or herself on his or her own card.

Suggested Reflection Questions

Content/Thinking

- Why is it important to be able to make positive statements about others?
- What are two positive statements that you made to others/they made to you?

Social

- How can making positive statements to each other help us work together better?

Personal

- How did you feel when you knew someone else was writing on your card?
- How did you feel when you read the comments on your card?
- Do you ever compliment yourself?
- Make a plan for complimenting yourself at least once every day.

Appreciation

Invite statements of appreciation:
- "I'm glad you notice that I..."
- "I felt good when..."

Boasters

Something I Cherish

Grades:	2-adult
Time:	20 minutes
Grouping:	community, tribes
Materials:	none

Objectives

1. To increase communication skills
2. To build inclusion

Instructions

1. Ask the community to meet in tribe.
2. Ask each tribe member to take a turn sharing "one thing that I cherish," explaining why it is so special or why she or he wants others to know, etc.
3. To draw the tribes back into the community, have each tribe member share with the community one item that another member of his or her tribe cherishes. Make sure each tribe member speaks of and is spoken about by another member of his or her tribe.

Suggested Reflection Questions

Content/Thinking
- What type of things do your tribe members cherish?
- Why is it important to share what you cherish with each other?

Social
- How well did your tribe members listen when others shared?

Personal
- How did you feel about sharing something you cherished?
- How can this type of sharing help your own family?

Appreciation

Invite statements of appreciation (to tribe members):
- "I liked it when..."
- "I felt good when..."
- "I was interested when..."

"I'm Proud" Appreciation Circle

Grades: 2-adult
Time: 30 minutes
Grouping: community, or tribes
Materials: none

Objectives
1. To encourage sharing good feelings about oneself
2. To encourage acceptance and appreciation of others
3. To build inclusion

Instructions
1. Discuss the difference between stating appreciation of oneself and bragging.
2. Invite one person of the community or one person in each tribe to sit in the middle as the focus person.
3. Have the focus person make an "I'm proud" statement. Examples:
   • "I'm proud that I am..."
   • "I'm proud that I am able to..."
   • "I'm proud that I..."
4. Have the other tribe members give positive feedback or make statements of appreciation to the focus person.
5. Continue the process until each person takes a turn being the focus person.

Suggested Reflection Questions
Content/Thinking
   • How did you choose your "I'm proud" statement?
   • What did you learn about your tribe members?
Social
   • Why is it important to be able to acknowledge what we are proud of?
   • How supportive was the tribe when you made your "I'm proud" statements?
Personal
   • How did you feel when you made your "I'm proud" statements?
   • How did you feel when you gave/received statements of appreciation?

Appreciation
Invite people to make statements of appreciation:
   • Is there anyone who would like to make a statement to anyone else in the class?

Option
Use the strategy in a community circle.

All In The Family

Grades:	2-adult
Time:	20 minutes
Grouping:	subgroups
Materials:	none

Objectives

1. To build inclusion
2. To promote awareness of how other family members feel

Instructions

1. Ask the students to form groups in different parts of the room according to their birth positions in their families: (eldest, youngest, in-betweens, only child).
2. Have each student share with the other members of his or her group:
   - How does it feel to be [*firstborn, etc.*]?
   - What are the responsibilities he or she has?
   - What are the advantages he or she has?
3. Merge the groups so that the eldest are with the in-betweens, and the only children are with youngest (or mix the groups together whichever way you want).
4. Now ask these groups to share:
   - Who do you think has the most power in your family?
   - How do you feel toward other siblings?
   - Who gets attention in your family and how do they get it?

Suggested Reflection Questions

Content/Thinking
- What did you learn about birth order and power in a family?
- What generalizations can you make about birth order?

Social
- What social skills did you use to make this activity successful?
- How well did you participate?

Personal
- How did you feel when you were with others in the same birth position as you?
- What did you feel about those in the same birth position/ different birth position?
- What did you learn about yourself?

Appreciation

Invite statements of appreciation:
- "I'm a lot like you when..."
- "I felt good when..."

What's In My Name?

Grades: 3-adult
Time: 20 minutes
Grouping: tribes
Materials: "What's In My Name?" worksheets

Objectives

1. To initiate tribe inclusion
2. To encourage tribe members to share feelings
3. To practice attentive listening

Instructions

1. Ask each student to complete the following "homework" assignment: Find out from your parents how you were named. Were you named after someone? How was your name picked? You may want to send home the instruction sheet for younger students (see next page). Allow a few days for the students to complete the assignment.
2. Have the students meet in tribes or the community circle.
3. Ask the students to take turns sharing how their names were selected, what nicknames may have happened, and how they feel about their names or nicknames.

Suggested Reflection Questions

Content/Thinking
- What similarities did you notice about how people's names were selected?
- Why is it important to know how you got your name?

Social
- How well did your tribe members participate in this activity?
- Why can this type of activity help tribe members feel better about each other?

Personal
- How did you feel when you learned how your name was selected for you?
- Would you consider changing your name? Why?

Appreciation

Invite statements of appreciation:
- "[*name*], I liked what you said about your name because..."
- "[*name*], I like your name because..."
- "[*name*], I felt that you understood when I said..."

Name_____

What's In My Name?

Instructions:
Answer the following questions about your name. Interview your parents if you do not know all the answers.

1. Why did your parents choose your name?

2. If you were named after someone, who was it?

3. What nicknames do you have, and how did you get them?

4. Do you like your name? Why, or why not?

5. If you could choose another name, would you, and what would it be?

Self-Esteem Cards

Grades: 3-adult
Time: 15 minutes
Grouping: tribes
Materials: 3 x 5-inch cards

Objectives

1. To build self-esteem
2. To reinforce the concept of appreciation
3. To foster positive feelings among tribe members
4. To build inclusion

Instructions

Note: This strategy should not be used until tribe members know one another fairly well.

1. Have the community meet in tribes; pass out cards.
2. Instruct each tribe member to write his or her first name in an upper corner of the card.
3. Tell the tribe members to place all their cards in a center pile. Have each tribe member draw a card (not divulging whose card he or she has), and write a thoughtful, warm statement on the card about the student whose name is on the card.
4. Have the students return all of the cards to the central pile when done writing and repeat the process of drawing and writing four or five additional times. If anyone draws his own card, begin the drawing again or have the students exchange cards.
5. After the final writing, return all cards and draw again. This time have each tribe member read the remarks on the card to the student whose name is on the card, delivering the tribe's message as warmly and sincerely as possible while the rest of the tribe listens.

Suggested Reflection Questions

Content/Thinking

- What did you learn by doing this activity?
- How did you choose the statements you wrote for your tribe members?

Social

- How does making thoughtful, warm statements to each other bring your tribe closer together?
- Why is it important to receive positive statements from others?

Personal

- How did you feel while your card was being read to you?
- How do you feel about your tribe now?

Appreciation

Invite statements of appreciation:

- "I felt good when..."
- "Thank you for..."

Objectives

1. To build self-esteem
2. To encourage giving statements of appreciation
3. To build inclusion

Instructions

1. Give each student a large piece of paper, a felt marker, and two pieces of masking tape.
2. Ask each student to print his or her name at the top of the paper.
3. Have the students attach the papers to each others' shoulders so that they hang down like capes on their backs.
4. Have the students stand and circulate so that each person in the group can write statements of appreciation on other people's paper capes. Emphasize that the statements need to be positive.
5. When each student has several written statements on his or her cape, ask the community to sit in a circle or have them form tribes. Have the students read their statements aloud or have them exchange papers and read to each other.
6. Encourage people to save their papers, perhaps to use as posters for their bedroom walls.

On My Back

Grades:	3-adult
Time:	20 minutes
Grouping:	community, tribes
Materials:	large paper, tape, markers

Suggested Reflection Questions

Content/Thinking
- What were some of the neat things people wrote?
- What similarities did you see in what people wrote?
- How did the fact that this activity was anonymous help you to be honest?

Social
- How did you take care of each other?
- How did you take turns?
- Why don't you offer positive statements to others more often?

Personal
- What feelings did you have when people were writing on your paper cape?
- What feelings did you have while your statements were being read aloud or while you were reading your statements?

Appreciation

Invite statements of appreciation:
- "I like it when..."
- "I felt good when..."

Option

Use as a learning strategy for well known-characters in history, politics, current events, literature, etc.

People Hunt

Grades: 3-adult
Time: 40 minutes
Grouping: community
Materials: "People Hunt" worksheets, pencils

Objectives

1. To promote community inclusion
2. To introduce oneself to others
3. To encourage sharing information

Instructions

1. Give one third of the students worksheet I, one third worksheet II and one third worksheet III.
2. Have the students circulate around the room, stopping to introduce him or herself, and asking different students the questions listed on his or her worksheet. Tell them to write down the names of those who fit the descriptions.
3. After ten to fifteen minutes, ask the community to meet in tribes or form groups of five for reflection questions.

Suggested Reflection Questions

Content/Thinking
- What did you learn that impressed or surprised you?

Social
- How well were group members participating in this task and how could you tell?
- What social skills were used to be successful with this task?

Personal
- How did you approach this task, did you go to people or did you wait for people to come to you?
- Do you feel any different now from when you first walked into the room?

Appreciation

Invite statements of appreciation:
- "I liked it when you..."
- "I felt good when..."
- "I'm like you when..."

Option

- Personalize the "People Hunt" by looking at students' permanent folders and making up relevant questions.
- Use the strategy to review academic subjects by writing appropriate questions.

People Hunt Worksheet I
FIND:

1. A person who does not own a TV

   His or her name is_____

2. A person whose birthday is within a month after yours

   His or her name is_____

3. A person who can cross his or her eyes

   His or her name is_____

4. A person who traveled over 2,000 miles last summer

   His or her name is_____

5. A person who lives in a house where no one smokes

   His or her name is_____

6. A person who owns a horse

   His or her name is_____

7. A person who is new to this school

   His or her name is_____

8. A person who likes brussels sprouts

   His or her name is_____

9. A person who is an artist

   His or her name is_____

10. A person who has more than six brothers and sisters

   His or her name is_____

People Hunt Worksheet II
FIND:

1. A person who can speak two languages

    His or her name is_____

2. A person who has been to a concert

    His or her name is_____

3. A person who has two different colored eyes

    His or her name is_____

4. A person with a new baby in his or her home

    His or her name is_____

5. A person whose birthday is the same month as yours

    His or her name is_____

6. A person who can roll his or her tongue

    His or her name is_____

7. A person who has been ice skating this past year

    His or her name is_____

8. A person not born in this country

    His or her name is_____

9. A person who has more than four animals in his or her home

    His or her name is_____

10. A person who woke up with a smile this morning

    His or her name is_____

People Hunt Worksheet III
FIND:

1. A person not born in California (New York, Texas, etc.)

   His or her name is_____

2. A person who stayed home last summer

   His or her name is_____

3. A person whose birthday is one month before yours

   His or her name is_____

4. A person who is the oldest child in his or her family

   His or her name is_____

5. A person who can touch his or her nose with his or her tongue

   His or her name is_____

6. A person who likes to invent things

   His or her name is_____

7. A person who jogs for exercise

   His or her name is_____

8. A person who has four dogs in his or her home

   His or her name is_____

9. A person who has been horseback riding in the past three months

   His or her name is_____

10. A person who has planted a tree

   His or her name is_____

Extended Nametags

Grades:	3-adult
Time:	15-25 minutes
Grouping:	community, triads
Materials:	5 x 8-inch cards, pencils, clock

Objectives

1. To promote inclusion
2. To share personal history, interests, beliefs
3. To enhance communication skills

Instructions

1. Distribute 5 x 8-inch cards.
2. Ask each student to print his or her first name or nickname in the center of the card, and directly under it the quality he or she most values in people.
3. Then have each student write the following in the corners:
   - upper left—a place where he or she spent his or her happiest summer
     option: his or her favorite place on earth
   - lower left—the name of a person who taught him or her something important
     option: the name of his or her best friend
   - lower right—the year he or she last spent three great days in a row
     option: the year he or she went on a big trip
   - upper right—three things he or she does well
     option: a goal that he or she has for the future
4. Have the students meet in triads. Explain that the triad will talk about the upper left corner of their cards for three minutes, which means each person has one minute to talk. Ask them to keep track of their time and to share equally.
5. After three minutes, have the triads give statements of appreciation. Allow two minutes for the statements.
   Examples:
   - "I liked it when..."
   - "You're a lot like me when..."
6. Have the students form new triads three more times, sharing the other three corners and giving statements of appreciation after each round. Use the same time periods as suggested in steps four and five above.
7. Form a community circle and invite each student to share something special he or she learned about a class member.

Suggested Reflection Questions
Content/Thinking
- Why is it important for the members of a community to have opportunities to share information about themselves?
- Are there other good questions we could ask?

Social
- How did you know that others were listening well when you spoke?

Personal
- What were your feeling when you were speaking? What were you feeling when you were listening?
- How did this activity help our class community get better acquainted?

Appreciation
Suggest people make statements of appreciation:
- "I liked hearing..."
- "I admire your..."

Open Forum

Grades: 3-adult
Time: 30 minutes
Grouping: tribes, subgroup
Materials: none

Objectives

1. To encourage acceptance of diverse feelings, beliefs, and cultures
2. To build inclusion

Instructions

1. Have the community meet in tribes or subgroups.
2. Tell the students that you will write a discussion question on the chalkboard, and each tribe member is to take a turn responding to the question. Discussion or questions are not allowed until each tribe member has had an opportunity to respond to the question. After all tribe members have had a chance to speak, students may ask one another follow-up questions and ask for clarification of what was said.
3. Remind the groups about the tribe agreements, especially "attentive listening."
4. Examples of inclusion questions:
   - What is the best book you ever read? Why did you like it?
   - How do you select your friends?
   - What guides your life?
   - If you could be an animal for a day, what would you be? Why?
   - What goal do you have for your future?

Option: Use the strategy for academic questions.

Suggested Reflection Questions

Content/Thinking
- What was something you learned from your discussion?

Social
- What social skills did you use to make this activity successful?
- How could you tell that your tribe members were being good listeners when you shared?

Personal
- Why would you be uncomfortable answering some of the questions?
- How did you feel when it was your turn?
- How did you participate? Are you happy with the way you participated? Why?

Appreciation

Invite statements of appreciation:
- "I liked it when..."
- "I'm a lot like you when..."
- "You're a lot like me when..."

This Is Me

Grades:	4-adult
Time:	30 minutes
Grouping:	community
Materials:	"This Is Me" poster worksheet, pins, pencils

Objectives
1. To build self-esteem
2. To build inclusion

Instructions
1. Explain to the community that they will be introducing themselves positively to each other by using "This Is Me" posters which they will create themselves.
2. Give each student a copy of the "This Is Me" poster worksheet (see following page), a straight pin, and pencil.
3. Allow five to ten minutes for everyone to complete their posters. Remind them to write positive things. Tell them that no self-put-downs are allowed.
4. Have the students help each other pin the posters to their own backs; then tell everyone to circulate and read each other's posters and share their own.
5. Have the community sit in a circle.
6. Discuss and reflect upon the activity.

Suggested Reflection Questions
Content/Thinking
- What did you learn about your tribe members?
- Why is sharing personal information sometimes important?

Social
- How did the poster theme of the activity help you to participate?
- How did you help others to feel OK about their posters?

Personal
- What section of the poster was the most difficult for you to complete? Why?
- How did you feel milling around the room?
- How do you feel about yourself now?

Appreciation
Invite statements of appreciation:
- "I liked it when..."
- "I appreciated that..."

"This Is Me" Poster

Name

I am always

I need

I value

A slogan I live by

Reasons And Alternatives

Grades:	4-adult
Time:	45-60 minutes
Grouping:	tribes
Materials:	large paper, markers

Objectives

1. To explore motives and alternatives concerning the use of cigarettes, alcohol, or drugs
2. To develop peer support for non-use of alcohol and other drugs
3. To build inclusion and influence in tribes

Instructions

1. Have the community meet in tribes. Ask each tribe to appoint a recorder. Pass out two large sheets of paper and a marker to each tribe.
2. Tell the students that they will be brainstorming; review the rules of brainstorming.
3. Ask the tribes to brainstorm for five minutes on the subject: "Why do people smoke, drink alcohol, or use drugs?" Ask each recorder to jot down all ideas as quickly as they are called out.
4. After five minutes, stop the brainstorming and have the recorders take new sheets of paper. Ask the tribes now to brainstorm about another subject: "What are some alternatives to using cigarettes, alcohol, or other drugs?"
5. Stop the brainstorming after five minutes. Have the recorders report back to the tribe or community.
6. Ask the students to write in their personal journals what they intend to do about using chemical substances and how they would like to live their lives. Have them share their commitments with their tribe members.
7. Next ask the tribes to discuss what they are willing to do to help friends say "no" to the use of cigarettes, alcohol, or other drugs. Have each tribe make a list and report back to the community.

Suggested Reflection Questions

Content/Thinking

- What did you learn about substance abuse?
- Why was this an important activity to do today?
- How can this knowledge change your behavior?

Social

- Why is brainstorming a good structure for this lesson?
- How can your tribe have improve its brainstorming process?

Personal

- How do you feel about your tribe members?
- What will help you to live the commitment you have made?

Appreciation

Invite statements of appreciation:

- "It helped me when..."
- "I appreciated..."

Kitchen Kapers

Grades:	3-adult
Time:	25-30 minutes
Grouping:	tribes, subgroups
Materials:	3 x 5-inch cards, paper clips, tooth picks, pencils, envelopes

Objectives

1. To build inclusion and influence
2. To experience the creative power of brainstorming as a problem-solving technique
3. To promote creativity and fun

Instructions

1. Prepare packets containing two 3 x 5-inch cards, two paper clips, four toothpicks, and one pencil in a sealed business-sized envelope.
2. Have the community meet in tribes or form subgroups. Review the agreements.
3. Give each tribe a packet. State that they will have twelve minutes to invent and build "one kitchen utensil every household simply must have." Encourage bizarre, zany, and unique ideas. State that all tribe members need to participate.
4. Stop the "inventors" at twelve minutes.
5. Ask each tribe to then prepare a short, three minute commercial advertising its product. All members need to take part in the commercial.
6. Have each tribe present their commercial to the community.

Suggested Reflection Questions

Content/Thinking

- What inventions did the tribes create?
- How did the purpose of the utensil change as you built it?
- What did you learn from this activity?

Social

- How did leadership in your tribe evolve?
- How can building project like this help build tribe spirit?

Personal

- How did you feel before your tribe knew what it would build?
- How did you feel when you completed the invention?

Appreciation

Invite statements of appreciation (to tribe members):

- "I felt good when..."
- "I liked it when..."

Life Map

Grades:	3-adult
Time:	30 minutes
Grouping:	tribes
Materials:	large paper, crayons or markers

Objectives
1. To build inclusion
2. To create a visual illustration of one's life
3. To encourage attentive listening

Instructions
1. Ask the community to meet in tribes.
2. Give each student a piece of paper and crayons or markers and have him or her draw a visual illustration of "my life to date," the significant trends and patterns in the form of a map.
3. Invite each student to share his or her "Life Map" with his or her tribe members, explaining the rationale for "road signs," "place names," ups and downs, and so on.
4. Ask the students to give their full, undivided, caring attention to the speakers; after each student's presentation ask his or her tribe members to draw out more details, ask questions, and express their mutual feelings or concerns.

Suggested Reflection Questions
Content/Thinking
- Why is it important to be able to draw a "Life Map?"
- How were the maps in your tribe the same?

Social
- How could you tell if your tribe members were being good listeners when others shared their "Life Maps?"

Personal
- How did you feel as you made your "Life Map"/as you shared with your tribe?

Appreciation
Invite statements of appreciation:
- "I felt good when..."
- "I like it when..."

What's Your Bag?

Grades: 3-adult
Time: 60 minutes
Grouping: tribes
Materials: paper bags, glue, magazines, scissors, stapler

Objectives
1. To build inclusion
2. To present uniqueness of oneself

Instructions
1. Have the community meet in tribes.
2. Give each tribe a pile of magazines, scissors and glue, and one bag per member.
3. Instruct the students to use pictures and phrases from magazines to create personal collages, using the outside of the bag for public image and interests and the inside for private world or less shared world.
4. Tell the students that they may staple their bags shut if they want to ensure privacy for their inside worlds.
5. Invite tribe members to take turns sharing with each the outside of their bags and offering the rationale for some of their choices. Tribe members may choose to share a part of the inside world at the time of activity, or this could be done in a separate activity.

Suggested Reflection Questions
Content/Thinking
- What type of things did you share about your outside worlds?
- Why is it important to have both an outside (public image) world and an inside (personal beliefs) world?

Social
- What social skills did your tribe members use during this activity?
- How did you help each other during this activity?

Personal
- How did you feel while making your bag?
- What did you learn about yourself/your tribe?

Appreciation
Invite statements of appreciation:
- "I felt good when..."
- "I like your bag because..."

Slip Game

Grades:	3-adult
Time:	varies
Grouping:	community, tribes
Materials:	question slips, paper bags

Objectives

1. To build inclusion
2. To promote personal sharing

Instructions

1. Pre-prepare a bag for each tribe containing slips of paper with questions on them.
   Examples:
   - "When are you really happy?"
   - "What is the most special positive quality about you?"
   - "When have you felt very proud?"

   (See more sample questions on the next page.) Make sure each bag contains the same number of question slips as the number of tribe members, plus a few extra.
2. Instruct the community to meet in tribes. Review the agreements. Pass out bags.
3. Everyone has the "right to pass" if they do not like the question that they draw and may select an alternative one from those that remain in the bag. They must put the original slip back after taking an alternative one. Ask tribe members to each draw a slip with their eyes closed; tell them about right to pass and option for drawing alternative questions.
4. Have tribe members take turns reading and answering their questions.

Suggested Reflection Questions

Content/Thinking
- What's one thing someone shared that you found interesting?

Social
- Why is "right to pass" such an important agreement for this activity?
- How did having the opportunity to choose another question slip help you and your tribe be successful?
- Did you feel more comfortable about sharing as the activity progressed?

Personal
- Why could it be difficult for you to share?
- How did you feel when you were answering the question you drew?

Appreciation

Invite statements of appreciation:
- "I'm a lot like you when..."
- "I admired you for..."

Option

Use the strategy for discussion on lesson topic questions.

SLIP GAME: Sample Questions

What makes you angry?

What makes you happy?

What makes you sad?

What do you do for fun?

Do you have any pets?

What is your favorite food?

What is your favorite place?

What is your favorite animal?

What is your favorite sport?

What is your favorite song?

What is your favorite TV program?

What do you and your friends do for fun?

If you could have one wish, what would it be?

What famous person would you like to be?

In what period of time, past or future, would you choose to live in?

What foreign country would you like to visit?

What would you like to be really good at?

What is your favorite story?

What is one food you don't like?

What do you do when you feel lonely?

What would you do with one million dollars?

Would you rather be rich, famous or happy?

What would you do if you were the president?

What would you do to improve school?

What qualities do you look for in a friend?

Who is the best person in the world?

What do you do when you get really angry?

Objectives

1. To build inclusion
2. To give students an opportunity to create visual illustrations of themselves from four time perspectives

Instructions

1. Ask the community to meet in tribes.
2. Give each student a "Look at Me!" worksheet, a pencil, and crayons or markers. Have each student draw himself or herself as a baby, as a small child, now, and five years from now. (Use your own worksheet to illustrate.)
3. Ask the tribe members to share their four drawings, explaining any anecdotes or details that seem appropriate.
4. Remind listeners to give full, undivided, caring attention to the speakers.

Suggested Reflection Questions

Content/Thinking

- What similarities/differences did you notice in your "Look at Me!" worksheets?

Social

- How could you tell that tribe members were using good listening skills when your tribe shared?

Personal

- How did you feel as you drew yourself?
- What did you learn about yourself?

Appreciation

Invite statements of appreciation:

- "I felt good when..."
- "I understand how you felt when..."

Look At Me!

Grades:	4-6
Time:	45 minutes
Grouping:	tribes
Materials:	"Look at Me!" worksheets, crayons or markers, pencils

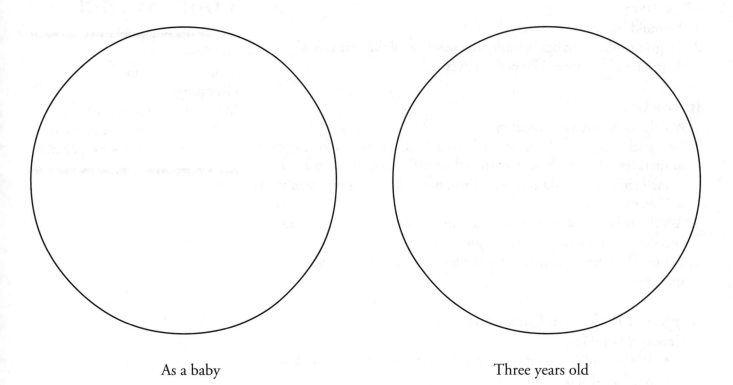

As a baby   Three years old

LOOK AT ME!

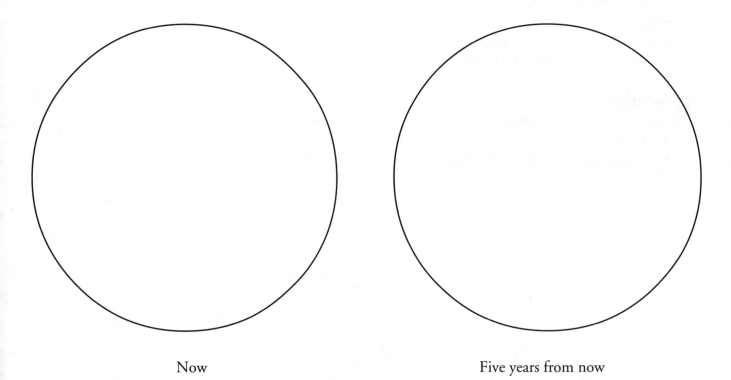

Now   Five years from now

Novel in an Hour

Grades:	3–adult
Time:	depends upon material
Grouping:	tribes
Materials:	a short story or novel

Objectives
1. To comprehend a novel, story or chapter of a book
2. To work cooperatively in small groups to retell the story by using drama, pictures, storytelling or other multiple intelligences
3. To practice listening, respecting and working together creatively

Instructions
1. Divide the chapters of a novel or short story into 5–10 sections, numbering each section.
2. Divide the class into the same number of groups.
3. Introduce the novel with an appropriate personal *inclusion question* for discussion.
4. Create interest in the novel by sharing something about the characters, theme or dilemma.
5. Describe the structure and process of Novel in an Hour:
   * the novel has been divided into sections (same number as groups);
   * everyone is actively involved;
   * everyone takes turns reading the material aloud;
   * the group plans multiple ways to share their part of the material with the whole community by using their multiple intelligences (drama, music, illustration, etc.).
6. Have each group appoint a time keeper (example: planning—20 minutes, and presentation—30 minutes).
7. Have the groups make their presentations to the community in the order of the sections of the novel.

Suggested Reflection Questions
Content/Thinking
* Which character was most important in how the story ended?
* What do you think the author's message is?
Social
* What was difficult for your group in planning your presentation?
* What was most helpful?
Personal
* What feelings did you have during your group's presentation?
* What makes this a good way to learn about a novel or story?

Appreciation
Invite statements of appreciation:
* "I liked it when…"
* "I appreciated the way that our group…"

Urgent!

Grades: 4-adult
Time: varies
Grouping: community, tribes
Materials: none

Objectives
1. To build inclusion and influence
2. To provide students an opportunity to think of significant other persons in their lives
3. To encourage communicating with a special person
4. To promote caring and acceptance for the concerns of others

Instructions
1. Have the community sit in a circle. Review the agreements.
2. Invite each student who cares to participate to send a verbal message to a person in his or her life with whom he or she feels an urgent need to communicate. Messages can involve suggestions for change in a person's life, a reaffirmation of caring and friendship, and so on.
3. Explain that the format for a message is: "Dear [*name*], I urge you to..." Have each student end his or her message by saying: "Your [*adjective*] friend, [*name*]." Model a message yourself.
4. There is no follow-up discussion after this activity. All messages are sent in an atmosphere of total acceptance.

Appreciation
Invite statements of appreciation:
- "I liked it when..."
- "I felt good when..."
- "I appreciated it when..."

One-Minute History

Grades:	2-adult
Time:	20-30 minutes
Grouping:	community, tribes, triads
Materials:	none

Objectives
1. To give each student an opportunity to share his or her background
2. To build inclusion

Instructions
1. Have the community sit in a circle or meet in tribes or triads.
2. Instruct the students that each student will have one minute in turn to tell his or her personal history. Remind the listeners to give full attention without interrupting.

Suggested Reflection Questions
Content/Thinking
- What did you learn about someone else?
- Why is it important to be able to summarize your life?

Social
- How could you tell that others were using good listening skills?
- Why was a minute enough/not enough time to share?
- Did the students who shared later in the activity share more or less? Why?

Personal
- How did you feel about sharing?

Appreciation
Invite statements of appreciation:
- "I liked it when you said..."
- "I felt good when..."
- "I was particularly interested when you..."

Tribe Graffiti

Grades: 2-adult
Time: 60 minutes
Grouping: tribes
Materials: large paper, crayons or felt pens

Objectives

1. To encourage the sharing of feelings and beliefs
2. To gather and appreciate many points of view
3. To review subject matter in cooperative learning groups
4. To build inclusion and promote influence

Instructions

1. Ask the community to meet in tribes.
2. To each tribe, distribute pens and a large piece of paper (at least 2 x 6-feet long) labeled with one of the following subjects (or an academic topic) on each:
   - pet peeves
   - what I wonder about
   - ambitions
   - favorite moments
   - things that scare me a lot
   - things that excite me
3. Invite the tribes to write "graffiti" on their paper for three to five minutes, all tribe members writing at once.
4. At the end of three to five minutes, ask the tribes to stop writing and exchange papers. Have the tribes now write on their new graffiti papers for the next three to five minutes. Repeat this procedure until all the tribes have had a chance to write graffiti on all the papers.
5. Return original papers to tribes and allow the members time to read the graffiti and discuss similarities in what people wrote.
6. Have each tribe report its findings back to the community.

Suggested Reflection Questions

Content/Thinking
- What general things did the community write?
- Why did you exchange papers?

Social
- How did your tribe members cooperate?

Personal
- What did you write that told something about yourself?
- How did you feel during this activity?
- Which graffiti topic meant the most to you?

Appreciation

Invite statements of appreciation:
- "It was helpful when you..."
- "I liked it when you wrote..."

Objectives
1. To build inclusion
2. To foster positive feelings in the community
3. To build self-esteem

Campaign Manager

Grades:	3-adult
Time:	60 minutes
Grouping:	tribes
Materials:	small circles with 6-inch diameter, 3 x 5-inch cards, pencils, small bags

Instructions
1. Have students meet in their tribes.
2. Pass out paper circles, cards, and a small bag to each tribe.
3. Instruct each tribe member to write his or her name on a slip of paper and drop it into a bag. Then have each member draw a name out of the bag (making sure he or she doesn't draw his or her own).
4. Tell the students that each is to be the "campaign manager" for the person whose name he or she drew a person who has been nominated for "Wonderful Person of the Year."
5. Explain that each student will design a campaign button on the circle of paper, and list three good campaign statements on the card to promote his or her nominee. The campaign manager may interview their candidate if they need more information on special qualities.
6. Have the campaign managers deliver the campaign speeches (using the cards) and present their nominees with their campaign buttons. Lead applause and cheering.

Suggested Reflection Questions
Content/Thinking
- What similarities did you notice between the campaign buttons and the presentations?
- Why is it important to make a good campaign speech?
Social
- What social skills did you need to make this activity successful?
Personal
- How did you feel when your manager was presenting your campaign?
- How did you feel when you were presenting your candidate's campaign?
- Would you ever like to manage a campaign for someone?

Appreciation
Invite statements of appreciation:
- "I liked it when..."
- "I felt good when..."

Personal Journal

Grades: 3-adult
Time: ongoing
Grouping: tribes, individuals
Materials: notebooks

Objectives
1. To allow time and privacy for reflecting on personal learning
2. To provide a method for noting personal goals, commitments, hopes, and growth
3. To facilitate sharing of personal observations
4. To build inclusion

Instructions
1. Plan regular time throughout the week for students to write about personal learning and school experiences. Tell the class that personal journals are a way to reflect on their own progress, hopes and goals; and that no one has access to another's journal without permission.
2. Urge the students to periodically review and compare their recent entries with former ones, and to congratulate themselves for signs of growth or learning. Suggest that they write "I Learned" statements.
3. Have tribe members share things from their personal journals when they choose to do so.

Suggested Reflection Questions
Content/Thinking
- What sort of information do you imagine most of you are writing in your journals?
- Why is keeping a personal journal good for you?
- How can keeping a journal show you your personal growth?

Personal
- How does it feel to have a personal data bank?
- What changes have you noticed in yourself?
- What are you learning about yourself through your journal?

Appreciation
Invite statements of appreciation:
- "I appreciate your need for privacy because..."
- "I liked it when you..."
- "I think it's neat that you..."
- "I value who you are because..."

Tribe Mimes/ Role-Play

Grades:	2-adult
Time:	45 minutes
Grouping:	tribes
Materials:	none

Objectives

1. To build self-esteem
2. To promote inclusion and influence
3. To act out or role-play dilemmas or problem situations

Instructions

1. Have the students meet in their tribes.
2. Ask if anyone knows what a "mime" is or how circus clowns communicate with an audience. Explain that "mime" means acting out a message or image without speaking any words.
3. Give each tribe a written message or image to act out.
    Examples:
    • harnessing a horse
    • baking a cake
    • fixing a bicycle tire
4. Have each tribe decide how they will portray the message or image without speaking.
5. Have each tribe present its mime to the class, and have the other students guess what is being portrayed.
6. Then explain "role play" which means adding speech to what is being acted out. Give the tribes prepared cards that contain problem situations that may be confronting students. Example: Terry and Aaron are approached by two friends who ask them to go with them after school to smoke cigarettes they just found. Act out how Terry and Aaron could handle the situation so that they feel proud of themselves.
7. Give the tribes time to plan how to role play the problem cards, and invite them to present their role plays.
8. Be sure to follow all presentations with reflection questions.

Option: Rather than defining the problem situations yourself, have the tribes define them. They can write their situations on cards and exchange them with other tribes to act out.

Note: This strategy can be used very effectively with lesson topics.

Suggested Reflection Questions

Content/Thinking
• What did you learn from the mime presentations?
• Why is acting out a situation using mime a good way to learn?

Social
• What social skills did you need to do mime?
• How did leadership in your tribe develop during this activity?

Personal
• How did you feel while you were acting your part?
• How did you feel as you watched others acting their parts?

Appreciation

Invite statements of appreciation:
• "I really liked it when..."
• "I enjoyed most seeing..."

The Week In Perspective

Grades: 4-adult
Time: 10-15 minutes
Grouping: triads, pairs
Materials: none

Objectives

1. To give each student an opportunity to reflect on recent experiences
2. To increase communication skills and sharing
3. To build inclusion and influence

Instructions

1. Ask the community to form triads or pairs.
2. Tell the students that they will take turns interviewing each other. Ask them to decide who will be the first person to be interviewed, the second, and the third (if using triads).
3. Urge the students to listen attentively to the person being interviewed and not discuss anything he or she is saying.
4. Provide the students with questions to ask. Examples:
   - "What new and good thing happened to you this past week?"
   - "What was hard about your week?"
   - "Is there something you meant to do this week but put off?"
   - "What one thing did you do that you enjoyed?"

Suggested Reflection Questions

Content/Thinking
   - What did you learn by doing this activity?
   - Why is answering questions about your week easy/difficult?

Social
   - Why is interviewing a difficult skill to master?
   - Why are being the interviewer and the interviewee both important skills?

Personal
   - How did you feel while you were being interviewed?
   - How do you feel as a community now?
   - What did you learn about yourself in this activity?

Appreciation

Invite statements of appreciation (to partners):
   - "I liked it when you said..."
   - "I felt good when..."

Live Wire

Grades:	4-adult
Time:	15 minutes
Grouping:	community, tribes, triads
Materials:	wire

Objectives
1. To create a visual illustration of one's life
2. To encourage attentive listening
3. To promote inclusion

Instructions
1. Have the community form tribes or triads.
2. Give each student a three-foot-long piece of wire with which to construct a visual illustration of his or her "life to date:" the significant trends, patterns, and events of his or her years thus far.
3. Invite each student to share his or her "Live Wire" with other tribe members, explaining the rationale for its design.
4. Review the agreements. After one student shares, the others may ask questions, express their mutual feelings or concerns.

Suggested Reflection Questions
Content/Thinking
- What did you learn in this activity?
- What similarities/differences were there among your experiences?
Social
- Why is the right to pass important for this activity?
- How well did your group members listen to/help each other?
- How can you improve your listening skills?
Personal
- How did you feel as you *made/shared* your lifeline?

Appreciation
Invite statements of appreciation:
- "I felt good when..."
- "I like it when..."

Client-Consultants

Grades: 3-adult
Time: 30 minutes
Grouping: tribes
Materials: none

Objectives

1. To encourage active listening
2. To experience group support for a concern
3. To assist a peer, colleague, or friend to resolve a problem
4. To promote influence

Instructions

1. Have the class sit in their tribes.
2. Tell the students that each will have a turn expressing a concern or a problem that he or she may be experiencing at school. Each person will have a turn at being a "client" while the other tribe members are listening as "consultants." Explain that the consultants:
   * are to be non-judgmental
   * are not to tell the client what to do
   * are to offer alternative suggestions to the client for solving the problem
   * and may ask for additional information if it seems helpful or necessary.
3. Review or remind the students about their caring listening skills (especially paraphrasing).
4. Allow approximately 10 minutes for each client's turn.

Suggested Reflection Questions

Content/Thinking
   * What solutions did the consultants find for your problem?
   * Why is having a consultant helpful to you sometimes?

Social
   * What social skills did you need to be a good consultant?
   * How well did the consultants listen? How could you tell?
   * How does this activity affect the feeling tone in your tribe?

Personal
   * How does it feel to share your own concern with others?

Appreciation

Invite statements of appreciation (to tribe members):
   * "I felt [*feeling*] when you..."
   * "I cared a lot when you said..."
   * "I feel I would like to help you..."

Cooperation Squares

Grades:	4-adult
Time:	30 minutes
Grouping:	tribes
Materials:	puzzle sets (see next page for directions)

Objectives

1. To encourage cooperation
2. To help students become aware of their own behaviors that may help or hinder community effort
3. To build inclusion and influence

Instructions

1. Begin the strategy with a community circle discussion of the meaning of cooperation. List on the chalkboard the requirements for cooperation as generated by the community.
   Example: Everyone has to understand the problem.
   Everyone needs to believe that he or she can help.
2. Ask the community to meet in tribes. Describe the activity as a puzzle that only can be solved through cooperation.
3. Hand out one puzzle set (see next page for instructions) to each tribe.
4. Read or state the following instructions aloud:
   "Each tribe should have an envelope containing pieces for forming five squares of equal size. Each square contains three puzzle pieces. Each tribe needs to select five students who each get three puzzle pieces; the other tribe members can be observers. The strategy is complete when each of the five tribe members has formed a perfect square. While doing this, the five tribe members may not speak or signal for puzzle pieces, but they may give puzzle parts to others in the tribe if they think they might help them complete their squares."
5. Now ask each tribe to distribute the puzzle pieces equally among its five chosen members.
6. Have the observers share their observations after the puzzles are completed.

Suggested Reflection Questions

Content/Thinking

- What did you learn about nonverbal cooperation?
- Why did you do this strategy without talking?

Social

- What social skills did you need to make this activity successful?
- Why is "giving" a social skill?

Personal

- How did you feel when someone finished his or her square and then sat back without helping others solve their puzzles?
- How did you feel when someone held a puzzle piece and did not know you needed it or did not see the solution?

Appreciation

Invite statements of appreciation:

- "I liked it when..."
- "I felt good when..."

Directions For Making A Puzzle Set

A puzzle set consists of one envelope containing fifteen cardboard pieces that are cut in the design below. When properly arranged they form five separate squares of equal size. Each square contains three pieces. Prepare one puzzle set for each group of five persons.
To prepare a puzzle set:

1. Cut out five six by six-inch cardboard squares.
2. Line them up in a row and mark them as illustrated below, penciling the letters a, b, c, etc. lightly, so that they can be easily erased later.
3. Cut each square as marked.

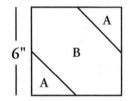 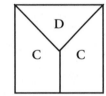 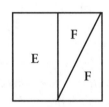

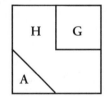

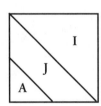

4. Mark 5 envelopes A, B, C, D and E.
5. Place the 15 cardboard pieces, a-j, on top of the five envelopes as follows:

    A: pieces i, h, e
    B: pieces a, a, a, c
    C: pieces a, j
    D: pieces d, f
    E: pieces g, b, f, c

6. Before inserting the pieces into the envelopes, erase the penciled letters and write the appropriate envelope letter on each piece. This will make it easy to return the pieces to the envelopes so that the activity may be used again.

Objectives

1. To encourage active decision-making
2. To build appreciation for another's point of view
3. To share a concern or problem anonymously, and have peers suggest solutions
4. To promote influence

Dear Abby

Grades:	4-adult
Time:	30-45 minutes
Grouping:	tribes
Materials:	5 x 8-inch cards

Instructions

1. Have the community meet in tribes, and give each tribe a pile of cards on which you have previously written a concern or problem (real issues) appropriate to your students' age level.
2. Ask tribe members to each take a turn at reading a problem out loud from a card to rest of the tribe. Then have them say, "If I were Dear Abby I would suggest this person [*advice*]."
3. Later (that day or a different one), distribute blank cards to the tribes and ask each tribe member to write one real concern or problem on the card, addressing it to the fictitious news columnist, "Dear Abby."
4. Collect the cards and redistribute the cards back to tribe members to suggest what they, as "Dear Abby," would advise the person to do.

Suggested Reflection Questions

Content/Thinking

* What type of problems seemed to be the most frequent?
* Why is being able to solve problems an important skill?

Social

* How well did your tribe members listen? How could you tell?
* What is the link between good listening and good solutions to problems?

Personal

* What did you feel when you listened to other students' concerns?
* How did you feel when you were giving a solution?

Appreciation

Invite statements of appreciation:

* "[*name*], you were a good listener..."
* "[*name*], I liked it when you said..."

Unfinished Fantasies

Grades: 2-adult
Time: 30 minutes
Grouping: tribes, triads
Materials: none

Objectives
1. To promote inclusion
2. To develop greater self-awareness
3. To encourage the development of imagination

Instructions
1. Have the community meet in tribes or triads.
2. Present an unfinished fantasy.
   Examples (or create one of your own):
   - You are eating lunch in a school cafeteria. You get your lunch and walk into the lunchroom. The lunchroom is crowded and noisy with lots of students laughing and shouting and having a good time. Off in a corner is a boy sitting all alone at a table. What do you do? What happens?
   - You are sitting in a class. Several students in the class are making belittling comments to another student. That student is obviously having her feelings hurt. She catches your eye and looks at you. What do you do? What happens?
   - You are sitting in a classroom. A student whom you don't know has constantly bugged the teacher and caused trouble ever since the class began several months ago. Although he is often funny, everyone is fed up with his behavior. He comes into the room and takes a seat next to you. What do you do? What happens?
3. Have each tribe member think about her or his ending to the fantasy situation and then share it.
4. Have the tribe decide which endings would be the kindest, most helpful, or most positive.

Suggested Reflection Questions
Content/Thinking
- What choices do you have when your feelings are hurt by others?
- Which endings were the kindest, most helpful, or most positive?
- Why is finishing a fantasy a powerful tool for learning?

Social
- How well did group members participate in this activity? How could you tell?

Personal
- How do you feel about the way you ended your fantasy?
- How do you feel about the others in your tribe or triad?

Appreciation
Invite statements of appreciation:
- "I liked it when..."
- "I'm like you when..."

Personal Contract

Grades:	4-adult
Time:	15 minutes
Grouping:	tribes
Materials:	5 x 8-inch index cards, pencils

Objectives
1. To reflect upon personal situations
2. To commit to new attitudes, behaviors or achievements
3. To experience support from peers
4. To build influence

Instructions
1. Have the community meet in tribes. Ask each tribe member to identify a personal behavior, attitude or achievement they would like to accomplish.
2. Explain how writing a "personal contract" makes change easier. Explain that a contract is a commitment that is specific, believable, and attainable in a certain period of time.
3. Give students time to consider, then have each write a personal contract as follows:

   "I, [*name*], will [*describe specific commitment or action*] by [*specific date*].

   Signed:_____

   Witnessed:_____

   Witnessed:_____
4. Have each student ask two tribe members to sign as witnesses and be supportive of the change to be made.
5. Suggest each student ask tribe members to check on progress of the contract's completion.
6. Keep contracts in tribe envelopes for periodic review.

Suggested Reflection Questions
Content/Thinking
- For what personal behavior, attitude, or achievement did you write a contract?
- Why is developing a personal contract difficult?
- How can a personal contract help you make the change you want to make?

Social
- What role did the witnesses play in this contract?
- What support did you get from your tribe members?

Personal
- How does having a contract make you feel?
- How did you feel as a witness?
- How will this help you change?

Appreciation
Invite statements of appreciation (to tribe members):
- "I felt good when..."
- "I like my contract because..."

Space Pioneers

Grades:	4-adult
Time:	35 minutes
Grouping:	tribes
Materials:	pencils, paper

Objectives

1. To give practice in assessing different qualities and opinions
2. To encourage sharing
3. To encourage understanding and acceptance of others' perspectives
4. To provide an opportunity to look at evolving styles of communication and leader-behavior within the group
5. To encourage influence

Instructions

1. Tell "Space Pioneers" story (on next page) while students are seated in tribes.
2. Write the list of "Advisors" (or a similar list of your own selection), on the blackboard for all to see.
3. Ask each participant to identify the five advisors they would want to help settle the newly discovered planet.
4. Discuss the difference of a group of people making a decision by consensus in contrast to voting.
5. Announce that the tribes have fifteen minutes to reach a consensus on which five advisors to take into space.
6. Ask the tribes to appoint a recorder to take notes.
7. After fifteen minutes have the recorders report the final consensus lists to the community.

Note: Use the strategy "Consensus Building" prior to having the class community do this strategy.

Suggested Reflection Questions

Content/Thinking
- What do you see as the main purpose of Space Pioneers?
- Why would you want to, not want to, go on this trip?

Social
- What did you have to do to reach consensus on who you would take? Was it an effective way to come to an agreement?
- How did different group members provide leadership for this activity?

Personal
- How did you feel about your tribes choice?
- What did you contribute to help your group make the selection?

Appreciation

Invite statements of appreciation:
- "I liked it when..."
- "I admired you for saying..."
- "I'm much like you when..."

Options

Have the students...

- agree on a name for the new planet
- share one personal possession each would take on the trip
- brainstorm and agree on what supplies and equipment they would need

Use the strategy for academic topics

- people to design a model city
- people to work on a national policy for children

Space Pioneers

A new planet has been discovered in our solar system. This planet resembles Earth in every way, except that there are no human beings living there. Our government wants the students of this class to be the first pioneers to settle on the newly discovered planet. They want you to select five adult advisors who you think would be valuable on the new planet. Select from the following list of ten people:

1. Zelda Learner, age 45, elementary school teacher.
2. Oroville Oates, age 41, farmer.
3. Clara Kettle, age 34, cook.
4. Dr. Margarita Flowers, age 27, botanist.
5. Woody Hammer, age 56, carpenter.
6. Flo Nightingale, age 37, registered nurse.
7. Betty Bechtel, age 32, engineer.
8. Melvin Melody, age 24, musician.
9. Reverend Adam Goodfellow, age 51, minister.
10. Barry Bonds, age 26, professional baseball player.

Tower-Building

Grades: K-adult
Time: 20-30 minutes
Grouping: tribes, subgroups
Materials: 8½ x 11-inch paper, masking tape

Objectives

1. To promote an awareness of influence issues
2. To explore nonverbal communication
3. To build tribe cohesiveness

Instructions

1. Have the community meet in tribes. Pass out fifteen to twenty pieces of paper and one roll of masking tape to each tribe.
2. Tell the tribes that they are to nonverbally construct a tower or castle using only the given supplies, and that they will have ten minutes to complete the task.
3. At the end of the ten minutes, stop the action.
4. Have all the tribes view each others' buildings.
5. Ask tribe members to return to their tribes for discussion and reflection.

Suggested Reflection Questions

Content/Thinking

- What was the purpose of this activity beyond building a tower?
- Why might nonverbal communication be as important as verbal communication?

Social

- What social skills did you need to successfully build your tower?
- How did leadership in your group develop while you were building your castle? Did all your tribe members participate?
- What were the feelings among tribe members?

Personal

- What did you learn about yourself?
- Is this your usual style of working with others?
- How would you change the way you work in a group?

Appreciation

Invite statements of appreciation:
- "I appreciated it when..."
- "I thought that [name] was very..."
- "Our tribe is..."

Options

- Give the tribe three to five minutes to plan their towers before they start building.
- Stop the action after five minutes and let the tribes talk for thirty seconds. Then have them continue nonverbally for the last five minutes.

Resentment/ Appreciation

Grades:	K-adult
Time:	10 minutes
Grouping:	community
Materials:	none

Objectives

1. To practice "I-Messages"
2. To develop oral language skills
3. To learn to express feelings and give feedback on behavior

Instructions

1. Have the community sit in a circle.
2. Explain the terms resentment (negative feelings concerning something that happened) and appreciation (positive feelings concerning person or event).
3. Review the "I-Message" framework for expressing either negative or positive feelings. Write the sentence framework on the blackboard. I am [*name the feeling*] when [*name the behavior or event*].
   Examples: "I am angry, when I cannot have my turn."
   "I appreciate Cary's thoughtfulness in making hot chocolate for all of us."
4. Review the Tribe agreements.
5. Ask for volunteers who wish to express an appreciation or resentment.

Note: It is important to follow up with a student privately if any statements of resentment are expressions of a serious concern; handle statements concerning the whole class with the community. Lead the class to solve problems that may pertain to all by using problem-solving strategies.

Suggested Reflection Questions

Content/Thinking

- What appreciations/resentments did you share?
- Why might sharing resentments/appreciations be positive for you?

Social

- Why does trust need to be developed before people will share resentments?
- How could you tell that students were listening?
- Why is sharing feelings helpful to a community?

Personal

- How do you feel now that you were able to say what you felt?

Appreciation

Invite statements of appreciation:
- "I admire you for..."
- "I learned..."

Note: Use the next activity, "Confrontation," as a possible follow-up.

Confrontation

Grades: K-adult
Time: 15-40 minutes
Grouping: full group
Materials: none

Objectives
1. To provide a way to work out problems
2. To enhance self-awareness
3. To reduce tattling
4. To teach communication skills
5. To encourage influence

Instructions
1. One day when a problem between two students comes to your attention, invite the community to sit in one community circle. Ask the two students for permission to share the problem with the community.
2. State the problem or have the two students involved describe it.
   Example: Tanya: "Dawn keeps moving ahead of me when we are supposed to take turns."
   Dawn: "No, I don't. Tanya is always pushing people."
3. Review the agreements carefully, and ask everyone to listen attentively without comment.
4. Have the two students involved sit facing each other in the center of the circle.
5. Ask each to tell the other what he or she is feeling about the problem by using "I-Messages;" help them phrase the "I-Messages" if you need to.
6. Ask each to repeat exactly what the other has stated.
7. Then ask each what he or she could do to help resolve the problem.
8. If they have difficulty, turn to the rest of the community for suggestions. Tell the students not to judge who is right or wrong.
9. If the discussion wanders, ask leading questions to redirect the students to the problem. If the problem cannot be solved, set a time to work with the pair privately.
10. When a solution is reached, have the two students write a contract with each other.

Suggested Reflection Questions
Content/Thinking
- Why is it important to tell someone you are upset with him or her?
- What do you think will happen now?

Social
- What kind of listeners were you?
- Why is listening important when you're involved in a conflict?

Personal
- How do you feel right now?
- What feelings did you have as the discussion was going on?

Appreciation
Invite statements of appreciation:
- "I admire you for..."
- "I learned..."

Objectives

1. To enhance the abilities of students to think constructively by developing the capacity to investigate, analyze, solve-problems and construct meaningful knowledge
2. To enable students to take responsibility for their own learning
3. To practice the collaborative skills of team planning, project management and assessment
4. To enable students to discover and believe in their own unique abilities

Instructions

Pre-class preparation: Select an academic theme or topic for group exploration and assemble a list of resources applicable to the investigation or project to be carried out by student groups. Define the objectives and outcome tasks for the learning groups.

1. **Engage (teacher leadership):** Define an *inclusion question* or strategy that links the topic to students' interests or personal experiences. Connect the topic to past learning. State the objectives, task and the time for the tribes to accomplish their explorations or projects. Describe your role as a "guide on the side" who is available to suggest resources, to clarify the process as necessary and to review the tribes' progress.

2. **Explore (student leadership):** Transfer responsibility to the tribes to review the four Tribes TLC agreements, and then to discuss and list several questions about the topic that they would like to explore. Each tribe selects one question and informs the class community what they will research. Each group decides how they will research their selected question (interviews, Internet, library, videos, books, articles, conduct experiment, etc.). Each tribe makes an action plan (who will do what) and initiates their investigation.

3. **Explain (student leadership):** The tribes discuss their discoveries, plan presentations (how they will teach the class); they confer with the teacher-guide and present their discovery to the class community. They share their action steps and justify conclusions from researched information.

4. **Elaborate (student leadership):** The tribes involve the class (other tribes) to expand on concepts, connect to real-world issues and think of questions for further exploration.

5. **Evaluate (student leadership):** Each tribe asks reflection questions they have prepared. They complete assigned individual or group reports.

The Five E's for Discovering Learning

Grades:	3–adult
Time:	depends upon material
Grouping:	tribes
Materials:	academic theme/ information

Suggested Reflection Questions:

Content/Thinking
- What was the most important thing that your tribe learned?
- How can your tribe's discovery be applied elsewhere?

Social
- What was difficult for your group to do?
- What was most interesting?

Personal
- What feelings did you have during your tribe's presentation?
- What makes this a good way to learn about a topic?

Appreciation

Invite statements of appreciation:
- "I liked it when...."
- "I appreciated the way our group...."

Family Camp Trek

Grades: 2-8
Time: 45 minutes
Grouping: tribes
Materials: "Family Camp Trek" worksheets

Objectives

1. To promote critical thinking
2. To learn to assess and set priorities
3. To have students share special things about themselves
4. To promote respect for individual differences
5. To experience influence

Instructions

1. Ask the community to meet in tribes, and pass out the "Family Camp Trek" worksheets to each student.
2. Tell the students that they are to imagine that each of their families has been invited on a special three-month camping trek next summer in Canada. Tell them that each person may carry one backpack. All the other supplies (food, medicines, tents, sleeping bags, etc.) are being provided. Say that each trek group will consist of three families (about twenty people) and an experienced guide. Explain that each student is to make a list of important or satisfying things to have in his or her backpack, because he or she will be away from home for such a long time.
3. Allow the students ten minutes to make their lists. Then have them share their lists with their tribes.
4. Next have each student decide which three items would be the most important and note them with a star.
5. Again have the students share their lists with their tribes, explaining why these items are more important to them than others.

Suggested Reflection Questions

Content/Thinking
- What were some of the things you took in your packs?
- What was similar/different?
- Why is it important in life to set priorities?

Social
- What social skills do you need when a group is setting priorities?

Personal
- What did you learn about yourself during this activity?
- How did you feel about having to leave some things out of your pack?

Appreciation

Invite statements of appreciation:
- "I liked it when..."
- "Thank you, [*name*], for..."

Family Camp Trek Worksheet

1.

2.

3.

4.

5.

6.

7.

8.

9.

10.

Third-Party Mediation

Grades:	K-adult
Time:	varies
Grouping:	community, tribes
Materials:	none

Objectives

1. To provide a process for conflict resolution that helps both parties arrive at a mutually agreeable solution
2. To model a third-party-mediator role as one who does not make judgments or take sides
3. To develop trust and acceptance of individual differences
4. To build inclusion yet allow influence (a sense of value)

Instructions

1. Call together two students who are in conflict and tell them that it is likely a mutually agreeable solution can be worked out. Ask if they would like that to happen. Make it clear that you will not take sides or set yourself up as a judge.
2. Ask each student, one at a time, to describe the conflict; say the other is not to interrupt. Encourage each student to focus on what is going on now rather than list past grievances. If they try to interrupt each other or are not listening, ask each to summarize the other's position.
3. Ask each student in turn to state how the situation makes him or her feel. Encourage use of "I-Messages." Reflect back their feelings. Have each person rephrase the other's feelings.
4. Have both students in turn state what they would like as an outcome to the conflict. As mediator, encourage both to modify their "ideal states" and decide what they would be willing to give up and work toward. Help them look at alternatives.
5. Have both students acknowledge what changes they each are willing to make in a specific period of time.
6. Have the students draw up a list of the steps each agrees to take and have them make an appointment to check back with the mediator.

Note: This method can be used with groups as well as individuals.

Suggested Reflection Questions

Content/Thinking
- What specific steps did the mediator use to help the two students resolve their conflict?
- Why is having a third-party mediator helpful in some conflicts?

Social
- What social skills did you use as you observed the conflict?

Personal
- What did you feel as we worked through your conflict?
- Observers: What were you feeling for the students in conflict? How can this help you in the future? At home?

Appreciation

Invite statements of appreciation:
- "It was helpful when you..."
- "I appreciated..."

Thumbs Up, Thumbs Down

Grades: K-adult
Time: 5-10 minutes
Grouping: community
Materials: none

Objectives
1. To encourage active decision-making
2. To encourage the expression of opinions
3. To accept individual differences
4. To encourage influence

Instructions
1. Have the community sit in a circle.
2. Demonstrate three different ways the students can vote or express their opinions on an issue:
   * thumbs up—agree
   * thumbs down—disagree
   * thumbs sideways—no opinion or pass
3. Then, in rapid-fire sequence, ask controversial questions appropriate to the age level and interests of the community and have students vote. Examples:
   "How do you feel about eating at McDonalds?"
   "Playing soccer? Skateboards? Jumping rope?"
   "People helping each other in tribe learning groups?"

Note: This activity can be related to lesson topics by having the students vote on decisions made by characters in books or history, or by having the students express their opinions on lessons, activities, etc.

Suggested Reflection Questions
Content/Thinking
* What other issues could you vote on?
* How did this type of voting differ from other voting you've done?
* Why is discovering different ways to vote important?

Social
* How is this type of voting helpful to our community?

Personal
* How did you feel about making your opinions known in public like this?
* Why might you have been tempted to change your vote as you looked around?

Appreciation
Invite statements of appreciation:
* "I felt good when..."
* "One thing I like about this group is..."

Put Yourself On The Line

Grades: 2-adult
Time: 15 minutes
Grouping: community, tribes
Materials: none

Objectives
1. To practice taking a stand among peers
2. To build appreciation for the different opinions
3. To use a structure to promote critical thinking on curriculum topics and issues
4. To experience influence

Instructions
1. Ask the community to stand up.
2. Describe an imaginary line down the center of the room. Say the imaginary line may be called a "continuum." Identify the two positions at either end of the line as "strongly agree" and "strongly disagree." State that the middle position is for those who have no opinion, choose to pass, are non-risk-takers, or are "moderates."
3. Tell the students to move to places on the line that express their feelings or opinions when you call out statements. Examples:
   - It's OK to talk to strangers on the street.
   - It's important to always please the teacher.
   - One should never climb dangerous mountains.
   - Always do what your friends do so you won't be left out.
   Have students suggest topics; use for lesson topics and current events.
4. When the students take their place on the line have the ones near each other discuss why they are there. Pick one representative from each area of the line to report to the community.
5. Have the community meet in tribes to share feelings on a particularly controversial topic.

Suggested Reflection Questions
Content/Thinking
- What did you learn?
- What did you see happen?
- Why is making your opinion public sometimes important?
- Why is recognizing individual opinions important?

Social
- Why is it important not to put down other people's opinions?
- Why might you not want to "take a stand" on a topic?

Personal
- How did you feel about publicly taking a stand?
- Why might you have been tempted to change your position after you looked around you?

Appreciation
Invite statements of appreciation:
- "I felt good when..."
- "One thing I like about this group is..."

Where Do I Stand?

Grades:	3-adult
Time:	15-40 minutes
Grouping:	community, tribes
Materials:	animal signs, string, tape

Objectives

1. To encourage sharing
2. To encourage respect for individual differences
3. To experience inclusion and influence

Instructions

1. On large cards, print four animal names: lion, deer, fox, dove.
2. Suspend the animal signs from the ceiling in four areas of the classroom.
3. Ask each student to stand under the sign for the animal that they are most like when in their tribe. Encourage people to talk among themselves while they are deciding where to stand.
4. When all the students have chosen animals and have taken their places under the signs, ask them to share why they placed themselves where they did.
5. Continue the activity by repeating steps 3 and 4 with other situations. Examples:
   • How you are with your friends?
   • How you are with your family?
   • How are you by yourself?
   • How are you in a social situation with people you don't know?
6. Ask the students to meet in tribes and talk about their choices—why they stood where they did.
7. Have all write in their Personal Journals what they learned.

Suggested Reflection Questions

Content/Thinking
   • What are the qualities of a lion/fox/dove/deer?
   • What did you learn about other students in the community/yourself?

Social
   • Why would you find it difficult to take a stand?
   • How is taking a stand an important skill for all of us?

Personal
   • How did you feel when you took your stand?
   • How did you feel sharing your reasons with the community?
   • What did you learn about yourself?

Appreciation

Invite statements of appreciation:
   • "I was interested when..."
   • "I felt good when you said..."

Alternate Signs

   • Mountain, river, ocean, meadow
   • Piano, trumpet, drum, flute
   • Have students suggest signs

One, Two, Three

Grades: 3-adult
Time: 10-15 minutes
Grouping: community, tribes, subgroups
Materials: pencils, paper

Objectives
1. To make choices between competing alternatives
2. To allow students to affirm and explain their choices
3. To practice decision-making
4. To promote influence

Instructions
1. Ask the students to meet in tribes, form groups of four to six, or meet as a community.
2. State that you will ask a question and then offer three alternative answers. Tell the students that you will be asking them to make some choices by ranking the three alternatives in the order of their importance or preference. Tell each student to write down the three alternatives and then put a number 1, number 2 or number 3 after each item according to his or her first, second and third choice.
Examples:
Where would you rather be on a Saturday afternoon?
   • at the beach?
   • in the woods?
   • window shopping downtown?
Which do you consider most important in a friendship?
   • honesty?
   • loyalty?
   • generosity?
3. Have the students share their choices with each other and explain why they made the selections.

Suggested Reflection Questions
Content/Thinking
   • How did your choices compare to choices made by others?
   • Why are some choices harder to make than others?
Social
   • What choices might be more difficult/easier to make?
   • Why is being able to make a choice an important skill?
Personal
   • What feelings did you have when you had difficulty choosing?
   • What have you learned about yourself?

Appreciation
Invite statements of appreciation:
   • "I liked it when..."
   • "I appreciated your dilemma when..."

Objective

1. To enable a large group to identify shared goals and concerns
2. To structure interest-related work groups
3. To experience influence

Goal-Storming

Grades:	3-adult
Time:	60 minutes
Grouping:	community, tribes
Materials:	large paper, markers, tape

Instructions

1. Decide upon a relevant question for the full community to address: Example: "Where would we like to go on a field trip?"
2. Ask the community to form small groups or meet in tribes.
3. Review the rules for "Brainstorming:"
   - D defer judgment
   - O offbeat, original
   - V vast number
   - E expand, elaborate
4. Ask each tribe to choose a recorder and then brainstorm for five minutes, listing all ideas.
5. Ask the recorders to read all the ideas to the community. Discuss consensus and how to form a consensus. (See "Consensus-Building")
6. Instruct each tribe to form a consensus on three ideas.
7. Record the three ideas from each tribe on a single sheet of paper or the chalkboard.
8. Discuss the ideas as a full community. Combine and/or eliminate ideas that are similar or repetitive.
9. At this point choose among several options:
   - Form task or interest groups around listed concerns
   - Sticker vote as individuals to determine highest priority

Suggested Reflection Questions

Content/Thinking

- Why is this a good way to find out what a group wants?
- What makes goal-storming difficult?
- Why are the DOVE brainstorming guidelines important?

Social

- What social skills did you need to make brainstorming successful?
- How could you tell if your tribe worked well together?

Personal

- How do you feel about the group's priority?

Appreciation

Invite statements of appreciation:
- "I liked it when you..."
- "I felt good when..."

"Goal-Storming" is a variation of "Brainstorming." The group should first become familiar with the Brainstorming process.

Our Treasury

Grades: 3-6
Time: 60 minutes
Grouping: tribes
Materials: none

Objectives
1. To allow for individual influence
2. To practice group decision-making

Instructions
1. Ask the community to meet in tribes.
2. Give each group a fictitious sum of money (or paper money), which is to be its tribe treasury.
3. Tell each tribe to brainstorm about the best uses of this money. (Review the brainstorming process if necessary.) Have the tribes make a list of their ideas.
4. Have each tribe decide what four things on its list it would spend its treasury on.
5. Ask each tribe to report its decision to the community.

Suggested Reflection Questions
Content/Thinking
- What were some of the things you listed?
- What did you learn about making choices?
- Why is deciding how to spend money often difficult?

Social
- How did you resolve differences of opinion among tribe members?
- What are the most important social skills you need when making decisions as a tribe?

Personal
- How do you feel about the decisions you made?
- What have you learned about yourself?

Appreciation
Invite statements of appreciation:
- "I appreciated it when..."
- "I knew what you meant when you said..."
- "I liked it when..."

Consensus-Building

Grades:	3-adult
Time:	25-40 minutes
Grouping:	tribes, pairs
Materials:	5 x 7-inch file cards

Objectives

1. To reach a consensus or agreement on shared concerns, ideas, or priorities
2. To build tribe cohesiveness
3. To experience influence

Instructions

1. Have the students meet in tribes, and distribute 5 x 7-inch cards to each person.
2. Discuss the importance of groups having a way to make decisions together a way that gives every member a way to contribute his or her ideas.
3. State a question that students will try to come to an agreement on through discussion. Example: What field trip sites would be most interesting for our class?
4. Ask each student to write down five answers to the question.
5. Have two tribe members get together, compare lists and agree on four ideas eliminating all others.
6. Have two pairs get together, compare lists, agree on 4 out of their 8 combined ideas and eliminate the others.
7. Have the tribes report their four final ideas to the class. Keep a list on the chalkboard of all ideas.
8. Have the class discuss all of the ideas and eliminate those that seem unworkable or less possible. Then use "sticker voting" to give each student an opportunity to choose his or her three preferred ideas. (See "Group Problem Solving.")
9. Add up the value of the stickers to determine the final choice of the class. The value of the stickers are: Blue=15 points, Red=10 points and Yellow=5 points.

Suggested Reflection Questions

Content/Thinking
- What four ideas did your group come up with?

Social
- Why might making decisions this way be easier/difficult sometimes?
- How did your group come to a consensus?

Personal
- How did you feel when your tribe made their final choices?
- How did you influence your tribe's decision?

Appreciation

Invite statements of appreciation:
- "I like our choices because..."
- "I felt good when..."
- "Our tribe is cool because..."

Peer-Response Huddle

Grades:	K-adult
Time:	15 minutes
Grouping:	tribes
Materials:	none, or 5 x 7-inch cards

Objectives

1. To structure a cooperative learning experience
2. To develop energy and interest in curricula
3. To build pride
4. To promote influence

Instructions

1. Have the community meet in tribes.
2. Have the tribe members count off, beginning with the number one, or pass out numbered cards so that each tribe member has a number.
3. Tell the students that you will call out a question, and that each tribe has thirty seconds to huddle and decide upon one answer. Say you will then call out a number, and that each tribe member with that number will quickly stand up. Say you will ask one of the students standing to give the answer.
4. Keep the questions, huddle time, and responses going as rapidly as possible so that the energy takes on a "popcorn" effect. Don't call on the first person who pops up unless you intend to promote competition. After an answer is given, lead the applause.

Suggested Reflection Questions

Content/Thinking

- What did you learn that you didn't know before?
- Why is this a good way to review information?

Social

- What social skills did you need to be successful?
- How can your tribe improve the way it worked together?

Personal

- How did you feel when your number was called?
- How do you feel about your tribe now?

Appreciation

Invite statements of appreciation:

- "I liked it when..."
- "I want to thank you, [*name*] for..."

Acknowledgment to Spencer Kagan's structure, "Numbered Heads Together"

Objectives

1. To help slower learners understand or learn subject matter
2. To provide peer support for learning
3. To structure a cooperative learning experience
4. To build inclusion and encourage kindness
5. To experience influence

Tribal Peer Coaching

Grades:	K-adult
Time:	varies
Grouping:	tribes, triads, pairs
Materials:	vary

Instructions

1. Have the community meet in Tribes. Ask tribe members to share which of them are very sure that they understand the concept or material from a lesson topic or unit.
2. Ask if those tribe members would be willing to be "coaches" for a short time to the other tribe members who are not quite as sure.
3. Have tribe members form pairs or triads, with one coach in each subgroup.
4. Tell the coaches that their goal is to have their students be able to repeat back or explain to them the information or concept being learned. Suggest some ways, that the coaches can be helpful.
5. Tell the students how much time will be allowed, and remind them of their attentive listening skills.
6. When time is up, ask those who were "students" to explain to their whole tribes what they learned from their coaches.

Suggested Reflection Questions

Content/Thinking
- What did you learn about coaching/being coached?
- Why is peer coaching a powerful way to help you learn?

Social
- What social skills does a peer coach need?
- What recommendations do you have for a peer coach?

Personal
- How did you feel as a coach/being coached?
- How did you help others during this activity?

Appreciation

Invite statements of appreciation:
- "I appreciated it when..."
- "[*name*], you really helped me when..."
- "Thank you, [name], I think you are..."

Jigsaw

Grades: K-adult
Time: varies depending on lesson task
Grouping: tribes
Materials: vary
Subject: any lesson topic

Objectives

1. To structure team learning/team teaching in tribes
2. To build the academic self-image of students
3. To develop tribe spirit and pride
4. To help each student feel valuable to others
5. To experience inclusion and influence

Instructions

1. Select a lesson that you consider appropriate for the following process.
2. Divide it into equal parts (or the number of members per tribe) and define study questions. Prepare sufficient materials for the study groups.
3. Explain the Jigsaw process to your class. Then ask the students to meet in their tribes.
4. If you have not already done so, engage them with an activity on the personal feeling level to awaken interest about a topic.
5. Give each tribe one set of lesson materials. Ask each tribe to decide who will become an "expert" for each part of the lesson.
6. Ask people responsible for Part l to move to a jigsaw study group; do the same for the other parts.
7. Tell the groups what their specific task is and the amount of time that will be allowed. Move from group to group, helping only as needed.
8. When all have finished, ask people to return to their own tribes.
9. Beginning with Part l, ask the "experts" to share the material that they prepared in their Jigsaw group; prepare a format for sharing if you think it will help them.
10. After each segment has been shared, take time for a full group discussion and in tribes to reflect on the experience.

Suggested Reflection Questions

Content/Thinking
- What did you learn?
- Why is this a good way to learn a lot in a short time?

Social
- What social skills did you need to make this activity successful?
- Why do you need good listening skills for this activity?

Personal
- How did you feel to have other students teaching you?
- How did you feel teaching others what you had learned? Why?

Appreciation

Invite statements of appreciation:
- "I liked it when..."
- "I want to thank, [*name*] for..."

Acknowledgment is made to Elliot Aronson's work (see "Resources")

Animal Triads

Grades:	2-5
Time:	20 minutes
Grouping:	tribes, subgroups
Materials:	"Animal Triads" sets
Subject:	science

Objectives
1. To encourage influence
2. To increase awareness of animal families

Instructions
1. Lead a community discussion about cooperation. Emphasize:
   - Each student wants all the people in the group to do well.
   - Each student believes that he or she can help the others.
   - Everyone must understand the task.
2. Ask the community to meet in tribes. Explain that the activity is to put a puzzle together, and that it can be solved only if everyone helps each other (cooperates).
3. Pass out an "Animal Triads" set to each tribe.
4. Read the following directions aloud: "Each tribe has an envelope containing twelve or fifteen triangles with the name (or picture) of an animal on each triangle. The triangles are blue, red and yellow. The task is complete when each tribe member has arranged three triangles with animals from the same family on them in a row. While doing this, follow the rules which are:
   - No one may speak
   - No one may signal for a triangle
   - You may give triangles, but you may not reach over and just take any."
5. Ask each tribe to distribute the triangles equally among tribe members giving each person, one of each color, but not in the same "family" (For example: fox, dolphin, koala).
6. The remaining member(s) are to be "Observers," who remain silent during the activity, and share their observations after the task is completed.
7. Each tribe works until the task has been completed.

Suggested Reflection Questions
Content/Thinking
- What did you learn about animal families?
- Why is it important to follow the rules in this activity?
Social
- What did you learn about communication skills and giving to others?
- What did you learn about cooperation?
Personal
- What was frustrating about this activity?

Appreciation
Invite statements of appreciation:
- "I liked it when..."
- "I felt good when..."

Option
Use other lesson topics in which sorting or categorizing is important (geography, arithmetic, parts of speech, history, etc.).

Animal Triads

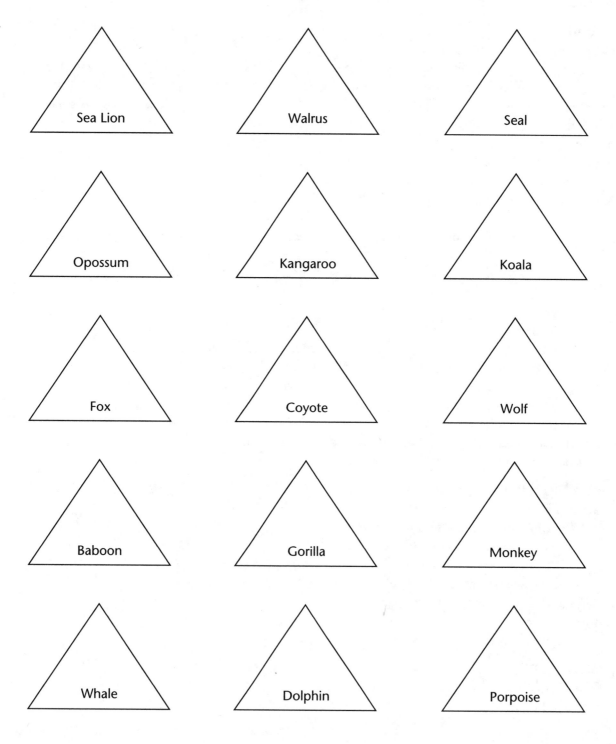

Shaping Up With Blocks

Grades:	1-5
Time:	20 minutes
Grouping:	tribes, subgroups
Materials:	colored blocks of various geometric shapes
Subject:	communication

Objectives

1. To develop observation and communication skills
2. To practice following directions
3. To understand spatial relationships
4. To learn geometric shapes
5. To experience influence

Instructions

1. Have the students meet in tribes.
2. Invite two members in each tribe to sit back to back in the center of the tribe. Give each partner the same number and colors of blocks.
3. Tell the tribes that the two members will be moving their blocks into a pattern, taking turns being the "director." The director gives instructions to the other member, the listener. They will switch roles when the pattern has been completed.
4. Tell the director to move one block and describe the placement of the block to the listener.
   Example: "Put the blue triangle in front of you pointing away from you." Tell the listener to place his or her colored block in the same position.
5. Have the director continue adding six to ten blocks and describing their positions until a pattern he or she is pleased with is completed.
6. Have the two partners compare patterns and see how similar or dissimilar they are.
7. After the partners' discussion, have the other students in each tribe reflect what they saw and heard.
8. Invite other tribe members to take turns doing this strategy.

Option

This method can be used for older students in geography, science, and art by giving the director different materials (maps, patterns, diagrams, etc.)

Suggested Reflection Questions

Content/Thinking
- What did you learn about giving directions to others?
- Why is this a difficult activity?

Social
- Why is listening and following directions important?
- How did the director and the listener work together?
- How can they improve working together?

Personal
- How did you feel about having to follow directions without seeing your partner's pattern?
- How do you feel about the importance of clear directions?

Appreciation
- "It was neat working with you because..."
- "You two were a good team because..."

Current Events Debate Circle

Grades: 4-adult
Time: 30 minutes
Grouping: community
Materials: none
Subject: history, social studies, politics, science

Objectives

1. To enable students to express their views
2. To encourage discussion of current events
3. To enhance the student's ability to see different sides of an issue
4. To provide a structure for learning or reviewing the curriculum
5. To experience influence

Instructions

1. Arrange six chairs in a circle.
2. Tell the community that you would like to have five volunteers sit in the circle to express their views on [topic]. Explain that the extra chair is for anyone who wants to come in briefly and add information to the debate (facts, dates, etc.), after which he or she must go back to his or her seat.
   Examples:
   - Should skateboards be allowed at school?
   - How important is it for people to learn to use computers?
   - How can people resist peer pressure to use cigarettes, alcohol, or other drugs?
3. Say that the remaining community members are to be silent until all the students in the circle have been heard.
4. After the circle members have debated the topic, invite the community to direct questions to the circle members.

Suggested Reflection Questions

Content/Thinking
- What did you learn about the topic?
- Why is the debate circle a good way to learn about a topic?

Social
- What social skills did you need to be good debaters?
- How did it help to have the "open" chair in the circle?
- How well did you listen to others?

Personal
- How did you feel being inside/outside the circle?

Appreciation

Invite statements of appreciation:
- "I felt good when you said..."
- "I liked it when..."
- "I am glad you said..."

Objectives

1. To structure a cooperative learning experience for a history topic
2. To enhance communication skills
3. To experience influence

Instructions

1. Give each tribe the name of a celebrity or historical character, and allow time for each tribe to learn as much as it can about the person.
2. Set up a row of chairs in front of the room facing the class.
3. Ask each tribe to select a tribe member to "be" their celebrity.
4. Have each celebrity sign in on the chalkboard and then take a seat in the row of chairs ("interview panel").
5. Ask each character to tell the other panel members about his or her prominence in history. After they have all done so, call time out and let tribe members huddle with their character to remind them of more data to present. After several huddles, invite the audience to ask questions of the "celebrity." Allow tribe members to help answer.
6. Lead rounds of applause after each character's performance.

Suggested Reflection Questions

Content/Thinking

- What did you learn about the different celebrities?
- Why is this an interesting way to learn new information?
- What values were reflected by the characters?
- In what other ways can you use this activity?

Social

- What did tribe members do to support their celebrity?

Personal

- How did you feel while you were portraying your character?

Appreciation

Invite statements of appreciation:

- "[name], I respect you for..."
- "[name], I liked the way you portrayed..."

Celebrity Sign-In

Grades:	4-adult
Time:	varies
Grouping:	community, tribes
Materials:	row of chairs in front of room
Subject:	history

Perception And Transmission Of Information

Grades:	5-adult
Time:	40 minutes
Grouping:	community
Materials:	copies of young girl/ old woman drawing
Subject:	perception

Objectives

1. To promote inclusion and influence
2. To promote an understanding of different points of view
3. To demonstrate how perceptual limitations can affect communications

Instructions

1. Have the community meet in tribes.
2. After an inclusion activity, hand out copies of the young girl/old woman drawing to each tribe. Instruct the tribe members to glance at the drawings briefly, without discussion. Then collect all copies immediately.
3. Ask people to share what they saw in the drawing. Emphasize the concept that people perceive differently; ask questions such as "would you talk to this person on the bus?" or "who in your family does this person remind you of?"
4. Give copies of the drawing to each tribe member and have the tribes continue the discussion.
5. Assist students who have difficulty identifying both aspects of the drawing.
6. Have the tribe members expand their discussions to other areas in their points of view might be limited by their perception of information.

Suggested Reflection Questions

Content/Thinking

- Why do some of you see a young girl while others see an old woman? Is there a correct way to see the picture?
- Why is this an important activity to do?

Social

- Why do conflicts arise between individuals who perceive information differently?
- How can you resolve conflicts based on different perceptions?

Personal

- What did you feel towards the students who saw the drawing the same way you did/differently than you did?
- How did you feel when you "discovered" the other aspect of the drawing?

Appreciation

Invite statements of appreciation:

- "I am a lot like you when..."
- "I felt good when you said..."

Note: Use prior to history curricula concerning warfare, debates, constitutional rights, different political views, viewpoint of parents versus teenager, etc.

Perception And Transmission Of Information

Tribe Portrait

Grades: K-adult
Time: varies (see note)
Grouping: tribes
Materials: paper, felt pens, pencils, erasers

Objectives

1. To develop self-awareness
2. To develop awareness of spatial relationships
3. To develop cooperative skills
4. To practice observation skills
5. To build inclusion and influence

Instructions

1. Explain to the community that each tribe will draw a self-portrait and that the portrait will include individual drawings of each tribe member.
2. Ask the community to meet in tribes, get their materials, and find a space to work.
3. Discuss possible put-downs that could occur and how to avoid them.
4. Each tribe member asks one other member to do a sketch of him or her.
5. "Artists" draw their subjects using pencils.
6. After completing portraits, artists check with subjects for additions or corrections.
7. After corrections and additions have been made, the artists use marking pens on portrait.
8. When the portraits of all the tribe members are finished, the tribe decides how to present their portraits to the rest of the class.

Suggested Reflection Questions

Content/Thinking

- Why did you draw a tribal portrait?
- Why was it easy/difficult to draw a tribal portrait?

Social

- How did this task require you to work together?
- How well did you work together?
- Did every member of your tribe participate in this activity?

Personal

- How did you feel when your portrait was being done?
- How did you feel when you saw your portrait?

Appreciation

Invite statements of appreciation (to "artists" and tribe members):

- "I like what you drew because..."
- "When I look at our tribal portrait I feel..."

Note: This project can best be done over a period of two to five days. Also, the teacher may move from tribe to tribe giving some instruction. Excellent opportunity to bring in outside art resource person to work with small groups.

Paraphrasing

Grades:	K-adult
Time:	30-45 minutes
Grouping:	community, tribes
Materials:	colored paper strips
Subject:	language therapy or bilingual education

Objectives
1. To build inclusion and influence
2. To teach and practice paraphrasing

Instructions
Version A:
1. Have the community stand or sit in a large circle.
2. Turn to the student on your left and ask a question.
   Examples:
   "What is your favorite color?"
   "What is your favorite holiday?"
   "What is your favorite fruit?"
3. The next student answers, and the first student who asked the question repeats back the answer. Example:
   Student #1: "What's your favorite color?"
   Student #2: "Red."
   Student #1: "Shawn's favorite color is red."
4. Have students continue the sequence around the circle.

Version B:
1. Give all the students colored paper strips prepared as follows:
   "_____'s favorite_____ is _____."
2. Have tribe members pair up and decide who is #1 and who is #2.
3. Have partner #1 ask a question and partner #2 give the answer.
4. Then have partner #1 fill in the blanks on his or her strip.
5. Have partners switch so that partner #2 now asks the question.
6. After all the students fill in the blanks on their colored strips have the tribes staple the strips together and display them.

Suggested Reflection Questions
Content/Thinking
- What similarities did you notice in people's answers?
- Why are we learning about paraphrasing?

Social
- Why is it important to take turns in this strategy?
- How could you tell people were cooperating during this activity?

Personal
- How did you like working with a partner?
- What did you contribute during this activity?

Appreciation
"I liked working with you, [name], because..."

Option
The activity can be used for various combinations of curriculum material. A variation on Version A is to have students ask each other across the circle or to integrate it with the "Spider Web" activity. In Version B, older students work in groups of three or four, asking and recording things they have learned on any lesson topic.

What Will Happen Next?

Grades: K-adult
Time: 20-30 minutes
Grouping: tribes
Materials: paper, pencils, crayons
Subject: reading comprehension

Objectives

1. To encourage critical thinking skills
2. To build inclusion and influence

Instructions

1. Have the students meet in their tribes.
2. Begin to read, or have students read, a story stopping at an interesting or suspenseful point.
3. Have each tribe discuss what they think will happen next. Each tribe can share their version by illustrating it on one large piece of paper, or they can role play it.
4. Ask the tribes to present their versions to the class.
5. Lead much applause after each tribe's presentation.

Suggested Reflection Questions

Content/Thinking
- How did your tribe go about writing your version together?
- How did your tribes' stories differ from one another?

Social
- How did you decide which ending to use?
- How could your tribe have improved getting everybody involved in deciding about the story ending?
- What's happening in your tribe now?

Personal
- How did you feel about your tribe's story?

Appreciation

Invite statements of appreciation:
- "I'd like to thank [*name*] for listening to me."
- "I felt good when..."
- "I was excited when..."

What's In A Name?

Grades:	4-adult
Time:	45-60 minutes
Grouping:	tribes
Materials:	large paper, colored pens
Subject:	social studies, history, or science

Objectives
1. To build inclusion and influence
2. To learn information

Instructions
1. Have the community meet in tribes.
2. Have each tribe choose the name of a well-known character who may be the subject of a history, social studies, or science lesson.
3. Have each tribe write the name vertically with colored pens on the left side of a large piece of paper.
4. Challenge each tribe to research and write a phrase or fact about the character's life after each letter of the name.
   Example:
   W as president from 1789 to 1797
   A lways told the truth, it is said
   S uffered at Valley Forge in 1778
   H ad 3,000 of his men die at Valley Forge
   I n no political party as the president
   N ever stopped drilling his soldiers in the winter
   G oing on for six years of war, the British were tired of it
   T wo years after Yorktown, British and Americans signed a treaty
   O n October 19, 1781, was surrendered to by Cornwallis
   N ever gave up in the Revolutionary War

Suggested Reflection Questions
Content/Thinking
- What did you learn about your character?
Social
- How did your tribe organize itself for the activity?
- How well did all your tribe members help in the research?
- How did you encourage all your tribe members to participate?
Personal
- How do you feel about your tribe now?

Appreciation
Invite statements of appreciation:
- "I appreciated [*name*]'s help and cooperation."
- "I liked it when..."

Find The Word

Grades: K-adult
Time: 20-30 minutes
Grouping: community
Materials: 3 x 5-inch index cards, safety pins, markers
Subject: social studies, history, reading or vocabulary

Objectives

1. To introduce a unit's vocabulary words and their meanings
2. To build inclusion and influence

Instructions:

1. Give each student a card with a word printed on it from the social studies, history, science, or language unit. (If the words have been only recently introduced, write a word list on the chalkboard.) Have kindergarten students do this activity with pictures rather than printed words.
2. Have each student pin his or her card on the back of another student without that student seeing it.
3. Tell the students to move around the room and ask each other questions that can be answered "yes" or "no" until each student determines what is written on the card on his or her back. Explain that they may ask each other student only one question and then must move along to the next student.

Suggested Reflection Questions

Content/Thinking

- What kind of questions did you ask?
- Why might this be a fun way to learn new vocabulary words?

Social

- What social skills did you need to make this activity work well?

Personal

- How did you feel when you found out what or who you were?
- How did you enjoy this activity?

Appreciation

Invite statements of appreciation:

- "I enjoyed it when..."
- "I liked it when..."
- "I'm similar to [*name*] because..."

Why Is This Word Important?

Grades:	4-8
Time:	60 minutes
Grouping:	tribes
Materials:	paper, pencils
Subject:	social studies, history, reading, or vocabulary

Objectives

1. To practice group decision-making skills
2. To study and learn the meanings of words
3. To build group inclusion and influence

Instructions

1. Have the community meet in tribes; give each student a card from "Find The Word" strategy. Have each student write down what he or she thinks is the significance or importance of the particular word in relation to the unit being studied.
2. Then have tribe members pass the cards to each other and add additional comments on the importance of the word or concept.
3. After all the tribe members have written their comments, have the tribe members read the cards aloud.
4. Ask the tribe members to decide on one sentence that best represents the significance of the word or concept on each card (by using voting, stickers or a point system).
5. Have the students read the cards to the community and display them so that others may review them.

Suggested Reflection Questions

Content/Thinking

- What vocabulary words did you learn?
- Why do you have different ideas about the importance of a word?

Social

- Why is building a consensus difficult sometimes?
- How well did your tribe work together?

Personal

- How did you feel when you had to write a comment about the importance of the word?
- What have you learned about yourself?

Appreciation

Invite statements of appreciation:

- "I liked it when..."
- "[name] really helped us when..."
- "Our tribe is..."

What's In Your Wallet?

Grades: 2-adult
Time: 30 minutes
Grouping: tribes
Materials: personal items

Objectives
1. To create tribal inclusion
2. To give the students an opportunity to share something of themselves

Instructions
1. Remind the students of the agreements.
2. Ask each student to select something from his or her desk, wallet, purse, or backpack that is special and symbolic of him or her.
3. Ask the students to meet in their tribes to share their special items.

Suggested Reflection Questions:
Content/Thinking
- What was the value of this strategy?
- What did you learn?

Social/Interpersonal
- How well did your tribe members listen to each other?
- What could you do to help each other listen better?

Personal
- Was it hard for you to select something special to share? Why?
- How did you feel after sharing your special object?

Appreciation
Invite statements of appreciation:
- "I liked it when..."
- "I appreciated..."

A Special Friend I Know*

Grades:	3-adult
Time:	30 minutes
Grouping:	community, tribes
Materials:	none

Objectives
1. To build community inclusion
2. To share feelings about an aspect of school
3. To experience the "Think-Pair-Share" structure*

Instructions
1. Have the community meet in tribes. Ask the students to think silently for a moment about the following questions:
   - When were you a special friend to someone?
   - What made you a special friend?
   - What did you do or say?
2. Invite each student to turn to a tribe and share his or her special qualities by speaking in the present tense.
   Example:
   "Margery, I would like you as my special friend because [*two or three of her special qualities*]."

Suggested Reflection Questions:
Content/Thinking
   - What qualities did you share that were similar?
   - Why is friendship important?
Social
   - Why is being a good listener important in being a good friend?
   - How did this strategy help you as a tribe/community?
Personal
   - What would you change about yourself if you wanted to be a better friend?

Appreciation
Invite statements of appreciation:
   - "I liked it when..."
   - "It helped me when..."
   - "I admired you when..."

---

*This is a structure from *Cooperative Learning Resources*, by Spencer Kagan

A Funeral For Put-Downs

Grades:	K-adult
Time:	35 minutes
Grouping:	community, tribes
Materials:	2-inch paper slips, pencils

Objectives

1. To promote awareness and sensitize the students to the hurt of put-downs
2. To involve the students in eliminating put-downs (good strategy for secondary students)
3. To create a positive community climate and inclusion

Instructions

1. Give each student a slip of paper.
2. Have each student write a hurtful put-down remark or behavior he or she never wants to hear or see again. (Have the teacher, aide, parent, or student helper write the slips for younger students.)
3. Have each tribe put their slips in a community box and ask three to four students to take turns reading the slips to the class.
4. Invite several students to share how they felt when put down by another person in the school.
5. Take the class outside and light a fire within a metal wastebasket or trashcan. Throw the box of slips into the fire. (Other options are to bury the slips or put them into a dumpster.)
6. Invite statements of good-bye to the put-downs.
7. Ask the students what they could do to help each other keep the painful statements dead.

Suggested Reflection Questions:

Content/Thinking
- What did you do?
- Why is it important to "burn, bury, or trash" the put-downs?
- What can the community do to keep the put-downs buried?

Social
- What can your tribe do to keep those put-downs buried?

Personal
- What can you do to keep those put-downs buried?
- How did it feel to burn or bury the put-downs?

Appreciation

Invite statements of appreciation:
- "I appreciated..."
- "It was great when..."

Objectives

1. To write a tribe poem using individual member contributions
2. To demonstrate synergism and inclusion within the tribe
3. To develop an appreciation of individual contributions to a tribe effort and to experience influence

Instructions

1. Have the community meet in tribes. Tell the students they will be writing a tribe poem.
2. Assign roles for each tribe member:

    Taskmaster: gets materials and monitors the time

    Recorder: makes a final copy of the poem

    Facilitator: ensures that each tribe member's ideas are heard and respected

    Reader: reads the final version of the poem to the community

3. Have the taskmasters obtain three cards for each tribe member and a different colored felt pen for each.
4. Write on the chalkboard the following sentence starters for use in the tribal poem:
    - I wish...I dreamed...
    - I used to be...But now I am...
    - I seem to be...But really I am...
5. Tell your students: "Here are a number of ways to start a tribe poem. Put your heads together in your tribes. Choose the sentence starter you like best or make up your own."
6. Ask each tribe member to take a piece of scratch paper and write as many versions of the completed sentence as possible during the time available (five to ten minutes).
7. Ask each tribe member to choose his or her two best lines and write one line on each of two cards.
8. Explain that each tribe will put together its poem as follows *(steps may be written on the chalkboard)*:
    - each tribe member reads his or her two cards to the tribe
    - the tribe gives positive feedback (feelings, words, etc. that they liked) after each tribe member shares

    When all the tribe members have shared, the tribe cooperates to:
    - pick at least one card from each tribe member
    - decide in what order the lines should go in the tribe poem (the tribe may decide to modify lines only with the consent of the author)
    - decide on a one- or two-word title

A Poem By Our Tribe

Grades: 2-12
Time: 50 minutes
Grouping: tribes
Materials: scratch paper, 3 x 5-inch cards, felt pens

9. When the tribe members have agreed on the order of the lines and the title, have the Recorder make a final copy and have all the tribe members sign the poem.
10. Ask the tribes to post their poems, and have each tribes' Reader take turns reading their poem to the class.

Suggested Reflection Questions:

Content/Thinking
- What did you learn about writing poetry?
- Why would you like to express your feelings using poetry?

Social
- How were your ideas encouraged and honored?
- Which agreement is the most important in an strategy like this?

Personal
- How do you feel about how you helped your tribe?
- How did you encourage other tribe members to contribute?

Appreciation
Invite statements of appreciation:
- "Thank you, [*name*], for..."
- "It was great when..."

Adapted from "Writing a Group Poem," by Nan & Ted Graves, *Cooperative Learning*, Vol. 11, No. 4, July, 1991

What's The Tint Of Your Glasses?

Grades:	6-adult
Time:	45 minutes
Grouping:	tribes
Materials:	poster paper and colored pencils/pens for each tribe

Objectives

1. To build understanding that our different backgrounds give us different perspectives
2. To show that seeing things differently is O.K.
3. To experience how different viewpoints help us to see the whole picture
4. To promote multicultural awareness, acceptance and understanding
5. To experience influence

Instructions

1. Have the community meet in tribes.
2. Have each student draw a pair of eyeglasses on a sheet of paper.
3. Ask each student to draw small designs or symbols on his or her glasses in response to the questions you will read.
   Examples:
   - What is your country of birth?
   - How many sisters and brothers do you have?
   - What language do your parents speak other than or in addition to English?
   - Have you ever lived on a farm or ranch? In a big city?
4. Have the tribe members compare glasses. Ask "Do any look the same?"
5. Discuss how different experiences give people different perspectives and opinions.
   Example: City person versus country person looks at pigs in a pen (pigs are dirty/pigs are great).
6. Ask each tribe to make a list of three other examples.
7. Have each tribe report their list to the community. Ask "What can happen when people believe everyone sees things the same way?" Discuss perceptions, assumptions, conflict, or respect for differences.

Suggested Reflection Questions:

Content/Thinking
- What did you learn about how different people see the same thing?

Social
- How well did your tribe work together during this activity?

Personal
- How did you feel when someone had a different point of view?
- How can you help others see your point of view?

Appreciation

Invite statements of appreciation:
- "Thanks, [name], for..."
- "I appreciate your..."

Building A Time Machine

Grades: 3-adult
Time: 45 minutes
Grouping: tribes
Materials: assorted junk

Objectives
1. To encourage tribe members to create something together
2. To have tribes present their creations to the community
3. To experience influence

Instructions
1. Ask the students if they have ever read any books or seen any movies about time machines.
2. Call on a few students to share what they know about time machines.
3. Let the students know that their tribes will have an opportunity to build a time machine.
4. Have the community meet in tribes. Give each group equal amounts of "junk" to build their time machine.
5. Give the tribes the next twenty minutes to construct their time machines.
6. Have the tribes take turns presenting their time machines to the class.
7. Have each student write a letter to someone in another time that could be delivered by his or her tribe's time machine.

Suggested Reflection Questions
Content/Thinking
- What decisions did your tribe have to make?
- Why is it important to use your imagination?
- What did you learn by doing this strategy?

Social
- How did your tribe make its machine?
- What did you do to help?
- How can your tribe work together better?

Personal
- How did you help your tribe build the time machine?
- How did you feel while you were working?

Appreciation
Invite statements of appreciation:
- "[*Name*], you helped when..."
- "I liked it when..."

Career Choices

Grades: 2-12
Time: 40 minutes
Grouping: community
Materials: career signs

Objectives
1. To help the students make choices and honor each other's choices
2. To give the students an opportunity to share some of their career views
3. To experience influence

Instructions
1. Make two signs with a career choice such as "chemist" and "marine biologist" (or use two other occupations) written on each of them and put them up on different sides of the room.
2. Tell your students that they are going to be asked to make a choice about occupations related to the field of science or health.
3. They will make their choice by moving to one side of the room or the other, to stand under the sign of the occupation of their choice. Example: Point out the sign "chemist" on one side of the room and "marine biologist" on the other side of the room.
4. Have students discuss in groups of 3 or 4 why they chose the occupation.

Suggested Reflection Questions:
Content/Thinking
- Why is it important to make choices?
- What other occupations did you consider?

Social
- How well did the community honor the agreements?
- Which agreement might be the most important in an strategy like this?

Personal
- Why did you make the choice you did?
- How did you feel about making your choice public?

Appreciation
Invite statements of appreciation:
- "I appreciated it when..."
- "It was great when..."

Community Circle Metaphor

Grades: 2-adult
Time: 40 minutes
Grouping: community, pairs
Materials: sentence strips for younger students

Objectives
1. To build community inclusion
2. To share feelings about an aspect of school

Instructions
1. Begin with everyone in a community circle. Explain that the students will be completing the following sentence:
   "When I am working on [*name a subject, such as math, writing, reading, art, music*] I am most like a [*name an animal*] because I [*name a behavior or quality*]."
2. After brief thinking time, have the students form pairs. Ask the partners to face each other and discuss their answers to the question. Give the partners two to five minutes to share.
3. Ask several pairs to share their answers with the community.

Suggested Reflection Questions
Content/Thinking
   • What did your answers have in common?
Social
   • Why is sharing with a partner easier than sharing with the community?
Personal
   • Did you share a fully as you could? Why or why not?
   • How did you help your partner?
   • How did you feel about sharing with your partner?

Appreciation
Invite statements of appreciation:
   • "It felt good when..."
   • "One thing I liked about what you said was..."

Dream Quilt

Grades:	3-adult
Time:	40 minutes
Grouping:	community, pairs
Materials:	squares of paper: a size which works for your room and age group

Objectives

1. To build community inclusion
2. To share a personal goal for the year

Instructions

Note: This is an excellent strategy to start the year or the semester.

1. Have the community sit in a circle.
2. Ask each student to think of a goal for the year, something he or she wants to accomplish.
3. Ask students to choose a partner and take turns sharing their goals.
4. Now pass out squares of paper to the students and ask them to write or illustrate their goals.
5. In a community circle, ask the students to share their goals with the class.
6. After all the students have shared their goals, have them decorate their square, sign their name, and post all the squares together on a bulletin board in the form of a quilt.

Suggested Reflection Questions

Content/Thinking
- What did you learn?
- What type of goals did most of you have?
- Why are goals important?

Social
- What could you do to improve this strategy?

Personal
- How did you feel about putting your goal down on paper?
- What other goal didn't you put down that you might want to share?

Appreciation

Invite statements of appreciation:
- "Thanks, [*name*] for..."
- "I appreciated your sharing..."

Family Changes— Comparing/ Contrasting

Grades: 3-adult
Time: two class periods
Grouping: community
Materials: photos of a parent—mounted on cardboard

Objectives

1. To give students an opportunity to share something about their parents
2. To have students compare and contrast the differences between their parents when they were younger and now

Instructions

1. Ask each student to find two pictures of one of their parents—one as a child and one current. Ask him or her to mount the photos together on cardboard and bring them to school. Give the students a few days to gather the photos.
2. Have the community meet. Have each student share his or her parents' photos with the community.
3. When everyone has shared, explain the meanings of compare and contrast (compare is to look for the similarities, contrast is to look for the differences). Then ask for a volunteer to compare and contrast his or her parents' photos.

Suggested Reflection Questions:

Content/Thinking

- What did you learn about comparing and contrasting?
- What did you learn about your parents or someone else's parents?
- Why is this strategy difficult?

Social

- What social skills were important during this strategy?
- How can you improve this strategy?

Personal

- How did you feel sharing your parents' pictures?
- How did you feel listening to others as they shared?

Appreciation

Invite statements of appreciation:

- "It helped me when..."
- "I liked it when..."

Finding All We Have In Common

Grades:	2-adult
Time:	35-45 minutes
Grouping:	community, pairs
Materials:	none

Objectives
1. To give students an opportunity to introduce themselves
2. To give students an opportunity to work in pairs and find commonalities
3. To build inclusion

Instructions
1. State that we are a unique group about to start an exciting journey together, and that, like any people coming together, we need to learn about each other.
2. Have each student find a partner he or she does not know at all or does not know very well. Say "In the next five minutes find out all the things that you have in common with your partner (likes, dislikes, qualities, skills, goals or whatever)."
3. Have the community sit in a circle. Have each partner introduce himself or herself and tell what he or she discovered.

Suggested Reflection Questions:
Content/Thinking
- What are things many of you have in common?
Social
- Why is finding out what you have in common a good way to get to know somebody?
- Why is attentive listening so important for this strategy?
Personal
- How did you feel about finding out all that you and your partner had in common?
- How did you feel about sharing what you and your partner have in common?

Appreciation
Invite statements of appreciation:
- "I really liked..."
- "It was great when..."

Flies On The Ceiling

Grades: 2-adult
Time: 35 minutes
Grouping: tribes
Materials: paper, pencils

Objectives

1. To identify the dynamics of group interaction
2. To process a sequence of learning activities and behaviors
3. To practice reflecting on systems and situations
4. To experience influence

Instructions

1. After students have been working together on a task, have them set aside their books and papers.
2. Ask the students to close their eyes and pretend they had been flies on the ceiling watching their tribe work together during the last few minutes or hours. Tell them to "run the movie backwards now" and think what the flies saw happening.
   - Who did what to get you started?
   - What did you do while your tribe was working together?
   - What did other tribe members do?
   - What helpful things happened?
   - Who did them?
   - Did everyone participate?
   - How did you help each other?
3. After a few minutes, have the tribe members share what they as flies saw happening. It is helpful to have each tribe choose a recorder to make a list of behaviors, positions, acts, interactions, etc.
4. Have the tribes give their report to the community.
5. Then ask each tribe to make a list of "things what we could do to have our tribe work better next time."

Suggested Reflection Questions:

Content/Thinking
- These questions were handled in #2 above.

Social
- Why is it important to look at how groups are working together?

Personal
- How could you use this strategy in other groups and relationships?
- How can you help your tribe to work together better?

Appreciation

Invite statements of appreciation:
- "Thanks for..."
- "It helped me when..."

Objectives

1. To build interdependence
2. To practice reading with a partner
3. To experience influence

Instructions

1. Have the students get some identical reading (history, social studies, or other).
2. Ask the students to line up (without talking) across the room according to their birth dates, beginning with January on one side of the room.
3. Starting on one side, have each student in turn state his or her birth month and date.
4. Create two lines by leading the last person, so that each student is facing a partner. Have the partners stand an arm's length apart.
5. Have one partner read the first paragraph of the text. The other partner paraphrases what was read.
6. Next have the other partner read the next paragraph. Partners alternate reading and paraphrasing until they finish reading the selection you assigned.

Suggested Reflection Questions

Content/Thinking
• What did you learn from the material you just read?

Social
• Why is reading together helpful?
• Why is choosing partners using a lineup fun?

Personal
• How did you help make this strategy successful?
• How do you feel reading to another person?

Appreciation

Invite statements of appreciation (to partners):
• "I liked your reading because..."
• "Thanks for helping me..."

Fold The Line Reading

Grades:	3-adult
Time:	30 minutes
Groupings:	community line-up, and pairs
Materials:	textbook or handout reading material

Paraphrase Passport*

Grades:	2-adult
Time:	20 minutes
Groupings:	community, triads, tribes
Materials:	none

Objectives
1. To follow up on the "Reflecting Feeling" strategy
2. To practice listening
3. To practice paraphrasing while discussing a topic

Instructions
1. Review the strategy "Reflecting Feelings" with the community. Have the students discuss how they felt when they played the roles of speaker, feeling reflector, and observer.
2. Tell students they will be discussing topics by using "paraphrasing passports," which is a way to learn how to be a good listener. In "Paraphrase Passport" no one has permission to speak until he or she correctly restates (paraphrases) the idea of the previous speaker. Example:
   John: "I am concerned that violence is increasing in many cities, and believe that unemployment is a major cause."
   Sarah: "John, you are concerned about the increase in violence and attribute it to unemployment."
3. Have students again form the triads they were in for "Reflecting Feelings" and choose who will be the first speaker. Explain that the first student contributes an idea and the second student must restate it correctly before contributing his or her idea.
4. Topic to discuss:
   Older students: "How does good listening help to develop caring and learning in a community?"
   Younger students: "How does good listening help our tribe?"

Suggested Reflection Questions:
Content/Thinking
* What did you learn from your discussion about listening?
* Why is listening an important social skill?
Social
* How well did you paraphrase what the person before you said?
Personal
* How might "Paraphrase Passport" help you to listen to others?
* How could good listening help you to be a better friend?

Appreciation
Invite statements of appreciation:
* "I liked it when you said.."
* "It felt good when..."

---

*This structure is from *Cooperative Learning, Resources for Teachers*, by Spencer Kagan

Objectives

1. To graph and review information gathered by tribes
2. To develop an appreciation of differences
3. To develop a sense of community
4. To experience influence

Instructions

1. Prior to initiating this strategy, select some different types of graphs (Venn diagram, bar graph, line graph and/or picture graphs) to teach the recording of statistical information. Sketch the graph models on newsprint or the blackboard. Set aside large sheets of paper, one for each tribe.
2. Have the students meet in their tribes, and explain that each tribe will graph information on the large sheets of paper about the members of their tribes (heights, eye colors, numbers of siblings, distance from school, shoe sizes, head circumferences, etc.).
3. Have tribe members choose roles: recorder, reader, measurer, taskmaster. Review the responsibilities of each role.
4. Ask each tribe to discuss and choose which graph model they will use.
5. Invite a tribe to use you as an example, measuring your height and recording the information.
6. Have the tribes present their graphs when completed to the community.

Graphing Who We Are

Grades:	4-12
Time:	30 to 60 minutes
Grouping:	tribes
Materials:	wall graph formats, large paper, tape measures, rulers, maps

Suggested Reflection Questions:

Content/Thinking
- Why is it important to be able to read graphs?
- What did you learn about graphing in this strategy?

Social
- What social skills did you need to be successful in this strategy?

Personal
- How did you help your tribe?
- What else might you have done to help your tribe?

Appreciation

Invite statements of appreciation:
- "I appreciated..."
- "It was great when..."

Adapted from "All About Us," by Nan & Ted Graves, *Cooperative Learning*, Vol. 11, No. 2, December, 1990

I Used To Be; We Used To Be

Grades: 2-adult
Time: 45 minutes
Grouping: tribes
Materials: paper, pencils

Objectives

1. To give the students an opportunity to look at personal changes
2. To give tribes an opportunity to look at how they have changed
3. To share personal and tribal changes
4. To experience influence

Instructions

1. Have the community meet in tribes.
2. Ask each student to (silently) compare the following things about himself or herself today, and his or her old self in the past: physical appearance, favorite things to do, behavior, hobbies, beliefs, fears, friends, etc.
3. Have each tribe member write a poem, using the following format:
   > I used to be...
   > But now I am...
   > I used to be...
   > But now I am...
4. Ask the tribe members to share their finished poems.
5. While students are still in their tribes ask each tribe member to create a poem about his or her tribe, using the following format:
   > We used to be...
   > But now we are...
   > We used to be...
   > But now we are...
6. Ask the tribe members to share their finished poems.
7. Ask each tribe to share one or two of its "we" poems with the community.

Suggested Reflection Questions:

Content/Thinking
- What did you find out about your tribe members?
- What changes have your tribe members made?

Social
- How well did your tribe honor the agreements during this strategy?
- How do your tribe members feel about each other now?

Personal
- How do you feel about how you have changed?
- What other changes do you want to make?

Appreciation

Invite statements of appreciation:
- "I appreciated it when..."
- "Thank you, [*name*] for..."

Objectives

1. To learn how to use a point system for evaluating choices
2. To involve students in evaluating choices
3. To create a positive decision-making process
4. To experience influence

Instructions

1. Have the students meet in tribes, and give each tribe the handout "Making A Choice."
2. Have tribe members read the problem aloud, discuss the advantages and disadvantages of the alternatives and make a choice.
3. Tell them to rate the criteria for each alternative by writing one, two or three in the appropriate boxes. Then add up the totals in each column. The tribe choice is the alternative with the highest rating.
4. After the tribes have made their choices, have them present their choice to the class. Point out how often people can have the same information and come up with different solutions.

Suggested Reflection Questions:

Content/Thinking

- What have you learned about making choices?
- How could a "weighted" point system help you or your tribe made a choice?

Social

- How did your tribe members help each other?
- What social skills did you need to make a choice this way?

Personal

- How did you feel when your tribe came up with your solution?
- How did you help your tribe?

Appreciation

Invite statements of appreciation:

- "I appreciated it when..."
- "You helped when..."

Making A Choice

Grades:	4-adult
Time:	45 minutes
Grouping:	tribes
Materials:	"Making A Choice" handouts

Making A Choice Handout

Introduction

When we have a problem, we have a choice between alternative ways to solve it. One aspect of making a choice is to identify and compare the advantages and disadvantages of the alternatives. A systematic approach can be used to make the comparison. Study and complete the model chart below so that you can learn to use it to make good choices.

Problem

You are a playground equipment committee for a brand new elementary school, grades K-6. You have been given the task of deciding which piece of playground equipment you will put in first. Your total budget for this year is $500. The money must be spent within the next two months. You want good quality and something that will have the widest possible use. It must also be attractive and you want students to be able to use it as soon as possible. There is no chance of more money this year.

Alternatives	Advantages	Disadvantages
Three tetherball poles	Cost would be within budget	Contractor can't do it for seven weeks
Two basketball poles, backboards, and hoops	Several students can play at a time	It might cost a bit more than $500
Large sandbox	Younger students have been asking for one; it would cost $400	Uncertain if older children would use it
Two swings	Everybody likes swings and contractor could install within two weeks	Only two students at a time could use them

Rate the criteria for each: 3 = good or high, 2 = medium, 1 = low or poor

Criteria	Tetherball	Basketball	Sandbox	Swings
Low cost to install				
Low maintenance				
In use soon				
Attractive				
Appeals to all ages				
TOTAL				

Newspaper Scavenger Hunt

Grades:	3-12
Time:	45 minutes
Grouping:	tribes
Materials:	one complete newspaper for each tribe, "Newspaper Scavenger Hunt" worksheets, colored pencils

Objectives

1. To learn how to find information in a newspaper
2. To work together to find the needed information
3. To experience influence

Instructions

1. Explain to the students that they will have ten to twenty minutes to find all the items in the paper described on the "Newspaper Scavenger Hunt" sheet, circle them in the newspaper with their colored pencil, and write the page numbers next to the items on the sheet. Say that everybody in the tribe is expected to participate and locate items.
2. Have the community meet in tribes. Assign roles in each tribe:
   Taskmaster: gets the materials and monitors the time
   Facilitator: ensures that each tribe member works his or her section of the paper
   Spokesperson: reads the page numbers to the community when called upon
3. Have each taskmaster pick up one copy of the newspaper, one worksheet for his or her tribe, and a different colored pencil or pen for each tribe member.
4. Have each tribe divide the newspaper up between tribe members.
5. When time is up, ask the spokesperson from each tribe to share how many items his or her tribe was able to find. Randomly ask tribes to share what they found for various items on the worksheet.

Suggested Reflection Questions:

Content/Thinking
- What did you learn about using a newspaper?
- What are the sections of a newspaper?

Social
- How did you participate during this strategy?
- Which agreement is the most important in an strategy like this?

Personal
- How did you help your tribe members?
- How did you feel when you found your items in the newspaper?

Appreciation

Invite statements of appreciation:
- "I liked it when..."
- "Thanks, [*name*] for..."

Adapted from "Lesson Plan: Scavenger Hunts," by John Myers, Cooperative Learning, Spring, 1992

Newspaper Scavenger Hunt Worksheet

Look through your newspaper and locate the information asked for below. Circle the item in the paper with a colored pencil. Write in the page number where you found the information. When you are finished, fold the newspaper back into its original condition.

1. a comic where two people are arguing _____
2. an ad for a job in local or state government _____
3. a map _____
4. a picture of a famous person _____
5. the word "business" _____
6. an editorial article criticizing local, state, or federal government _____
7. an article about an environmental problem _____
8. the word "conflict" _____
9. an article about a conflict in sports _____
10. an advertisement for a used car made in 1987 _____
11. news about some aspect of education _____
12. a cartoon making a political statement _____
13. a letter to the editor about local government _____
14. an ad for a movie related to law enforcement _____
15. an article about a foreign country _____
16. a story which has to do with children _____
17. the word "defense" _____
18. an article relating to guns _____
19. a birth or death notice _____
20. the circulation (number of papers sold daily) _____

What strategy did your tribe use?

_____

_____

Make up four more questions:

_____

_____

_____

_____

Adapted from "Lesson Plan: Scavenger Hunts," by John Myers, Cooperative Learning, Spring, 1992

One Special Thing About Me

Grades:	K-adult
Time:	35-45 minutes
Grouping:	community, pairs
Materials:	none

Objectives

1. To give students an opportunity to introduce themselves
2. To give students an opportunity to work in pairs before sharing
3. To promote inclusion

Instructions

1. Have the community sit in a circle. State that we are a unique group about to start an exciting journey together and, like any people coming together, we need to learn about each other.
2. Say: "Think about yourself and something about you that people would remember. Think about something that makes you special. It doesn't have to be something big, but it needs to say something about you. It can be silly, fun, sentimental, or kind."
3. State that there will be one minute of quiet time before sharing with a partner.
4. After the minute, ask each student to share with a partner for two to three minutes.
5. After the students have shared with their partners, ask them to re-form the community circle.
6. Then go around the circle, inviting each student to state his or her name and what makes him or her special. Start with yourself to provide good modeling.

Suggested Reflection Questions:

Content/Thinking
- Why is it difficult to think of something that makes you special?
- What type of things makes you feel special?

Social
- Why is it easier to share with a partner?
- What social skills did you need to use to be successful in this strategy?

Personal
- How did you feel sharing with one other person?
- How did you feel sharing in the community circle?

Appreciation

Invite statements of appreciation:
- "I liked it when you said..."
- "Thank you for sharing..."

Our World Is Changing

Grades: 3-adult
Time: 45 minutes
Grouping: community, tribes
Materials: paper, pencils

Objectives
1. To create a tribe list of changes in the world
2. To give individuals an appreciation of change
3. To practice brainstorming

Instructions
1. Have the community meet in tribes and have the tribe members greet each other.
2. Review the rules for brainstorming (see "Brainstorming" strategy).
3. Have each tribe select a recorder. Have the recorders raise their hands so you can be certain each recorder is ready.
4. Have the tribes brainstorm and write lists of how the world has changed since their parents (or grandparents) were born. Give the tribes five minutes to brainstorm.
5. Have the community meet. Have tribes report one or two changes that have made an impact on their lives. (Suggestion: Ask the student with the shortest hair in each tribe to report.)

Option: Have the tribes cut pictures from magazines and make collages that show how the world has changed since their parents were born.

Suggested Reflection Questions
Content/Thinking
* What do you feel are the most important changes that have happened?
* Why is it important to know how the world has changed?

Social
* Why is brainstorming a good strategy to use?
* What social skills did your group need to be successful at this strategy?

Personal
* How did you feel sharing the changes you recognized?
* What did you do to help your tribe?

Appreciation
Invite statements of appreciation:
* "I liked it when you said..."
* "Thank you for..."

Partner Introduction

Grades:	2-adult
Time:	35-45 minutes
Grouping:	community, pairs
Materials:	none

Objectives

1. To give students an opportunity to introduce themselves
2. To give students an opportunity to work in pairs before sharing
3. To experience inclusion

Instructions

1. State that we are a unique group about to start an exciting journey together, and, like any people coming together, we need to learn about each other.

2. Have each student find a partner he or she does not know at all or very well. Have the partners decide who will be the interviewer and who will be the interviewed. For one minute the interviewer will tell his partner all the things that he does not know about him. The interviewee is only to listen and not respond. For example, an interviewer might say, "I don't know your name," "I don't know how many people are in your family," etc.

3. The partner being interviewed then responds for two minutes giving information that they would be willing to have shared with the whole community.

4. Have the partners switch roles and repeat the strategy.

5. Have the community form a circle and have each student introduce his or her partner to the community, and share one thing they learned about their partner.

Suggested Reflection Questions:

Content/Thinking
- What did you learn about your partner?
- What are the most common things you shared?

Social
- Why might interviewing be a good way to get to know somebody?
- Why is attentive listening so important for this strategy?

Personal
- How did you feel to interview your partner?
- How did you feel to have your partner share what you said?

Appreciation

Invite statements of appreciation (to partners):
- "One thing I liked was..."
- "Thank you for..."

Put Down The Put-Downs

Grades: 2-adult
Time: 40 minutes
Grouping: tribes
Materials: paper, pencils

Objectives

1. To build community inclusion
2. To list put-downs and the feelings they cause
3. To share the personal experience of receiving a put-down
4. To practice brainstorming

Instructions

1. Have students meet in tribes.
2. Lead a brief discussion about put-downs (hurtful names and behaviors).
3. After reviewing the rules for brainstorming, have each tribe select a recorder.
4. Ask the tribes to brainstorm put-downs that people use in the class or school.
5. Then have each tribe make a list of the feelings they have when they receive a put-down. Give each student time to share a time when a put-down really was hurtful.
6. Ask the tribes to brainstorm: "What could we do to help each other put-down the put-downs?"
7. Have each tribe present their list to the class, and ask reflection questions.

Option: Have the community select two or three ideas for ending put-downs. Use sticker voting (Group Problem-Solving) to do so.

Suggested Reflection Questions

Content/Thinking

- What were some of the "feeling words" you shared?
- What were some of your solutions for dealing with people who use put-downs?

Social

- Why do put-downs hurt your feelings?
- What are some important social skills to use when you brainstorm?

Personal

- How did you feel when you remembered getting a put-down?
- How do you feel when you put-down another person?
- How do you feel about your solutions?

Appreciation

Invite statements of appreciation:

- "Thanks for..."
- "One thing I liked about what you said was..."

Reflecting Feelings

Grades:	4-adult
Time:	40 minutes
Grouping:	triads
Materials:	"Feeling Statements" worksheets

Objectives

1. To build community inclusion
2. To teach and practice listening skills
3. To share ideas and feelings about a given topic

Instructions

1. Discuss with the community how person's feelings can be identified by the tone of his or her voice (harsh, friendly, concerned), body language (leaning forward, withdrawn), or words.
2. Ask the students to form triads and decide which triad members will be A, B, or C. Ask for a show of hands of all A's, all B's and all C's to avoid confusion.
3. Explain that the triad members will play the following roles in each round (post a chart, if necessary):

	A	**B**	**C**
Round 1	Speaker	Feeling Reflector	Observer
Round 2	Feeling Reflector	Observer	Speaker
Round 3	Observer	Speaker	Feeling Reflector

4. Distribute a set of three feeling statements to each triad, and have each member draw one slip.
5. First, have the speaker tell the reflector who is speaking the statement, then they are to role-play their statements with much feeling. The "reflectors" will rephrase the feeling back to the speaker. Example: Speaker: "A father is speaking to his son. He says, 'I am delighted that we can go fishing together on Saturday.'"
   Reflector: "You feel excited and very happy that we will be able to fish together all day on Saturday."
   The Observer then tells the Speaker and Reflector what he or she heard and saw during the role-play.
5. Rotate the roles so that everyone has a turn in each of the three roles.

Suggested Reflection Questions

Content/Thinking
- What did you learn about reflecting feelings?

Social
- Why is listening such an important skill?
- Why is the observer's role important?

Personal
- How well did you play the different roles?
- How are you going to use this information tomorrow?

Appreciation

Invite statements of appreciation:
- "Thanks for..."
- "I liked it when..."

Feeling Statements

Friend: Just because I don't wear name brand clothes like the other kids treat me like I don't exist!

Friend:

- -

Student: I don't get this assignment. I don't see how this is going to help me.

Teacher:

- -

Mom: Your room is a mess! This is driving me crazy!

Son/Daughter:

Feeling Statements

Friend: My mother won't let me talk on the phone for more than five minutes. She's even making me pay part of the phone bills.

Friend:

- -

Student: I never say anything in class because it doesn't come out right.

Friend:

- -

Friend: My mother dragged me to a discount store and made me buy three outfits! I'm not going to wear them anyway!

Friend:

Feeling Statements

Student: I wish you wouldn't make me wait when I want your help. You are always helping somebody else.

Teacher:

- -

Friend: My parents always complain about what I don't do, but they never notice when I do something right!

Friend:

- -

Friend: I wanted to go to the movies with all of you Friday night, but my parents just told me I'm grounded.

Friend:

- -

Snowball I-Messages

Grades:	2-adult
Time:	45 minutes
Grouping:	community, tribes
Materials:	paper and pencils

Objectives

1. To create community inclusion and energize the class
2. To give individuals practice in writing I-Messages

Instructions

Note: Use the strategy "Teaching I-Messages" prior to using this one.

1. Ask each student to bring one piece of paper, a pencil and something firm to write on and sit in a community circle.
2. Review the elements of an "I-Message" and the difference between an "I-Message" and a "You-Message."
3. Give examples of an "I-Message" and a "You-Message" and ask the students to think of an example of each.
4. Ask several students to model an "I-Message" and then a "You-Message."
5. Ask each student to draw two lines that divide the paper into four squares, and to write a "You-Message" in one square.
6. After the students have done so, tell them you will give them two commands: "crumple" and "toss." Explain that when you say "crumple," they will crumple their papers into "snowballs," and when you say "toss," they will toss the "snowballs" into the center of the circle.
7. Then have the students pick up a "snowball," read the "You-Message," and change it into an "I-Message." Have the students write the "I-Message" in another square.
8. Repeat the process one more time.
9. Have each student take a snowball back to his or her tribe, and have the tribes critique the messages.

Suggested Reflection Questions

Content/Thinking

- Why is it important to know the difference between a "You-Message" and an "I-Message?"
- What kind of messages do you get/give in "You-Messages?"

Social

- Why is this strategy a good way to learn about "I-Messages?"

Personal

- How did it feel to change a "You-Message" into an "I-Message"?
- How can you use "I-Messages" in your life?

Appreciation

Invite statements of appreciation:

- "I liked..."
- "I enjoyed it when..."

Student-Developed Lesson Plans

Grades:	4-adult
Time:	90 minutes
Grouping:	tribes
Materials:	copies of "Tribes Lesson Plan"

Objectives

1. To promote tribal influence
2. To have students develop their own lesson plans

Instructions

1. Have tribes meet for two or three minutes and create their own inclusion.
2. Give each tribe a copy of the "A Tribes Learning Experience."
3. Discuss the elements that make up the plan:
   - an inclusion activity to awaken interest or connect to previous experiences
   - an academic learning goal
   - a social learning goal
   - a tribal strategy or cooperative learning structure (or a sequence of the same)
   - instructions
   - reflection questions
   - time for statements of appreciation
4. Have each tribe plan a twenty-minute lesson on a theme or academic topic for younger students or the community.
5. When finished, the lessons can be presented or taught to the class by the tribes.

Suggested Reflection Questions

Content/Thinking
   - What was the most difficult thing about this strategy?
   - What did you learn by doing this strategy?

Social
   - How well did your tribe work together?
   - What can your tribe do to work together even better next time?

Personal
   - How do you feel about developing lesson plans now?
   - What could you do to help your tribe be even more successful next time?

Appreciation

Invite statements of appreciation (to tribe members):
   - "I liked it when..."
   - "I appreciated..."

Give Me A Clue

Grades:	4-12
Time:	20-30 minutes
Grouping:	tribes, subgroups
Materials:	clue cards, colored cubes, colored pencils or crayons

Objectives:

1. To demonstrate understanding geometric vocabulary terms
2. To use spatial reasoning to think in three dimensions
3. To learn that accomplishing a group task depends upon each member contributing their skills and knowledge

Instructions

1. Have students meet in tribes or small groups of four to six members.
2. State the objectives and the task: to build a three dimensional figure with colored cubes, using the information on the "Build It" clue cards.
3. Distribute eight colored cubes (two blue, two green, two red, and two yellow) to each tribe. Have each tribe member draw one clue card.
4. State the rules:
   - the clue card is theirs alone and no one else may touch it
   - the blocks may be touched only when it is a member's turn
   - students share their clue by reading its information aloud
   - help may be asked in reading the information
   - if a question arises, ask tribe members before asking the teacher
5. Tell students to:
   - read the clues on their cards to their tribe
   - share their thinking to help the tribe come to an understanding of each vocabulary term
   - analyze the clues until a solution seems to have been found
6. Tell the students that they will recognize the correct solution when everyone agrees that the three dimensional figure matches with the clues.
7. Have the tribes record their solution by drawing it.

Suggested Reflection Questions

Content/Thinking
- Which vocabulary words needed to be clarified by your tribe? What do they mean?

Social
- What did tribe members do to help your tribe be successful?
- What did tribe members say or do that opened up your thinking?
- Describe the benefits of working as a tribe rather than alone.

Personal
- What did you do that was helpful?

Appreciation

Invite statements of appreciation:
- "It was helpful when..."
- "I liked it when..."

This strategy is adapted from "Get It Together—Math Problems for Groups 4-12." Lawrence Hall of Science, Berkeley, 1989. (See "Resources" for additional information)

Build It #1

There are six blocks in all.
One of the blocks is yellow.

Build It #1

The green block shares
one face with each of the
other five blocks.

Build It #1

The two red blocks do not
touch each other.

Build It #1

The two blue blocks do not
touch each other.

Build It #1

Each red block shares
an edge with the
yellow block.

Build It #1

Each blue block shares
one edge with each of
the red blocks.

Objectives

1. To encourage attentive listening
2. To experience group support for a concern
3. To assist a peer, colleague, or friend to resolve a problem
4. To experience individual problem-solving in the influence stage

Instructions

1. Have the community form a circle.
2. Review the agreements. Choose a recorder who will write down the suggestions made by the community.
3. Ask for a volunteer to share a concern or problem that he or she is experiencing and for which he or she would like some suggestions for resolving.
4. Tell the community that they are to listen without judgment or comment while the problem is being shared, but they may ask for additional information, if necessary, when the student has finished sharing.
5. Invite the students to make a suggestion, one at a time, to the person who shared. Encourage them not to repeat what someone else has already suggested.
6. Have the recorder give the list of possible solutions to the person who shared the problem.

Suggested Reflection Questions

Content/Thinking
- Why did we do this strategy?
- What type of suggestions were offered?

Social
- Why is it important to get ideas for solving problems from others?
- Which social skills did you use during this strategy?

Personal
- How did you feel to give suggestions?
- How could this type of a process help you?
- Where else could this strategy be used?

Appreciation

Invite statements of appreciation:
- "Thanks for..."
- "What made a difference for me was..."

Suggestion Circle

Grades:	2-adult
Time:	30 minutes
Grouping:	community
Materials:	none

Teaching I-Messages

Grades: 3-adult
Time: 50 minutes
Grouping: tribes
Materials: large paper and felt pens

Objectives

1. To give tribes practice in brainstorming and to introduce words to express feelings
2. To show the link between "feeling words" and "I-Messages"
3. To practice giving "I-Messages"

Instructions

Note: Teach this strategy before using "Snowball I-Messages."

1. Have the community sit in tribes and explain that they will be brainstorming (see "Brainstorming" strategy).
2. Have each tribe select a recorder.
3. Discuss various "feeling words" (happiness, anger, upset, love). Ask the tribes to brainstorm as many "feeling words" as they can in five minutes. Have the recorder write them down.
4. After five minutes, ask the tribes to take turns calling out the "feeling words" they wrote down. As teacher, record the words on the blackboard. Discuss how sharing feelings is important for clear communication.
5. Then ask, "Why is it also important to have a way to let people know how their behavior affects us?" Explain that "I-Messages" are a way to share feelings but not blame.
6. Use the formats in chapter five to write three to four examples of "I-Messages" and "YOU-Messages" on the board. Explain the difference between an "I-Message" and a "YOU-Message." Ask the class to contrast the impact the two different types of messages have.
7. Have each tribe member write four "I-Messages" using the feeling words they listed earlier. Each person should write to a friend, a relative, a classmate and a teacher. Allow ten minutes work time.
8. Then have the tribes review the "I-Messages" written by their tribe members. Have them help each other change any statements that are "YOU-Messages" to "I-Messages."
9. Ask the students to practice using "I-Messages" during the next few days, and to report back to their tribe on what happened.

Suggested Reflection Questions

Content/Thinking
- Why is it important to use "I-Messages?"

Social
- How can "I-Messages" help you to lessen conflict with friends?

Personal
- How does it feel to receive a "YOU-Message?"/"I-Message?"

Appreciation

Suggest people make statements of appreciation:
- "It helped me when..."
- "It felt good when..."

Objectives

1. To build community inclusion
2. To teach and practice the listening skills paraphrasing and reflecting feelings
3. To share ideas and feelings about a given topic

Instructions

1. Have the students form pairs and have the partners decide who is #1 and who is #2.
2. Have the partners sit "knees to knees" and "eyes to eyes."
3. Demonstrate how to paraphrase a statement.
   Example: Heidi says, "Sometimes I think I'd like to be an airline pilot."
   Paraphrase response: "Now and then you wonder about becoming a pilot."
4. Ask the #1 partners to speak briefly on the topic: "A time when I listened carefully." Partners #2 are to listen and then paraphrase the statement they heard. After three minutes have the partners switch roles.
5. Ask the community, "What is the importance of paraphrasing?"
6. Demonstrate how to reflect feelings along with paraphrasing.
   Example: Heidi says, "Becoming a airline pilot would be exciting because there still are not many women pilots."
   Paraphrase: "You feel excited whenever you imagine being one of the few women pilots."
7. Ask the #2 partners to speak briefly on the topic: "A time that I found my work a challenge." Partners #1 are to listen and then paraphrase the key statement and feelings. After three minutes have the partners switch roles.
8. Have the partners share what each felt during the activity.

Suggested Reflection Questions

Content/Thinking
- What listening skills did you use during this strategy?
- How does good listening help to build community?

Social
- How does reflecting feelings help you communicate better?

Personal
- How would you feel if someone listened to you like this?
- How can you use these skills?

Appreciation

Suggest people make statements of appreciation:
- "I could tell you were listening when..."
- "I appreciated your..."

Teaching Paraphrasing/ Reflecting Feelings

Grades:	4-adult
Time:	30 minutes
Grouping:	pairs
Materials:	none

Teaching Agreements

Grades: 2-adult
Time: two class periods
Grouping: tribes
Materials: large paper, felt pens, poster paint

Objectives

1. To have each tribe create a lesson to help teach an agreement to the community
2. To transfer responsibility to tribes for lesson development
3. To experience influence

Instructions

1. Review the agreements of attentive listening, right to pass, no put-downs, and mutual respect (and any others you've created for your class).
2. Explain to the students that you are looking for new and creative ways to teach these agreements and would like their help.
3. Have each tribe choose (or assign) one of the agreements. Explain that each tribe will create a lesson to teach that agreement to the community. Explain that they can use butcher paper, felt pens, and paint (or other art media you have available) to make any posters or signs needed to teach the lesson. Emphasize that you want them to be creative. Let them know they will have the rest of the period and one other period to create their lessons and share them with the community.
4. When the tribes are finished, have them present their lessons to the community.

Suggested Reflection Questions

Content/Thinking
- What did you learn about creating a lesson?
- Which agreement do you think is the most important? Why?

Social
- What social skills did your tribe need to be successful at this strategy?

Personal
- What did you contribute to your tribe to help it be successful?
- How did you feel when your tribe presented its lesson?
- What would you have done differently?

Appreciation

Invite statements of appreciation:
- "You helped a lot when..."
- "I liked..."

That's Me— That's Us!

Grades:	2-adult
Time:	40 minutes
Grouping:	community, tribes
Materials:	none

Objectives
1. To build community inclusion
2. To help the students identify personal or community skills, interests, or achievements

Instructions
1. Tell the students that you will call out a series of questions, and those who identify or agree are to jump up and say, "That's me!"
2. Start with a few simple topics that are appropriate to the students' age level and interest.

   Examples:
   - How many people have moved in the last two years?
   - How many people have green eyes?
   - How many people like broccoli?
3. Use this strategy to learn how the tribes are working together. Ask the tribes to stand and say, "That's us!"

   Examples:
   - Which tribes had no put-downs today?
   - In which tribe did everyone participate on the task?
   - Which tribe figured out why the rain forest in the Amazon is threatened?

Suggested Reflection Questions
Content/Thinking
- What did you find out about your tribe members/community members?
- What's one more question you might add?

Social
- Why was listening important?

Personal
- How did you feel about jumping up?
- How could you tell that your entire tribe would stand up?

Appreciation
Invite statements of appreciation:
- "It helped me when..."
- "Thanks for..."

Group Inquiry

Grades: 4-college
Time: varies
Grouping: tribes
Materials: dependent upon content resources and extent of research

Objectives:
1. To practice constructive thinking skills (accessing information, interpreting, synthesizing and applying)
2. To practice collaborative team skills
3. To transfer responsibility to students

Instructions
1. Inclusion: Build inclusion within the tribes by using the structure, write/pair/share. Ask people to take 5-10 minutes to write down the skills, talents and abilities that they bring to the group. You may want to list and discuss the various collaborative skills (See chapter 5 for Tribes collaborative skill list). Have people share their lists first in pairs. Then share with the tribe.
2. Content and Objectives: Discuss the general subject content and sub-content areas to be researched by the tribes. It is optional whether the class or teacher defines the sub-content areas. List the objectives to be learned from the experience. Have the tribes choose or randomly draw slips of content areas. (See option.)
3. Resources: Detail resources they can use for their inquiry or research (books, articles, computer info, library, interviews, films, etc.).
4. Task: Describe the task to be accomplished (group report, presentation, role play, article, etc.) within a specific time; inquiry projects can run from one hour to several weeks or months.
5. Roles: You may want to use roles within elementary tribes (facilitator, encourager, materials manager, recorder, etc.). If so, have people choose their roles according to the skills and resources they believe they bring to the group.
6. Accountability:
   • For presentations to the whole class, a peer evaluation sheet may be used.
   • Your own observations of individual performance can be made by taking notes.
   • Group and individual reports can be made and graded.

Suggested Reflection Questions
Content/Thinking
   • What was the most important content (theory, information etc.) that can be applied to _____ today? Or help people to understand _____? (Discuss, share or write about this question.)

Social
- What was the value for our community in using this teaching method?
- What collaborative skills were demonstrated?

Personal
- What would you like to know more about?
- What skills did you notice in others that you would also like to learn?

Appreciation

Invite oral or written statements of appreciation to individuals or the tribes.

Option: Instead of using sub-topics within tribes, use the "Jigsaw" method and have individual tribe members research the subject in expert groups and then return to teach content to their tribe.

Peer Evaluation of Group Presentation

Group name:

Evaluation Criteria	Outstanding	Good	Improvement Needed	Poor
1. Content				
2. Organization				
3. Cooperation of tribe members				
4. Use of aids: handouts, video, etc.				
5. Involvement/Interest for class				

Specific Suggestions for Improvement:

I Appreciated Learning:

This chart is an adaption of one in the article "Using Jigsaw Groups for Research and Writing in High School," by Glory-Ann Drazinakis, *Cooperative Learning*, Vol. 13, No. 2. Winter 1993.
This page may be duplicated for classroom use.

Group Problem-Solving

Grades:	2-adult
Time:	40 minutes
Grouping:	tribes
Materials:	large paper, markers, colored stickers

Objectives

1. To teach a group problem-solving process
2. To analyze alternatives
3. To experience influence

Instructions

1. Have the class community meet in tribes.
2. Give each tribe five minutes to come up with three typical problems that a student might have with another student—or that a student might have with someone else at the school.
3. Have each tribe read their problem to the class. Make sure that the problems are well-defined.
4. Explain that each tribe will have ten minutes to brainstorm and list possible solutions. Review the "Brainstorming" strategy and post the brainstorming rules. Give each tribe a large sheet of paper, a felt pen and three colored stickers (red, blue and yellow).
5. Write the "Group-Problem Solving" process on the board.
   - Brainstorm for ten minutes. Have one person record all ideas.
   - Each person selects three top choices with colored stickers (1st choice blue=25 points; 2nd choice red=15 points; 3rd choice yellow=5 points).
   - Add up the total points for each idea.
   - Present your top solutions to the community.
6. If this strategy is used for real-time problems, you may want to teach the tribes how to make a "Tribe Action Plan" that will identify tasks, responsibilities and completion dates. See chapter 7 for the plan format.

Suggested Reflection Questions

Content/Thinking
- What is the value of this process?
- What other ways can decisions be made in the tribe?

Social
- How well did your tribe honor our tribe agreements?
- What social skills did your tribe use when doing this strategy?

Personal
- How do you feel about your tribe's work together?
- How do you feel about your participation?
- How do you feel about your action plan?

Appreciation

Suggest people make statements of appreciation:
- "Thanks for your help..."
- "You made a positive difference when..."

Roles People Play

Grades: 3-adult
Time: 20 minutes
Grouping: community, tribes
Materials: handout on roles

Objectives
1. To promote an awareness of helpful group roles
2. To learn how the accomplishment of group tasks depends upon helpful behaviors
3. To learn to collaborative skills

Instructions
1. Discuss the objectives of the strategy and ask students to review the Tribe agreements.
2. Distribute the handout on "Roles That People Play In Groups."
3. Ask the students to study the cartoon and decide which role (or roles) they usually play when working with others in their tribe.
4. Ask the students to write answers to the questions on the bottom of the handout. Allow five to ten minutes time.
5. Have them share their responses with a partner.
6. Ask the students to share with their tribe a new role that he or she will try for the day (or week).

   Option #1: A Role Play
   - Have each tribe plan and present a brief role play in which one person is playing an unhelpful role.
   - Ask the class to guess which role is being demonstrated.

   Option #2: For Adult and/or Multicultural Groups
   - Delete the "What People Say" right hand column on the role description handout before distributing it to the tribes.
   - Have the groups to brainstorm and list all the things that people of their own peer group culture may say.
   - Then proceed with steps three to six in the instructions above, or use role play option #1.

Suggested Reflection Questions
Content
- What happens in a group when even one person is acting in an unhelpful role?

Social
- What helpful roles do people play in your tribe?
- How do those roles make working together easier?
- Do people in your tribe always play the same roles? How helpful is that?

Personal
- What feelings did you have during this strategy?
- What did you learn about yourself?

Descriptions of Helpful Roles	What People Say
Encourager: Tells group positive things and keeps energy going well.	Right on! Good job! Yes! Let's do it. Keep going. Brilliant!
Organizer: Helps group stay on task and time; encourages management of materials and resources.	File the papers. We have one bottle of glue. First we should...
Peace Keeper: Helps members to solve problems, make decisions, express feelings and understand each other.	Time out. Let's talk about this! You both have a good point.
Idea Person: Gives and seeks helpful ideas. Initiates action and clarifies.	What if we looked at it this way? Another idea would be to... What ideas do you have? Let's brainstorm more ideas.
Helper: Is supportive and friendly, willing to listen and help others.	We need to hear from everyone. I'll help you. Let's work on it together.

Unhelpful Role Descriptions	What People Say
Joker: Claims attention by interrupting, goofing off, distracting and trying to be funny.	There's a spider on your head. At recess I'm going to... Look at this! Want some gum?
Boss: Takes charge. Knows it all. Tells people what and how to do things. Usually doesn't listen well.	Do it my way! That's not right. The best way is to...
Sitter: Doesn't participate. Sits on the side. Always claims the right to pass. Will not help others. Can seem judgmental.	I pass. Don't count me in.
Put-Downer: Ridicules others and their ideas.	That's stupid. You're so dumb. We tried that once. How can you be so oblivious?
Talker: Goes on and on talking. Ignores others also wanting time. Controls by not pausing between sentences.	Blah, blah, blah. And then he said to me... I also know that... Stop interrupting me.

Roles People Play In Groups

Encourager • Joker • Organizer • Boss • Peace Keeper • Talker • Idea Person • Sitter • Helper • Put-Downer

Questions

1. Which role do you usually play in a group?

2. Why do you think that it's the easiest role for you to play?

3. What other role or roles would you like to play to help your group?

4. How willing are you to try out a new helpful role today?

Energizers For Pairs

Mirrors

Partners face one another. One student begins the activity by moving his or her arm slowly enough so that the partner can "mirror" the action. The objective for the leader is not to trick the follower, but to enable his or her partner to follow successfully. The partners then change roles and repeat the activity. Once the students get the idea, let them move their knees, feet, legs, heads, etc., as well. Follow with reflection questions on being a leader and a follower.

Stand Off

Stand facing each other, one arm's length from your partner. Place open hands up and out a little from your shoulders. The object is to make your partner lose footing by pushing or hitting his or her hands only.

Stand Up

Sit on the ground back to back with your partner with knees bent and elbows linked. Now stand up together. Try it in threes and fours.

Trust Walk

Have everyone find a partner. One person of the pair volunteers to be led with his or her eyes closed or blindfolded. The other member of the pair leads the person for five minutes, taking very good care of the blind partner. After five minutes switch roles.

Changes

For directions, see "Energizers For Large Groups" section.

Energizers For Small Groups

Knots

Stand in a circle shoulder to shoulder. Ask everyone to reach out and grab two other hands. (You cannot have both hands of one person, and you cannot have the hand of persons on each side of you.) If possible, try not to criss-cross. Now untangle so that all are standing in a round circle again.

Trust Circle

Make a circle with your tribe or small group. Have one person stand in the middle with his or her eyes closed and feet planted firmly. Have the rest of the tribe members gently push on the shoulders of the person in the middle, making sure he or she does not fall but does keep moving. The group supports the person as he or she rotates.

Wink

Have the students stand in a circle with their eyes closed. One person walks around the circle and quietly taps the back of one person who will be the "winker." Everyone opens their eyes and begins to mill around the room. If a person has been winked at, she or he must count to ten silently and then make a scene to let others know she or he is out of the game. The object is to catch the winker before everyone loses. If a person suspects the winker's identity, she says "I have an accusation!" However, there must be two accusers to stop the game. When someone else becomes suspicious, she or he shouts "I have an accusation!" Then both accusers count to three and point to the player they think is the perpetrator (no discussion is allowed). If they both point to someone who is innocent or to different people, they are automatically out of the game. If, however, they both point to the true winker, the game is over.

Bubble Gum

Each group has a pair of mittens and a pack of bubble gum. From the pack, each member must open a piece of gum with the mittens on and then pass the gum and mittens to the next member to do the same. To incorporate curriculum, discuss how bubble gum often has pictures of famous people in it, (sports figures, musicians, etc.). Each group should choose a famous person from the unit being studied and prepare a report or project to present to the class.

Alligators

As many students as possible stand on a bench or in a marked area. They are told they are in a lifeboat and there are alligators in the water. If any of them fall in, the alligators will know they are there and they will all die. Their job: line themselves up in order of height, by birthdates, etc.

Alligator Attack

Each tribe or team is given a piece of cardboard just big enough for all group members to stand on. All teams are at one end of the field or gym. All members must have a hand in carrying the cardboard (their "boat"). The leader will have a choice of two commands: "Go" means the teams may advance forward, holding their boat, at any speed; "Attack!" means that the team must place their boat on the ground and all members must get aboard and stay there. If one member should fall off the boat, the whole team is a goner. The last team on their boat is eliminated or must take a chunk out of their boat before the next "Go" command. See how many teams make it to the end of the field or gym!

People Patterns

Discuss types of patterns (A B A B, A B C A B C, A B B A B B). Have the members of a tribe or small group establish themselves in a pattern and stand in front of the class in that order. For example, an A B A B pattern might be "stripes on shirt, no stripes on shirt" or "earrings, no earrings." The people pattern should tell the audience what type of pattern they are demonstrating (A B A B, etc.) Members of the class must try to guess who can go next in the pattern; they may not guess the pattern until they have named a person to stand next in the people pattern. The person to correctly identify the pattern will join his or her tribe or small group to establish the next pattern. Pattern criteria should be clearly visible to all.

Energizers For Large Groups

Zoom, Zoom, Brake!

Have everyone stand in a community circle, facing in, shoulder to shoulder. Introduce the sound "zoom" and say that the sound goes zooming around the circle whenever you say it. When you say it, look to your right. That person immediately says "zoom" while looking to their right and this continues quickly around the circle. After going around the circle once, say that the car was only in first gear. Shift up into second and then third gear, the "zoom" going faster each time with more power. Now introduce the "brake" by demonstrating a screeching noise along with a hand signal of pulling back the brake. Have everyone try it with their own screeching brake sound. Now the group is ready to play. The rules are that you only get to brake once. When someone "brakes" the zoom reverses direction and goes the opposite way around the circle. Eventually everyone will get a chance to "brake" or the facilitator can call an end to the noise. It's a lot of fun, especially for younger kids.

Three Ball Pass

This is a mini "group juggle." Using something that is easy to catch, establish a pattern around the room as follows: Leader says someone's name and tosses them the ball; they choose another person, say that person's name, and toss them the ball; continue in this manner until each person has caught and tossed the ball once. The ball will end the pattern in the hands of the leader. Repeat the pattern until it can be done quickly. Begin again, and after several people have caught and tossed the ball, throw in the second ball, using the same pattern sequence; then throw in the third ball. This is a great energizer for learning names. After the group has mastered "Three Ball Pass," have them reverse the pattern! For a real challenge, have your group try it silently (after the pattern is established).

Two Truths and a Lie

This energizer is great for building inclusion and re-entry after a school vacation. Have each person write down three things about themselves, what they did over vacation, etc. Of these three statements, two must be true and one must be a lie. Suggest that the lie should not be very obvious; it can even be a small detail. The rest of the class (or small group) must guess which one is the lie.

Lineup

Have students line up in order of birthdate, height, number of family members, number of the bus they ride to school, alphabetical order of middle name, etc. Have them do this without talking. This is a good energizer for getting your group focused, settled, and silent. The line-up is also a handy way to get your class into random cooperative groups.

Fork and Spoon

This is a hilariously confusing exercise in communication. Have everyone seated in a circle. The leader has a fork in the right hand and a spoon in the left hand. The leader turns to the person on the right and, holding up the fork, says, "This is a fork." The person being spoken to says, "A what?" The leader repeats, "A fork" and hands the fork over. The person with the fork says, "Oh, a fork!" Now, the person with the fork turns to the person on their right and says, "This is a fork." The person being spoken to says, "A what?" The person with the fork turns to the leader and asks, "A what?" The leader says, "A fork." Then the person turns to their right and says, "A fork" and hands over the fork to the next person. That person says, "Oh, a fork," turns to the person on the right and begins again with "This is a fork." When the person replies, "A what?" each person must go back up the line, one at a time, asking "A what?" until the leader tells them "A fork." Then "Oh, a fork" is said down the line until it reaches the person holding and then handing over the fork, beginning again with "This is a fork." Now that the fork is flowing smoothly to the right, start the process to the left with the spoon! The leader must now be alert for responding in both directions to the "A what?" questions, saying "A fork" to the right and "A spoon" to the left. Watch the fun when both the fork and the spoon reach the same person at once, usually midway around the circle.

Zap

Have all participants stand in a circle. The leader has everyone "create some energy" by rubbing their hands together, quickly, back and forth. Next the leader has everyone take a deep breath in, hold for two to three seconds, and breathe out. Do two more deep breaths, while continuously rubbing hands. Now the leader instructs, (while all are still rubbing hands), that on the count of three, everyone will make a sweeping point with their right arm to the center of the circle and yell "zzzzzzaaaappp!" This energizer really creates some energy, while at the same time allowing for the expenditure of energy. Try zapping a person (only if they ask to be zapped), or even social issues such as classroom put-downs.

Shuffle Your Buns

Have all participants seated in a circle with chairs pushed in tight. (All chairs should be of equal height.) The leader stands and moves to the center of the circle, leaving one empty chair. Model the directions by saying, "Shuffle to the right." Only the person with the empty chair to his or her right may "shuffle their buns" into the chair to the right. As each person moves, they vacate their chair for the next person to "shuffle their buns." This begins to move around the circle quite rapidly. Now the leader may say, "Shuffle to the left." At this command, the person that just completed a shuffle to the right must reverse and "shuffle their buns" into the empty chair to their left. The procession then follows; each time a chair is vacated, someone is shuffling into it. It must be understood that one cannot "shuffle their buns" unless they are moving into an empty/vacated seat. Once the group has mastered shuffling their buns, the leader speeds up the process by reversing commands frequently enough so as to confuse the action. The object now is for the leader to shuffle his or her buns into an empty seat. Having interrupted the flow, the person now in the middle giving the "shuffle" commands is the person who failed to shuffle fast enough and lost his or her seat to the leader. To really get things rolling, give each person in the group a one-time-only opportunity to automatically reverse the shuffle by slapping the empty chair next to them instead of shuffling into it. This "confusion" allows the person in the middle a better opportunity to find a seat, and keeps anyone from having to be the middle person for too long.

Changes

Have students get in pairs, or do in a full group by having five people come and stand in the front of the room. Instructions are to look at your partner or class volunteers and notice and remember as much as you can about their appearance. Partners turn back to back (volunteers leave the room) and change three noticeable things about their appearance. Students must guess what changes have been made. This energizer is easy to repeat, because as time goes on, the changes can be more subtle, specific, even scientific! (Change three things involving color, quantity, your torso, etc.)

Clap-Slap

Get a rhythm going: two claps, two slaps on lap. Go around the circle filling the blanks to the following chant: My name is (Karen), I come from (Kuwait), and I sell (Kleenex). The first sound must match the beginning sound in your name.

Hagoo

Divide into two teams and form two lines. Have people stand shoulder to shoulder facing a person on the other team. Stand a yard apart. One person from each team will volunteer to walk past each person in the row of the opposite team. The people on the team try to make the volunteer from the other team smile as he/she walks by. No touching is allowed. If the volunteer cracks up he/she must join the opposite team. If he/she makes it to the end straight faced, he/she goes back in the row with his/her original team.

Hug Tag

Play this in the same way people play any game of tag, except that when two people are hugging they are safe from getting tagged by the person who is "it."

I Like My Neighbors

Have all members seated on chairs in a circle, with one person standing in the middle as "it." The person in the middle makes a statement such as "I like my neighbors, especially those who are wearing running shoes" (wearing glasses, are over twelve, have a birthday in September, etc.). All those people who are wearing running shoes must jump up from their seats and scramble to find a chair; the person in the middle also scrambles for an empty chair. The one person left standing becomes the new "it."

Extension: Two or more people seated away from each other may make eye contact and nonverbally "plot" to change places. When they make the dash to each others' seats, the "leader" may try to beat them to it.

I Love You, Honey

Have everyone stand in a large circle. One person in the middle walks up to one person in the circle and says, "I love you, honey." The chosen "victim" is to respond, "I love you too, but I'm not allowed to smile," without smiling. It can be said twice to the same person in the same way. Guess what happens. They smile! Right! The smiler may then trade places with the person in the center or join the person in the center in tempting others to smile. The second option is generally easier on individuals in the group than the first option.

The Lap Game

Everyone stands in a long line behind each other and puts their hands on the waist of the person in front of them. On the count of "three" everyone sits down on the lap of the person behind them. This can also be done in a big circle.

Rain

Have everyone sit in a circle, facing the center. Ask all to close their eyes, pausing for a moment or two to become quiet while each person gets ready to hear the sound the person on the right will be making. Keep eyes closed as the rainstorm begins with the leader rubbing her palms together, back and forth. The person to the left joins her, and then the person to her left, and so on, around the circle. When the leader hears the drizzle sound being made by the person on the right, she starts snapping her fingers. When the snapping action has been picked up by everyone around the circle, the leader switches to hand clapping, then to thigh slapping, and finally to foot stomping. After foot stomping, the leader reverses the order of sounds, introducing thigh slapping, hand clapping, finger snapping and finally palm rubbing. For the last round, the leader stops rubbing her palms and takes the hand of the person on her left. Each person follows suit around the circle until there is silence once again.

Do After Me

Sit in a large circle. One person begins by entering the circle and making a gesture, sound, or movement (the more ridiculous, the more fun), and then points to someone else in the circle to succeed him. This person makes the same gesture, sound, or movement as the preceding person made, and then adds her own performance. She then chooses the next person, and this person need only repeat the preceding action and add one before choosing someone new. The game is over when everyone has had a chance in the circle.

Monkey, Elephant, Palm Tree

Form a large circle with one person standing in the middle as "it." The person in the center first demonstrates positions for people to take when he/she calls out one of the animals or the palm tree. They are illustrated below:

The person in the center then twirls around and points his or her finger at one of the people in the circle and shouts out: "Monkey," or "Elephant," or "Palm Tree." The person pointed to and the two people on either side of her take the appropriate positions with their bodies. The member of the trio that flubs up becomes the new "it" and goes into the center of the circle to continue on with the game.

Skin the Snake

Have people line up one behind the other. Reach between your legs and with your left hand grab the right hand of the person behind you. The person in front of you needs to reach back to grab your right hand with their left hand. Once the chain is formed, you're set to go. The last person in line lies down on his back. The person in front of him backs up, straddling his body and lies down behind him. Continue until the whole group waddles back.

People Machine

One person begins the activity by assuming a strange position and making a repetitive movement with a repetitive sound. The next person connects physically in whatever creative way he or she chooses, making a different movement and sound. People keep adding themselves to the machine. The result is a huge people machine making a lot of noise.

Electricity

Have everyone sit down in one large circle, cross-legged and knees touching. Hold hands. One person starts a squeeze on one side and the next person quietly passes it on around the circle. Variation: start it off by squeezing both sides. Watch it explode. Variation: send an "ooh" or an "aah" the other way.

Bumpety-Bump-Bump

Form a circle standing up, with a chosen "it" in the center. The "it" walks up to you and stands in front of you and says one of the following:

"Center, bumpety-bump-bump"

"Self, bumpety-bump-bump"

"Right, bumpety-bump-bump"

"Left, bumpety-bump-bump"

You must say his or her name, your name, or the person's name to the right or left of you before "it" completes saying "bumpety-bump-bump;" otherwise you become "it."

Name Wave

All stand in a circle. One person says their name and at the same time makes a motion or gesture. (Example: Beth, as she waves her hand.) The person to the right says "Beth" and waves her hand as Beth did. The name and motion spread around the circle in a "wave." When the circle is complete, the next person says their name and a different motion and that "waves" around the circle. Continue until all names are said and activated.

Snowball

Each student places his/her name on a piece of paper and wads it up. Students line up, half on either side of the room. At a signal they begin a snowball fight. At the end each gets a snowball, learns new information about the person whose snowball they found, and shares it with the class.

Pen Pals

Give each participant a 3 x 5 index card and tell them to write a little known fact about themselves on the card, something they won't mind the group eventually knowing. State that they are not to write their name on the card. Collect all cards, shuffle and redistribute. If someone gets his/her own card back, it is exchanged for another. When everyone has an unfamiliar card, have all stand and circulate, asking one another questions about the information on the card. For example, "Did you barrel race horses as a child?" When the person answering the description is found, he/she signs the card and puts it on a designated wall space. When you are finished, the community has an instant bulletin board of people and their accomplishments. This is a good full group inclusion energizer, good for parents on back-to-school night, too!

12
Resources

12

Resources

The History of Tribes and Tribes TLC®

The initial version of the Tribes process began to evolve in the early seventies, a time when concerned educators and parents again began groping for ways to motivate children's learning, to bring up test scores, to manage school behavior problems, and to stem the tide upon which many good teachers were leaving the teaching profession. National surveys were alerting the general public, industry leaders and the U.S. Congress that the majority of high school students did not have the knowledge or skills to do well in the world of work and social complexities that they would face in life. Twenty years ago? Or is it today?

At the same time, Jeanne Gibbs realized that her own childrens' achievements and behavior in school seemed to be influenced by the quality of the classroom and school environment. Being a student at heart, Jeanne began exploring studies on school climate, human development, child development, and the dynamics of organizational systems. In 1973 she was challenged by her employer, the Medical Services of Contra Costa County, California, to consult with the County Department of Education towards the prevention of substance abuse related problems within eighteen county school districts. There was little research at that time on prevention other than studies which confirmed that informational curricula alone did not deter problems. The author reasoned that since environment influences human behavior, building positive environments within schools and families not only would be preventive, but could be significant in promoting academic learning and social development. This was a pretty far out idea when scary films, talks by former addicts and information on the perils of drug use were the favored strategies.

Nevertheless, the concept made enough sense to some other visionaries at the California Department of Education who in 1974 funded a small grant that would enable twenty six elementary school teachers to meet one day a month for eight months to pilot a group development process that Jeanne had been using for many years within community settings. As the teachers began to experience the caring environment within their own work groups, they began to use the term, "tribe." Repeatedly they said, "We feel like a family...we feel like a tribe."

From 1975 through 1985 numerous applications of the group development process were made through a non-profit corporation which Jeanne organized. The "people process" proved to be valuable in alcohol recovery centers, juvenile facilities, convalescent homes, daycare centers, peer assistance and recreational programs. It was used to facilitate planning committees, conferences and university classes. California schools began to request training when they learned that the Tribes small group process decreased student behavior problems, increased self-esteem and improved teachers' energy and morale. Recently the Research Triangle Institute, under a U.S. Department of Education contract, identified Tribes TLC® as a program to teach Kindergarten to 12th grade students social skills.[1] The Council of the Great City Schools has cited Tribes as a model schools are using to prevent violence.[2]

By 1986 educators recognized the value of using small groups for the teaching of academic curricula. Some teachers who had training in cooperative learning methods discovered that the Tribes group process improved the capacity of students to work together. Based on the extensive research of the cooperative learning field and teachers' experience with the process, the book, *Tribes, A Process for Social Development and Cooperative Learning* was published in 1987. The demand for training accelerated throughout the country, and in 1991 quality materials incorporating new research, concepts and methods were designed by the author and her colleagues. The more comprehensive version of the Tribes process became known as "Tribes TLC®" and resulted in the writing and publication of, *Tribes, A New Way of Learning Together*, 1994, and several revisions including this 2001 edition.

The primary mission of Tribes TLC® as now defined is "to assure the healthy development of every child in the school community so that each has the knowledge, skills and resiliency to be successful in our rapidly changing world."

Indeed, this can happen when schools engage all teachers, administrators, students and families in working together as a learning community—a community dedicated to caring and support, active participation, and positive expectations for all of the young people in their circle of concern.

The Research Triangle Institute's In-Depth Study of Tribes as a Social Skills Program

We are proud that the respected Research Triangle Institute (RTI) chose to study the Tribes process as a social skills instructional program. Their new book, *A Resource Guide for Social Skills Instruction*, by Joni Alberg, Christene Petry, and Susan Eller, contains a seven-page description of Tribes based upon site visits conducted around the country during the last two years, material submitted to them by CenterSource Systems, and a review of the book *Tribes, A Process for Social Development and Cooperative Learning* (1987). Although the original intent of the RTI contract with the U.S. Department of Education was to identify programs for teaching social skills to students with disabilities, Dr. Alberg's staff and advisory committee quickly learned that educators were every bit as interested in knowing about programs that could teach social skills to all students.

The new *Resource Guide for Social Skills Instruction* describes the need for social skills instruction, how to select a program, and how to teach social skills. Their instructions on teaching social skills concur with concepts incorporated into this book and TLC® teacher training. Chapter 2 of the Research Triangle Institute's book is on social skills instruction and begins with concrete advice:

If social skills are to be learned they must be taught just as academic subjects are taught. You can apply the same effective teaching principles to social skills instruction as you apply to your teaching of academic content. Thus, no matter what the content, effective teachers:

- are clear about their instructional goals;
- are knowledgeable about their content and strategies for teaching it;
- communicate to their students what is expected of them and why;
- are knowledgeable about their students, adapting instructions to their needs and anticipating misconceptions in their existing knowledge;
- prepare students to share responsibility with the teacher for their own learning by providing students with the skills to learn independently;
- monitor students' understanding by providing regular feedback;
- integrate their instruction with that in other subject areas;
- understand that students are more likely to remember and use what they learn if they see a purpose beyond meeting school requirements; and
- accept responsibility for student outcomes.

RTI's site observations in schools using the Tribes process included both self-contained and mainstreamed settings with children who had learning disabilities, emotional/behavioral disabilities, communication disorders, hearing impairments, and severe mental and physical disabilities. Some of their observations and conclusions were:

1. Few program modifications were required for students with disabilities except for the use of sign language by a teacher with hearing impaired students, and adaptation of some activities to accommodate students with orthopedic disabilities.

   Tribes appeared less successful with students who had severe disabilities and those who are completely nonverbal and cannot participate in groups.

2. The five elements of cooperative learning were noted in Tribes classrooms: positive interdependence, face-to-face interaction, interpersonal and small group skills, individual accountability, and group processing.

3. Observers noticed situations where students demonstrated internalization of the norms (agreements) when they called their peer's attention to inappropriate behavior and related it to the norms. "For example, in one 5th grade class, student X overheard student Y make a derogatory comment to student Z. Student X told student Y that the comment was a put-down and the student should apologize (and did)."

4. The administrators, teachers, and support personnel that were interviewed expressed their beliefs that "teacher tribes" are important for successful implementation and providing necessary peer support.

5. The practice in Tribes of transferring some of the responsibility for behavior management from teachers to students was observed. A 5th grade teacher is reported as saying, "Tribes is my classroom management because it sets the stage for learning and builds a basis for support among the kids."

In addition to being selected as one of eight social skills programs studied in depth, the new Research Triangle Institute *Resource Guide* includes annotations for the use of Tribes in elementary, middle/junior high/ and senior high/postsecondary grade levels.

1. Alberg, J., Eller, S., Petry, C., Nero, B. *Resource Guide for Social Skills Instruction.* Researched and compiled under the contract: Approaches and Choices to Developing Social Competence in Students with Disabilities, U.S. Department of Education, 1991-3.

2. Newkumet, M.B. and Casserly, M. *Urban School Safety: Strategies of the Great City Schools.* Washington, D.C.: Council of the Great City Schools, 1994.

The Impact of Group Processing

Tribes has always emphasized the importance of using reflection or process questions after each group strategy or learning experience. The motto shared among Tribes teachers has been, "The activity alone is not enough!" Throughout the years, CenterSource Systems trainers have been helping teachers define three types of reflection questions (1) about the content [facts and concepts] of a lesson; (2) about the collaborative social and constructive thinking skills used by students within their tribes; and (3) about the personal learning and meaning that a lesson had for the students. Reflection questions were emphasized as a way to develop metacognition (learning about our learning) and responsibility among students to improve their learning groups (tribes). Empirical studies confirm that the time spent with students on "group processing" also leads to the greater retention of subject matter and academic achievement.

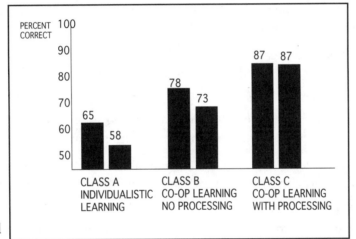

The study "The Impact of Group Processing on Achievement in Cooperative Learning Groups" by Stuart Yager, Roger Johnson, David Johnson, and Bill Snider describes three learning conditions assessed in three classes composed of 84 3rd graders. An intensive five-week unit on transportation was taught in all three classrooms but in different processes.

Classroom A used the conventional individualistic learning method whereby students study alone and fill daily worksheets. Classrooms B and C used cooperative learning groups (four students to a group) with students working together and each group completing the worksheets together. In addition, classroom C spent 5 minutes processing their work as a group and setting goals for improvement. A 50-item factual knowledge multiple choice test on the subject was given to all children prior to the unit and three weeks after the unit. A 25-item test was given after twelve instructional days and another 25-item test as soon as the unit was completed.

The graph was constructed from the research data. The first bar graph for each class shows achievement and the second bar graph indicates retention of knowledge after three weeks. Pretest scores for all students had averaged about 50%.

In classroom A, using the individualistic approach, marginal gains moved from 50 to 65% in achievement, with retention dropping to 58% three weeks after the unit was completed. In classroom B, using cooperative learning groups and no processing, gains moved from 50 to 78%, with 73% retention. Results in classroom C, using cooperative learning groups with processing are impressive, with higher achievement (87%) and *no* loss in the retention of knowledge after three weeks.

Other studies by the same researchers show comparably dramatic results from the contribution of group processing to learning and individual achievement. Interested readers can learn more by accessing these research articles: Stuart Yager, Roger Johnson and David Johnson, "Oral Discussion, Group-to-Individual Transfer, and Achievement in Cooperative Learning Groups," Journal of Educational Psychology 77:60-66, 1985. Stuart Yager, Roger Johnson, David Johnson, and Bill Snider, "The Impact of Group Processing Achievement in Cooperative Learning Groups," The Journal of Social Psychology, 126:389-397, 1986.

Initiating Classroom Parent Tribes

Time Required: 60 minutes
Facilitators: Two classroom parents trained by teachers
Materials: Tribes agreements posted on wall, 3 x 5-inch cards, pencils, large pieces of paper, felt tip pens

Objectives:

1. To develop participation and mutual support among the parents of the classroom
2. To provide parents with a satisfying initial experience in the Tribes process
3. To motivate parents to continue meeting throughout the year as a classroom learning community
4. To provide information on the goals of Tribes, its process, and collaborative agreements
5. To help parents learn how to foster resiliency in their children

Instructions

8 min.   **1.** As parents arrive the teacher and parent facilitators (PFs) invite the parents to sit in small groups of prearranged chairs or desks (four to seven in a group).

2. The teacher welcomes all, gives overview of the hour and tells why the Tribes process is being used within the class or school. He or she introduces the PFs, and briefly describes their role.

4 min.   **3.** The PFs share their names, students names, and their commitment to having the parents of the class become a supportive learning community.

4. The PFs then describe the Tribes agreements and ask the parents to honor them during their time together. They demonstrate the Tribes hand signal as a way to call attention.

5 min.   **5.** The parent facilitators discuss the importance of the Tribes agreements and attentive listening, and they demonstrate the skills.

1 min.   **6.** After asking each group to select a timekeeper, the PFs each ask the parents to share their name and one great quality about their student. Ask the timekeepers in each group to monitor the sharing time.

5 min.   **7.** The PFs ask the parents to think about, then share with one other person in the group, two things they hope for their child during the year. As one parent shares, the other notes down in one to three words the parent's hopes on a card. When the time is up, the PFs collect the cards.

5 min.   **8.** The teacher responds to some of the hopes listed, tying them to goals for the year.

5 min.   **9.** The PFs ask the following reflection questions:

- How many people enjoyed being able to talk with other parents tonight?
- How many would like to get together this way again?

5 min.   **10.** The PFs demonstrate and invite statements of appreciation in tribes.

5 min.   **11.** They invite everyone to close in a community circle, sharing, "I learned" statements.

A Tribes TLC® Learning Experience

Grade:

1. Provide for **inclusion**—a question, activity, or energizer.

2. Identify the **content objective** to be learned and the **collaborative/social skill** objective to be practiced.

Content Objective (write):

Collaborative Skills: (check)
- ❏ Participating fully
- ❏ Listening attentively
- ❏ Expressing appreciation
- ❏ Reflecting on experience
- ❏ Valuing diversity of culture/ideas
- ❏ Thinking constructively
- ❏ Making Responsible Decisions
- ❏ Resolving conflict
- ❏ Solving problems creatively
- ❏ Working on tasks together
- ❏ Assessing improvement
- ❏ Celebrating achievement

Social Skills:
- ❏ Sharing
- ❏ Listening
- ❏ Respecting
- ❏ No Put-Downs
- ❏ Empathizing

Other:

3. Identify the **strategy**(ies).

4. Ask **reflection questions** about what was learned.

5. Provide an opportunity for **appreciation**.

This form may be duplicated for classroom use.

Form A: A Teacher's Assessment

Attentive Listening

Date _____

Lesson_____

_____

_____

Tally each time the behavior is observed

Names of individuals or tribes

	Basic Skills					Advanced Skills				
	Faces speaker, leans forward	Maintains eye contact	Nods, smiles if appropriate	Does not interrupt the speaker	Encourages speaker to continue talking	Asks relevant questions to clarify and show interest	Paraphrases speaker's main ideas	Reflects the speaker's feelings	Summarizes for the group	TOTALS

This form may be duplicated for classroom use.

Form B: Student Assessment

Date _____

Participation in My Tribe

Name _____ Tribe _____

	Never	Sometimes	Mostly	Always
1. I listened to people in my tribe.				
2. I helped other people.				
3. I contributed ideas and information.				
4. I helped to clarify and summarize ideas and information.				
5. I encouraged others.				
6. I participated in making decisions.				
7. I expressed appreciation to others.				
8. I helped us to reflect on what we learned.				

Notes:

Form C: Student Assessment   Date _____

Our Tribe's Work Together

Tribe name _____

Using the numbers 1 (poorly), 2 (o.k.), and 3 (great!), rate how well your tribe did the following:

Rating	**Social skill or group interaction**
_____	1. We listened to each other.
_____	2. We checked our understanding of the task.
_____	3. We shared ideas and information.
_____	4. We encouraged and helped each other.
_____	5. We stayed on the task and used our time well.
_____	6. Other:

Total Score	

This material may be duplicated for classroom use.

- -

Form C: Student Assessment   Date _____

Our Tribe's Work Together

Tribe name _____

Using the numbers 1 (poorly), 2 (o.k.), and 3 (great!), rate how well your tribe did the following:

Rating	**Social skill or group interaction**
_____	1. We listened to each other.
_____	2. We checked our understanding of the task.
_____	3. We shared ideas and information.
_____	4. We encouraged and helped each other.
_____	5. We stayed on the task and used our time well.
_____	6. Other:

Total Score	

This material may be duplicated for classroom use.

Form D: Student Assessment   Date _____

My Constructive Thinking Skills

Name _____   Tribe _____

Instructions

Read the descriptions of constructive thinking skills below and estimate how well you do each skill. You can use a different color pencil or pen each week to evaluate your own progress in using these skills.

	Never	Sometimes	Mostly	Always
1. I am able to **access information** (using the library, computer, articles, interviewing, and working with others).				
2. I can **organize information** (using graphics, charts, note cards, computer data entry).				
3. I am able to **compare and summarize** facts and ideas.				
4. I can **plan and use** what I learn to solve problems and be creative.				
5. I am able to **reflect and evaluate** how well something is working and make improvements.				

Other comments:

Appendix

Notes

Chapter 1: A New Pattern of Interaction

1. These figures are from the *National Assessment of Educational Progress*, TA Document PR 502, Washington: National Parent Teachers Association, 1990.

2. *Action Plan for Improving Mathematics, Science, Language Arts, and Social Studies*, Honolulu: Department of Education, State of Hawaii, 1991.

3. David and Roger Johnson's extensive work has been an immense contribution to the development of cooperative learning and Tribes. The benefits of cooperation in education are summarized in their book *Cooperation and Competition, Theory and Research*. Edina, MN: Interaction Book Company, 1989, p. 169-179.

4. Ibid.

5. Claude M. Steele, "Race and Schooling of Black Americans," *Atlantic Monthly*, April 1992, p. 75. According to Steele, Philip Treisman, calculus professor at the University of California, Berkeley, offers evidence that cooperative effort is more likely to achieve excellence than is individual effort. In the typical competitive university setting, Treisman's African American students consistently were at the bottom of every calculus class. After he started using cooperative learning groups in which students had regular opportunity for study together, these same students "reversed their fortunes, causing them to outperform their white and Asian counterparts." In fact everyone's scores became higher.

6. The name "Tribes" has never denoted Native American tribes or any particular indigenous tribe. The term came into usage when teachers began to refer to their experience in the Tribes process. They connected their sense of community to what they imagined tribal communities were like. Richard Burrill, anthropologist, has written a commentary, "The Meaning of Tribes to Indigenous People," for this book. It is in Chapter 4.

   Beginning in 1991, Jeanne Gibbs began teaching and distributing materials based on the new Tribes TLC® process. Although the Tribes TLC® process incorporates certain elements of the cooperative learning method which has come to be known as Tribes over the years, the Tribes TLC® process and materials are significant improvements over traditional Tribes practices. Earlier Tribes materials, and materials from sources other than CenterSource do not embody the Tribes TLC® process.

   Educators, administrators, parents, and others interested in bringing Tribes TLC® programs to their organizations should take care to ensure that the trainers and the materials they are using are up-to-date and come from certified Tribes TLC® sources. Please contact CenterSource Systems in order to determine whether the training and materials you are considering constitute certified Tribes TLC® materials.

7. Peter Senge, "The Learning Organization Made Plain," *Training and Development*, Boston: October 1991, p. 38.

8. Alfie Kohn, "Choices for Children—Why and How to Let Students Decide," *Phi Delta Kappan*, Bloomington, IN: Phi Delta Kappa Foundation, September 1993, 75 (1), 8-19. The Shelley Berman side bar quote is also from this article, citing Berman: "The Real Ropes Course: The Development of Social Consciousness," *ESR Journal*, 1990, p. 2.

9. Ibid., p. 12.

Chapter 2: Finding Our Way to the Future

1. William Grieder, "Stand and Deliver, Alternatives Within Public Schools," *Utne Reader,* November/December, 1992, p. 76.

2. *What Work Requires of Schools, SCAN Report for America 2000,* Secretary's Commission on Achieving Necessary Skills, Washington, D.C., U.S. Department of Labor, 1991.

3. Ibid.

4. Cited by Harold Hodgkinson of the Institute for Educational Leadership, at Education and Work Conference: "Guess Who's Coming to Work," Northwest Regional Educational Laboratory, Portland, OR, 1990.

5. Mako Nakagawa, "Cooperative Pluralism," *Your Public Schools,* Olympia, WA: Office of Superintendent of Public Instruction, November, 1986, p. 2.

6. Bonnie Benard, *Moving Toward a Just and Vital Culture: Multiculturalism in Our Schools,* Portland, OR: Western Regional Center for Drug Free Schools and Communities, Northwest Regional Educational Laboratory, 1991, p. 9.

7. The fine phrase "habits of the heart" is credited to Robert Bellah, Professor of Sociology, University of California (Berkeley), author of *Habits of the Heart, Individualism and Commitment in American Life,* New York: Perennial Library, Harper & Row, 1985.

8. *Together We Can...Reduce the Risks of Alcohol and Other Drug Use Among Youth* is a multimedia planning kit coauthored and designed by Jeanne Gibbs and Sherrin Bennett for school community prevention planning groups. The meeting plans use the Tribes process to develop collaboration.

9. The work of the late Gerald Egan, Ph.D., Loyola University (Chicago) influenced the application of the Tribes process to many systems concerned with different population needs (juvenile facilities, alcoholism recovery facilities, convalescent homes, peer assistant and youth educator programs, parent educators and youth intervention groups). The book by Gerald Egan and Michael Cowan, *People in Systems: A Model for Development in the Human Service Professions and Education.* Monterey, CA: Brooks Cole, Publishers, 1979, though now out of print, is extremely helpful to system program planners who are able to track it down.

10. Urie Bronfenbrenner, *The Ecology of Human Development, Experiments by Nature and Design,* Cambridge, MA: Harvard 1979, p. 9.

11. This chart is based on a synthesis of stages described by child development theorists Jean Piaget and Erik Erikson. The "implications" column evolved out of many years of many teachers' experience and common sense.

12. C. Halverson and M. Waldrup, "Relations Between Preschool Barrier Behaviors and Early School—Measures of Coping, Imagination and Verbal Development," *Developmental Psychology,* v. 10, 1974, pp. 716-720.

13. Bonnie Benard, *Fostering Resiliency in Kids: Protective Factors in the Family, School and Community,* Portland, OR: Western Regional Center for Drug Free Schools and Communities, Northwest Regional Educational Laboratory, 1991, pp. 1-20. The primary researchers cited in Benard's documents are Norman Garmezy, Michael Rutter, and Emily Werner. Some of the source documents are:

Norman Garmezy, "Resiliency and Vulnerability to Adverse Developmental Outcomes Associated With Poverty," *American Behavioral Scientist,* 34(4), March/April 1991, 416-430.

Norman Garmezy and Michael Rutter, "How and Why Do Some Kids Flourish Against All Odds?" *Behavior Today,* Nov. 21, 1983, 5-7.

Michael Rutter, "Protective Factors in Children: Responses to Stress And Disadvantage," *Primary Prevention of Psychopathology: V. 3: Promoting Social Competence and Coping in Children,* Eds. Martha Whalen Dent and J.E. Rolf, Hanover, NH: University Press of New England, 1979, 49-74.

Emily Werner and Ruth Smith, *Vulnerable But Invincible: A Longitudinal Study of Resilient Children And Youth,* New York: Adams, Bannister, and Cox, 1989.

14. Bonnie Benard, "Resiliency Requires Changing Hearts and Minds," *Western Center News,* Portland: Western Center for Drug Free Schools and Communities, Northwest Regional Educational Laboratory, March 1993, p. 4.

15. Citing David and Roger Johnson's summary of studies in *Cooperation And Competition, Theory and Research.* Edina, MN: Interaction Book Company, 1989, p. 169-179.

16. Martin Wolins and Y. Wozner, "Revitalizing Residential Settings: Problems and Potential" in *Education, Health, Rehabilitation and Social Services,* San Francisco, CA: Jossey Bass Publishers, 1982, p. 10.

17. Ibid., Bronfenbrenner.

18. Miller, Ron, *What Are Schools For? Holistic Culture in American Culture,* Brandon, VT: Holistic Education Press, 1990.

Chapter 3: How Children Learn

1. "Digging for knowledge," *Wall Street Journal,* New York: September 11, 1992, B. 1.

2. Rachel Hertz-Lazarowitz and H. Shachar, "Changes in Teachers' Verbal Behavior in Cooperative Classrooms," *Cooperative Learning,* Santa Cruz: V. 11, Dec. 1990, No. 2. p. 13-14.

3. Ibid., p. 13.

4. Roger von Oech, *A Whack on the Side of the Head: How You Can Be More Creative,* New York: Warner Books, 1990, p. 24.

5. Stephen Schneider, "A Better Way to Learn," *World Monitor,* April 1993, p. 32.

6. "Gender Gaps—Where Schools Fail Our Children," was commissioned by the American Association of University Women as a follow-up to "How Schools Shortchange Girls," (1991). The updated study was researched by the American Institutes of Research (1998).

7. Miller, Ron, *What Are Schools For? Holistic Culture in American Culture,* Brandon, VT: Holistic Education Press, 1990.

8. Susan Kovalik, *Integrated Thematic Instruction: The Model,* Books for Educators, 4th ed., 1997, p. 4-6.

9. Howard Gardner, *Intelligence Reframed, Multiple Intelligences for the 21st Century.* New York, New York, Basic Books, 1999.

10. David Lazear, *Seven Ways of Teaching, The Artistry of Teaching with Multiple Intelligences,* Palatine, IL: Skylight Publishing Company, p. 109, 1989.

11. Lynn Stoddard, *Redesigning Education: A Guide for Developing Human Greatness*, Tucson, AZ: Zephyr Press, 1992.

12. Ronald Kotulak, *Inside the Brain: Revolutionary Discoveries of How the Mind Works*, Andrews & McMeel, 1997.

13. Eric Jensen, *Teaching the Brain with the Mind*, Association for Supervision and Curriculum, 1998.

14. Renata and Geoffrey Caine, *Making Connections: Teaching and the Human Brain*, Addison-Wesley Publishing Co., 1994.

15. Candace Pert, *Molecules of Emotion, the Science Behind Mind-Body Medicine*, New York: Simon & Schuster, 1997.

Chapter 4: What Tribes Are and How They Work

1. More than twenty-eight years ago two research reports led to the practice in Tribes of advocating long-term membership groups: Albert Lott and Bernice Lott, "Group Cohesiveness and Individual Learning," *Journal of Educational Psychology*, 57, p. 61-72, April 1966.

   Robert Fox, Margaret Luszki and Richard Schmuck, "Social Relations in the Classroom," *Diagnosing Learning Environments*, Chicago: SRA. Inc., 1966.

2. John McKnight, "Are Social Service Agencies the Enemy of Community?" *Utne Reader*, July/August 1992, p. 89-90.

Chapter 5: Creating The Learning Community

1. Stuart Yager, Roger Johnson and David Johnson, "Oral Discussion, Group to Individual Transfer, and Achievement in Cooperative Learning Groups," *Journal of Educational Psychology*, 1985, 77: 60-66.

   Stuart Yager, Roger Johnson, David Johnson and Bill Snider, "The Impact of Group Processing on Achievement in Cooperative Learning Groups," *The Journal of Social Psychology*, 1986, 126: 389-397.

2. We appreciate the permission to use this poem written by Gilbert Rees of Ontario, Canada. The poem is contained in an article by Jack Miller and Susan Drake: "Implementing A Holistic Curriculum," *Holistic Education Review*, Fall 1990, p. 30.

Chapter 6: Building Tribes

1. Alfie Kohn, *Beyond Discipline: From Compliance to Community*, Alexandria, VA: Association for Supervision and Curriculum Development, 1996, p. 76-77.

2. Peter Senge, *The Art and Practice of the Learning Community*, New York: Doubleday/Currency, 1991.

3. The Conflict Resolution Program of the San Francisco Community Board trains students as conflict managers for their schools. An elementary and secondary school curriculum is available. See "Suggested Resources" in Chapter 12 of this book.

Chapter 7: Calling Forth Power and Self Worth

1. Mara Sapon-Shevin and Nancy Schniedewind, "Cooperative Learning as Empowering Pedagogy," *Empowerment from Multicultural Education*, SUNY Press, 1991.

2. Ibid.

Chapter 8: Designing And Implementing Learning Experiences

1. Paulo Freire, *Pedagogy of the Oppressed*, New York: Herder and Herder, 1970.

2. Ursula Franklin, *Introduction to the symposium "Towards an Ecology of Knowledge,"* University of Toronto; As reported by Gordon Wells in *"Dialogic Inquiry in Education: Building on the Legacy of Vygotsky."* Toronto: Ontario Institute for Studies in Education, University of Toronto, p. 16, 1996.

3. Jacquelyn and Martin Brooks, *In Search for Understanding: The Case for Constructionist Classrooms*, Alexandria, VA: Association for Supervision and Curriculum Development, 1993.

4. Roger Bybee, *Constructivism and The Five E's*, Miami: The Biological Science Curriculum Study, Miami Museum of Science, 1997: Internet document: www.miamisci.org.

5. David and Roger Johnson, *Cooperation and Competition, Theory and Research*, Edina, MN: Interaction Book Company, 1989. R. Slavin, *Cooperative Learning: Theory, Research and Practice*, Englewood Cliffs, NJ: Prentice Hall, 1990. J. Pederson and A. Digby (Eds), Secondary Schools and *Cooperative Learning, Theories, Models and Strategies*, New York: Garland Publishing, p. 282, 1995.

6. Lynn Stoddard, *Redesigning Education: A Guide for Developing Human Greatness*, Tucson, AZ. Zepher Press, 1992.

7. Marion Brady, *What's Worth Teaching? Selecting, Organizing and Integrating Knowledge*, New York State University Press, 1989.

8. Ibid: Brady

9. Susan Kovalik, *Integrated Thematic Instruction: The Model*, Kent, WA: Books for Educators, 1993.

10. David Lazear, *Seven Ways of Teaching, The Artistry of Teaching With Multiple Intelligences*, Palatine. IL: Skylight Publishing, 1991.

11. Thomas Armstrong, *7 Kinds of Smart, Identifying and Developing Your Multiple Intelligences*, New York, New York Penguin Putnam, 1999.

12. Howard Gardner, *Intelligence Reframed, Multiple Intelligences for the 21st Century.* New York, New York, Basic Books, 1999.

13. The questions are based on Selma Wassermann's booklet *Asking the Right Questions: The Essence of Teaching*, Bloomington, IN: Phi Delta Kappan Educational Foundations, 1992, p. 10-17.

14. Eleanor Duckworth, *The Having of Wonderful Ideas on Teaching and Learning*, New York: Teachers College Press, 1987.

Chapter 9: Working With People Big and Small

1. To the best of the author's knowledge, the Flatland story comes from a small book written in the 1880s by a mathematician named Abbott. It has been used for more than 100 years to illustrate the difficulty of conveying the impact of a significant experience to others who have not as yet lived it.

2. John H. Lounsbury, "Perspectives on the Middle School Movement," *Transforming Middle School Education, Perspectives and Possibilities*, Ed., Judith Irvin, Boston: Allyn and Bacon, 1992.

3. Students 9-16 years of age were surveyed, and reported by G. Foster in the article, "Report of Student Needs: Fiske F/S/C/Partnership Program," Tallahassee, Fla.: Unpublished report, Florida State University, College of Education, 1989. Cited by: Koochan, F.K., *A New Paradigm of Schooling: Connecting School, Home and Community*, Ibid Irwin, 1992.

4. James Beane, *Middle School Curriculum from Rhetoric to Reality*, 1990, Ibid Irwin, 1992.

5. *Carnegie Council on Adolescent Development, Turning Points: Preparing American Youth for the 21st Century*, New York: Carnegie Corporation of New York, 1989.

6. R.T. Johnson, and D.W. Johnson, "Mainstreaming and Cooperative Learning Groups," *Exceptional Children:* 52: 553-561, 1986.

7. Johnson, R.T., and Johnson, D.W., Scott, L.E., and Ramolae, R.A., "Effects of Single Sex, and Mixed-Sex Cooperative Interaction on Science Achievement and Attitudes and Cross-Handicap and Cross-Sex Relationships," *Journal of Research in Science Teaching*, 1985, 22: 207-220.

8. J. Alberg, S. Eller, C. Petry, B. Nero, *Resource Guide for Social Skills.* Researched and compiled under the contract, "Approaches and Choices to Developing Social Competence in Students with Disabilities," to the Research Triangle Institute from the U.S. Department of Education. Book to be published by Sopers Publishers, Longmount, Colorado, 1994.

9. Laurie Olsen, *Embracing Diversity, Teachers' Voices from California Classrooms, A Publication of California Tomorrow Immigrant Students Project Research Report*, San Francisco, 1990..

10. Spencer Kagan is best known for his "structural approach" to cooperative learning. His philosophy and methods are described in his book *Cooperative Learning Resources for Teachers*, San Juan Capistrano, CA: Resources for Teachers, 1993.

11. The power of Group Investigation to increase academic achievement (particularly higher order thinking skills) is clearly demonstrated in Shlomo Sharan and Hana Shachar analysis of a year-long intervention in nine eighth grade classes in history and geography in a mixed ethnic Israeli school. *Language and Learning in the Classroom*, NY: Springer Verlag, 1988.

12. The basic book *Jigsaw Classroom* (Sage Publications, 1978) by Elliot Aronson is out of print. Spencer Kagan's book cited in the note above, provides a full discussion and specific strategies.

Chapter 10: Bringing It All Together

1. Everett Rogers, "Diffusion of the Idea Beyond War," *BreakThrough—Emerging New Thinking*, Walker & Co., New York: 1988, p. 240-248.

2. Juanita Brown and David Isaacs, "Conversation as a Core Business Process," *The Systems Thinker*, Pegasus Communications, Inc., Dec. '96/ Jan. '97.

3. P. Florin, and D.M. Chavis, *Community Prevention and Substance Abuse Prevention*, San Jose, CA: Bureau of Drug Abuse Services, County of Santa Clara, May 1990.

4. The quote by Marc Tucker of the National Center on Education and the Economy is contained in Edward Fiske's book, *Smart Schools, Smart Kids*, New York: Simon & Schuster, p. 259.

5. These recommendations are made by Bruce R. Joyce, "Cooperative Learning and Staff Development: Teaching the Method with Method," *Cooperative Learning Magazine*, Vol. 12, No. 12, Winter '91/'92, p. 10-13.

6. Anne Henderson, an associate with the National Committee for Education has cited forty-nine studies showing a positive correlation between family school collaboration and gains in student achievement. Cited in: Ibid, Fiske, p. 232.

7. The quote by Dr. James Comer is also cited in: Ibid, Fiske, p. 209.

Bibliography

Action Plan for Improving Mathematics, Science, Language Arts, and Social Studies, Honolulu: Department of Education, State of Hawaii, 1991.

Alberg, J., Eller, S., and Petry, C., *A Resource Guide for Social Skills Instruction,* Center for Research in Education, Research Triangle Institute (U.S. Department of Education, Office of Special Education Programs), Longmount, Colorado: Sopers Publishers, 1994.

Aronson, Elliot, *The Jigsaw Classroom,* Beverly Hills, CA: Sage, 1978.

Armstrong, Thomas, *In Their Own Way,* Tarcher Press, 1987.

Armstrong, Thomas, *7 Kinds of Smart, Identifying and Developing Your Multiple Intelligences,* New York, New York Penguin Putnam, 1999.

Short Changing Girls, Shortchanging America, A National Poll to Assess Self Esteem, Educational Experiences, Interest in Math And Science, And Career Aspirations, Association of University Women, 1991.

Bellah, Robert, *Habits of the Heart, Individualism and Commitment in American Life,* New York: Perennial Library, Harper & Row, 1985.

Benard, Bonnie, *Fostering Resiliency in Kids: Protective Factors in the Family, School and Community,* Portland, OR: Western Regional Center for Drug Free Schools and Communities, Northwest Regional Educational Laboratory, 1991.

Benard, Bonnie, *Moving Toward a Just and Vital Culture: Multiculturalism in Our Schools,* Portland, OR: Western Regional Center for Drug Free Schools and Communities, Northwest Regional Educational Laboratory, 1991.

Benard, Bonnie, *Resiliency Paradigm Validates Craft Knowledge,* Portland, OR: Western Center News, Northwest Regional Educational Laboratory, September 1993.

Benard, Bonnie, *Resiliency Requires Changing Hearts and Minds,* Portland, OR: Western Center News, Northwest Regional Educational Laboratory, March 1993.

Berman, Shelly, *The Real Ropes Course: The Development of Social Consciousness,* ESR Journal, 1990.

Brady, Marion, *What's Worth Teaching? Selecting, Organizing and Integrating Knowledge,* New York State University Press, 1989.

Brendtro, Larry, Brokenleg, Martin and Van Bockern, Steve, *Reclaiming Youth At Risk, Our Hope for the Future,* Bloomington, IN: National Educational Service, 1990.

Bronfenbrenner, Urie, *The Ecology of Human Development, Experiments by Nature and Design,* Cambridge, MA: Harvard 1979.

Brooks, Jacquelyn and Martin, *"In Search for Understanding: The Case for Constructionist Classrooms,"* Alexandria, VA: Association for Supervision and Curriculum Development, 1993.

Brown, Juanita and Isaacs, David, "Conversation as a Core Business Process," *The Systems Thinker,* Pegasus Communications, Inc., Dec. '96/Jan. '97.

Bybee, Roger, *Constructivism and The Five E's,* Miami: The Biological Science Curriculum Study, Miami Museum of Science, 1997. Internet document: www.miamisci.org.

Caine, Renata and Geoffrey, *Making Connections: Teaching and the Human Brain,* Alexandria, VA: American Association for Supervision and Curriculum Development, 1991.

Carnegie Council on Adolescent Development, *Turning Points: Preparing American Youth for the 21st Century,* New York: Carnegie Corporation of New York, 1989.

Caught in the Middle, Educational Reform for Young Adolescents in California Public Schools, Sacramento: Department of Education, 1987.

Cohen, Elizabeth, *Designing Groupwork: Strategies for the Heterogeneous Classroom,* Teachers College Press, 1986.

Conflict Resolution, An Elementary School Curriculum, San Francisco, CA: Community Board Program, 1990.

Conflict Resolution, A Secondary School Curriculum, San Francisco, CA: Community Board Program, 1990.

Cooperative Learning, The Magazine for Cooperation in Education, Editor: Liana Nan Forest. Santa Cruz, CA: International Association for the Study of Cooperation in Education, Volumes 1988-1993.

Cotton, Kathleen, *School Community Collaboration to Improve the Quality of Life for Urban Youth and Their Families, School Improvement Research Series,* Portland, OR: Northwest Regional Educational Laboratory, 1991.

Duckworth, Eleanor, *The Having of Wonderful Ideas on Teaching and Learning,* New York: Teachers College Press, 1987.

Egan, Gerald and Michael Cowan, *People in Systems: A Model for Development in the Human Service Professions and Education,* Monterey, CA: Brooks Cole, Publishers, 1979.

Fiske, Edward L. *Smart Schools, Smart Kids,* New York: Simon and Schuster, 1991.

Florin, P. and Chavis, D.M., *Community Prevention and Substance Abuse Prevention,* San Jose, CA: Bureau of Drug Abuse Services, County of Santa Clara, May 1990.

Foster, G., "Report of Student Needs: Fiske F/S/C/Partnership Program," Tallahassee, Fla.: Unpublished report, Florida State University, College of Education, 1989. In *Middle School Curriculum from Rhetoric to Reality,* Ed. Irwin, 1990.

Fox, R., Luszki, M. and Schmuck, R., *Social Relations in the Classroom: Diagnosing Learning Environments,* Chicago: SRA Inc., 1966.

Franklin, Ursula, *Introduction to the symposium, "Towards an Ecology of Knowledge,"* University of Toronto, as reported by Gordon Wells in *"Dialogic Inquiry in Education: Building on the Legacy of Vygotsky,"* Toronto: Ontario Institute for Studies in Education. University of Toronto, p. 16, 1996.

Freire, Paulo, *Pedagogy of the Oppressed,* New York, Herder and Herder, 1970.

Fullan, Michael and Miles, Mathew, "Getting Reform Right: What Works and What Doesn't," *Kappan Magazine,* Bloomington, IN: Kappan Educational Foundation, June 1992.

Gardner, Howard, *Intelligence Reframed, Multiple Intelligences for the 21st Century.* New York: Basic Books, 1999.

Gibbs, Jeanne and Bennett, Sherrin, *Together We Can, Reduce the Risks of Alcohol and Drug Use Among Youth,* Sausalito, CA: Interactive Learning Systems, 1990.

Goleman, Daniel, *Emotional Intelligence,* Bantam Books, 1995.

Grieder, William, "Stand and Deliver, Alternatives within Public Schools," *Utne Reader,* Nov./Dec., 1992.

Halverson, C. and Waldrup, M., "Relations between Preschool Barrier Behaviors and Early School Measures of Coping, Imagination and Verbal Development," *Developmental Psychology,* V. 10, 1974.

Hart, Leslie, *A Human Brain and Human Learning,* New York: Longman, 1983.

Henderson, Anne, *Correlation Studies: Family School Collaboration and Gains in Student Achievement,* National Committee for Education, 1987.

Hertz Lazarowitz, R. and Shachar, H., "Changes in Teachers' Verbal Behavior In Cooperative Classrooms," *Cooperative Learning,* Santa Cruz: V. 11, Dec. 1990.

Irwin, Judith L. (Ed.), *Transforming Middle School Education, Prospectives and Possibilities,* Boston: Allyn and Bacon, 1992.

Isaacson, Nancy and Bamburg, Jerry, "Can Schools Become Learning Organizations?" *Educational Leadership,* November 1992.

Jensen, Eric, *Teaching the Brain with the Mind,* Association for Supervision and Curriculum, 1998.

Johnson, David and Johnson, Roger, *Cooperation and Competition: Theory and Research,* Edina, MN: Interaction Book Company, 1989.

Johnson, R.T. and Johnson, D.W., "Mainstreaming and Cooperative Learning Groups," *Exceptional Children,* 52: 553-561, 1986.

Johnson, R.T., and Johnson, D.W., Scott, L.E., and Ramolae, R.A., "Effects Of Single Sex, and Mixed-Sex Cooperative Interaction on Science Achievement and Attitudes on Cross-Handicap and Cross-Sex Relationships," *Journal of Research in Science Teaching,* 22: 207-220, 1985.

Kagan, Spencer, *Cooperative Learning,* San Juan Capistrano: Kagan's Cooperative Learning Company, 1992.

Kaseberg, Alise, Kreinberg, Nancy and Downie, Diane, *EQUALS to Promote the Participation of Women in Mathematics,* Berkeley, CA: Lawrence Hall of Science, University of California, 1980.

Kohn, Alfie, *Beyond Discipline: From Compliance to Community,* Alexandria, VA: Association for Supervision and Curriculum Development, 1996, p. 76-77.

Kohn, Alfie, "Choices for Children—Why and How to Let Students Decide," *Phi Delta Kappan,* Bloomington, IN: Phi Delta Kappa, September 1993.

Kohn, Alfie, *No Contest: The Case Against Competition,* Boston: Houghton Mifflin, 1986.

Kotulak, Ronald, *Inside the Brain: Revolutionary Discoveries of How the Mind Works,* Andrews & McNeel, 1997.

Kovalik, Susan, *Integrated Thematic Instruction: The Model,* Village of Oak Creek, AZ: Books for Educators, 1997.

Lazear, David, *Seven Ways of Teaching: The Artistry of Teaching with Multiple Intelligences,* Palatine, IL: Skylight Publishing, 1991.

LeDoux, Joseph, *The Emotional Brain: The Mysterious Underpinnings of Emotional Life,* Touchstone Books, 1998.

Lott, A. and Lott, B., "Group Cohesiveness and Individual Learning," *Journal of Educational Psychology,* 57. April 1966.

Lounsbury, John H., *Perspectives on the Middle School Movement, Transforming Middle School Education, Perspectives and Possibilities,* Ed: Judith Irvin, Boston: Allyn and Bacon, 1992.

Maybury Lewis, David., Millennium: *Tribal Wisdom and the Modern World,* Meech Grant Productions Ltd./The Body Shop International, Viking Penguin Books, USA, 1992.

McKnight, John, "Are Social Service Agencies the Enemy of Community?" *Utne Reader,* July/August 1992.

Miller, Jack and Drake, Susan, "Implementing a Holistic Curriculum," *Holistic Education Review,* Fall 1990.

Miller, Ron, *What Are Schools For? Holistic Education in American Culture,* Brandon, VT: Holistic Education Press, 1990.

Miller, Ron, New Directions in Education: Selections from *Holistic Education Review,* Brandon, VT: Holistic Education Press, 1991.

Nakagawa, Mako, Cooperative Pluralism, *Your Public Schools,* Olympia, WA: Office Superintendent of Public Instruction, November, 1986.

Olsen, Laurie, *Embracing Diversity, Teachers' Voices from California Classrooms,* San Francisco: California Tomorrow Immigrant Students Project Research Report, 1990.

Pederson, J., and Digby, A., (Eds), *Secondary Schools and Cooperative Learning, Theories, Models and Strategies,* New York, Garland Publishing, p. 282, 1995.

Pert, Candace, *Molecules of Emotion, The Science Behind Mind-Body Medicine,* New York: Simon & Schuster, 1997.

Reich, Robert, *The Work of Nations,* New York: Alfred A. Knopf, 1991.

Tye, Kenneth A., "Restructuring Our Schools, Beyond the Rhetoric," *Kappan Magazine,* Bloomington, IN: Phi Delta Kappan Educational Foundation, September 1992.

Rogers, Everett, *Diffusion of the Idea Beyond War, Breakthrough—Emerging New Thinking,* New York: Walker and Company, 1988.

Sapon Shevin, Mara and Schneidewind, Nancy, "Cooperative Learning as Empowering Pedagogy," *Empowerment from Multicultural Education,* SUNY Press, 1991.

Sarason, Seymour, *The Predictable Failure of School Reform,* San Francisco: Jossey Bass, 1990.

SCANS Report for America 2000—*What Work Requires of Schools,* Washington, D.C.: Secretary's Commission on Achieving Necessary Skills, U.S. Department of Labor, 1991.

Senge, Peter, *The Fifth Discipline, The Art and Practice of the Learning Community,* New York: Doubleday/Currency, 1991.

Senge, Peter, "The Learning Organization Made Plain," *Training and Development,* Boston: Innovative Associates, Inc., October, 1991.

Slavin, R., *Cooperative Learning: Theory, Research and Practice,* Englewood Cliffs, NJ: Prentice Hall, 1990.

Steele, Claude M., "Race and Schooling of Black Americans," *Atlantic Monthly,* April 1992, p. 75.

Schneider, Stephen, "A Better Way to Learn," *World Monitor,* April, 1993, p. 32.

Schneidewind, Nancy, and Davidson, Ellen, *Cooperative Learning—Cooperative Lives: A Sourcebook of Learning Activities for Building a Peaceful World,* Boston: W.C. Brown Co., 1987.

Schneidewind, Nancy, and Davidson, Ellen, *Open Minds to Equality: A Sourcebook of Learning Activities to Promote Race, Sex, Class, and Age Equity,* Englewood Cliffs, NJ: Prentice Hall, 1989.

Stoddard, Lynn, *Redesigning Education: A Guide for Developing Human Greatness,* Tucson, AZ: Zephyr Press, 1992.

Von Oech, Roger, *A Whack on the Side of the Head: How You Can Be More Creative,* New York: Warner Books, 1990.

Vygotsky, L.S., *Mind and Society: The Development of Higher Psychological Processes,* Cambridge, MA: Harvard University Press, 1978.

Wassermann, Selma, *Asking the Right Question: The Essence of Teaching,* Bloomington, IN: Phi Delta Kappan Educational Foundation, 1992.

Werner, Emily and Smith, Ruth, *Vulnerable But Invincible: A Longitudinal Study of Resilient Children and Youth,* New York: Adams, Bannister, and Cox, 1989.

Wolins, M. and Wozner, Y., *Revitalizing Residential Settings: Problems and Potential in Education, Health, Rehabilitation and Social Services,* San Francisco, CA: Jossey Bass Publishers, 1982.

Bring your school to life with
TRIBES TLC®
Professional Development
from CenterSource Systems

Tribes is a community building process—one that should be experienced. You can make the Tribes process come alive for your district or school by scheduling training for your teachers and administration.

CenterSource Systems has a network of licensed trainers who conduct professional development training throughout the United States, Canada and the Caribbean. Schedule an overview presentation and classroom demonstration at your school where the key concepts of Tribes are explained and demonstrated through typical training strategies and our videos. Give your administration, school board and staff the information they need to consider whole school training. Schools and districts committed to the full implementation of Tribes TLC® can arrange training and support to teams and faculties through the following staff development opportunities:

TRIBES TLC®—Building Community for learning
The purpose of this training is to prepare teachers, administrators and support staff personnel to develop a caring school and classroom environment, and to reach and teach students through an active learning approach that promotes student development, motivation and academic achievement.

TRIBES TLC®—Achieving Excellence
This training builds upon "Building Community for Learning" by providing school personnel with additional in-depth knowledge and methods to intensify the use of the Tribes Learning Community process throughout school classrooms and the whole school community... and thereby achieve higher success for students and schools.

TRIBES TLC®—Discovering Gifts in Middle School
The purpose of this training is to provide a research-based approach for middle level school educators to focus their schools on the critical developmental learning needs of young adolescents. The training illuminates how to transform the cultures of middle schools into caring learning communities that support the full range of students' growth and development as well as establishing academic excellence.

Training-of-District Trainers
CenterSource Systems has designed a **capacity building model** for professional development so that your district or school can have your own certified Tribes TLC® trainers providing on-going training, coaching and support to teachers, administrators, resource personnel and parent community groups. The CenterSource Training-of-District Trainers provides in-depth skills, knowledge, experience and quality training materials to your own qualified personnel. A variety of training modules enable them to facilitate the Basic Tribes Course, support faculty groups, initiate parent community groups and conduct classroom demonstrations.

"What Tribes can bring to a class is dynamite—what it can bring to a total staff is spectacular!

—Leslie McPeak,
Principal
Modesto City
Schools

For additional information, please call or write:

CENTER SOURCE SYSTEMS

**7975 Cameron Drive
Suite 500
Windsor, CA 95492**

**Phone: 800 810 1701
Fax: 707 838 1062
e-mail: CentrSrc@aol.com
internet: www.tribes.com**

PROFESSIONAL DEVELOPMENT

Descriptions of the TRIBES TLC® Materials

TRIBES, a New Way of Learning and Being Together
by Jeanne Gibbs
Item 100 $32.95

This new edition shows teachers how to reach students by developing a caring environment as the foundation for growth and learning. Material details how to teach essential collaborative skills, design interactive learning experiences, work with multiple learning styles, foster the development of resiliency, and support school community change. 2001, 6th edition, 432 pages, 165 strategies/energizers, index and resources.

TRIBUS, una nueva forma de aprender y convivir juntos,
by Jeanne Gibbs, Item 120 $32.95

The same wonderful Tribes book has been translated into **Spanish!** 1998, 1st edition, 448 pages.

Guiding Your School Community,
by Jeanne Gibbs
Item 130 $14.95

In this 110-page book, written with school Administrators in mind, you will learn why and how the positive Tribes culture will develop community throughout an entire educational system. You will gain an understanding of how to initiate, support and sustain the Tribes process over time.

Discovering Gifts in Middle School,
by Jeanne Gibbs
Item 140 $32.95

This new book blends the philosophy and process of Tribes with an emphasis on adolescent development and middle school students. Learning about the contextual basis of human development and how the developmental focus leads to school renewal and student achievement is a major focus of this book. 2001.

Video: TRIBES, A New Way of Learning and Being Together
Item 151 $22.95

See and show others what Tribes looks like in a classroom. Hear what principals, teachers, parents, and kids say about the process. Revised 2000. 14 minutes.

Teaching Peace by Red Grammar
Item 153 (cassette) $10.00
Item 154 (CD) $15.00

A delightful set of 10 songs written, sung, and played by Red Grammar. The music supports the same caring principles and fun enjoyed in Tribes.

Teaching Peace Song Book and Teacher's Guide
by Kathy Grammar
Item 155 $15.00

Features piano, guitar, and vocal accompaniment to the Teaching Peace songs and contains activity and discussion ideas for each song. The guide also contains a bibliography of over 100 books that relate to the themes of the songs. 1993, 85 pages.

Video: Creating Futures of Promise
Item 161 $22.95

Bonnie Benard and students describe the concept of Resiliency and Protective factors. 15 minutes.

Energizer Box
Item 162 $21.95

This colorful desktop card file contains 101 tried and true energizers that are a great way to revitalize students throughout the day.

Tribes Buttons and Magnets
(2 ¼ Inches)
Item 165 (50 Buttons) $20.00
Item 166 (25 Magnets) $20.00

Assorted Tribes buttons in English, Spanish or Hawaiian. Please specify. We also put the agreements with the teddy bear on a magnet for your kids to take home for the fridge. Great for the whole school, parents nights, Tribes Celebration days and just for fun.

Warm Fuzzy
Item 167 $12.00

We were delighted to find these soft wooly creatures for preschool and kindergarten classrooms. They make "Warm Fuzzy" from the popular story told in this book, tangible for young children.

Video: TRIBES–Learning for the 21st Century
Item 170 $22.95

Looking at Tribes as a process for systemic change from classroom to the whole school community. 15 minutes.

Tribes Postcards
(Pack of 50, English or Spanish)
Item 173 $7.50

A full-color card to send to tribe members, other educators and parents to announce events, stay in touch and keep expressing appreciation.

Tribes Bookbag
15" L x 12" H
Item 175 $14.95

A wonderful way to tote your Tribes TLC® materials, vinyl lined with outside pocket. Blue and white with your favorite Tribes kids on the front. Great gift idea too!

The Tribes Assessment Kit: Reflecting on the Tribes TLC® Process
Item 400 $75.00

The Tribes Assessment Kit will help your Tribes school strengthen its implementation of the process and assess outcomes. The Kit includes four process assessment instruments and complete directions for use throughout classrooms of the school.

MATERIALS

TRIBES TLC® MATERIALS ORDER FORM

Item No.	Description	Price	Qty.	Cost
100	*Tribes, A New Way of Learning and Being Together* by Jeanne Gibbs	$32.95		
120	*Tribus, una nueva forma de aprender y convivir juntos* by Jeanne Gibbs	$32.95		
130	*Guiding Your School Community* by Jeanne Gibbs (Tribes Administrator's book)	$14.95		
140	*Discovering Gifts in Middle School* by Jeanne Gibbs	$32.95		
151	Video: *Tribes, A New Way of Learning and Being Together* by CenterSource Systems	$22.95		
153	*Teaching Peace* (audio tape) by Red Grammer	$10.00		
154	*Teaching Peace* (CD) by Red Grammer	$15.00		
155	*Teaching Peace Song Book and Teacher's Guide* by Kathy Grammer & colleagues	$15.00		
161	Video: *Creating Futures of Promise* (15 minute video on Resiliency)	$22.95		
162	*Energizer Box* (desktop card file with 101 Energizers)	$21.95		
165	*Tribes Buttons Assorted* (2¼ inches) Bag of 50 Specify: ☐ English ☐ Spanish ☐ Hawaiian	$20.00		
166	*Magnets* (Bag of 25) ☐ English ☐ Spanish	$20.00		
167	*Warm Fuzzy* (stuffed animal approx. 9" long)	$12.00		
170	Video: *Tribes–Learning for the 21st Century*	$22.95		
173	*Tribes Postcards* (Pack of 50) ☐ English ☐ Spanish	$7.50		
175	*Tribes Book Bag* (15" L x 12" H)	$14.95		
400	*Tribes TLC® Assessment Kit*	$75.00		

Method of Payment:
Check enclosed for $_____

Master Card, VISA or Amex
#_____

Expiration Date: MM/YY ____/____

Purchase Order #_____
Please attach purchase order to this form

Shipping Rates:	Continental USA	Hawaii, Alaska & Canada
Up to $39.99	=$5.00	=$5.00
$40.00 to $59.00	=$6.00	=$8.50
$60.00 to $349.99	=10%	=15%
$350 or more	=5%	=11%

All shipping is via UPS ground or USPS Priority Mail
Call for international or rush shipping rates

*California residents: include sales tax for your county

Subtotal	
Shipping	
Sales Tax*	
TOTAL	

SOLD TO Name _____

Organization _____

Address _____

City/State/Zip _____

Day Phone _____

SHIP TO Name _____

Organization _____

Address _____

City/State/Zip _____

Day Phone _____

MAIL, FAX OR PHONE IN YOUR ORDER TODAY!

Phone: 800 810 1701
707 838 1061
FAX: 707 838 1062

CenterSource Systems, LLC
7975 Cameron Drive, Suite 500
Windsor, CA 95492

OR ORDER ONLINE AT: www.tribes.com

Index

Notes

Notes

Notes

Notes